13 WOMEN

PARABLES FROM PRISON

13 WOMEN

EDITED BY KARLENE FAITH

WITH ANNE NEAR

Douglas & McIntyre
Vancouver / Toronto / Berkeley

Douglas & McIntyre Ltd.
2323 Quebec Street, Suite 201
Vancouver, British Columbia
Canada v5t 4s7
www.douglas-mcintyre.com

Library and Archives Canada Cataloguing in Publication
13 women : parables from prison / edited by Karlene Faith ; with Anne Near

ISBN 10: 1-55365-142-1 · ISBN 13: 978-1-55365-142-0

1. Women prisoners—Canada—Biography. 2. Women prisoners—United
States—Biography. 3. Female offenders—Canada—Biography. 4. Female
offenders—United States—Biography. I. Faith, Karlene. II. Near, Anne.
III. Title. IV. Title: Thirteen women
HV8738.T45 2006   365′.43′092271   C2005-905667-3

Library of Congress information is available upon request.

Editing by Barbara Pulling
Cover design by Jessica Sullivan
Text design by Lisa Hemingway
Cover photograph: Simon Watson/Getty Images
Printed and bound in Canada by Friesens
Distributed in the U.S. by Publishers Group West

We gratefully acknowledge the financial support of the Canada Council
for the Arts, the British Columbia Arts Council, and the Government of Canada
through the Book Publishing Industry Development Program (BPIDP)
for our publishing activities.

Dedicated to the women of SIS

(Strength In Sisterhood), especially:

Brenda Blondell, Sylvie Bouchard, Ann Hansen,

Gayle Horii, Christine Lamont and Kris Lyons,

and to the memory of Jo-Ann Mayhew.

Dedicated to every woman on the planet

who has survived prison with

her heart and mind intact.

CONTENTS

ACKNOWLEDGEMENTS

THIS BOOK IS BASED on interviews conducted between 1972 and 2004, a steady gathering of autobiographies of imprisoned women in the U.S.A. and in Canada. In the end, it was difficult to make final selections as to whose stories to include here. When the first stories in this collection were told to me, activists and researchers were just beginning to pay attention to imprisoned women. Most of the women we met in various prisons were keen to tell their own truths. Over the course of the past three decades, the brave candour of women who are or have been prisoners has contributed to a much more substantial body of knowledge about women, crime and punishment than existed in the early 1970s. My first thank you, then, is to all the women who have shared details of their lives so that others can better understand the circumstances of women sent to prison.

Anne Near was the inspiration for this book's conception, and she did the editing on several chapters. She set the tone with her insights, keen editorial eye and penetrating commentaries. Anne's three daughters also pitched in. Timothy gave helpful comments on an early draft of the manuscript. Holly helped with logistics, communications and arranging for outside opinions of the manuscript. Laurel has offered steady and much-needed support and perspective in the circuitous process of developing Chapter 12, on First Nations women. My heartfelt thanks to all the Near women for their help with this project.

I am grateful to Jean Gallick, my friend and indispensable work partner inside the prison who conducted the interview with Marie Elder, Chapter 7 in this book.

I extend deep thanks to Faith Nolan. Her insightful and encouraging reading of an early version of Chapter 8 (Mattie) was clarifying and gave needed direction to the revisions.

Thank you to Allison Campbell, community ally, who kindly and very efficiently transcribed a number of the tapes.

A special thanks to Charlotte Sheedy, whose astute, critical comments on an early version of the manuscript served as a guide for how best to present these women's engaging stories.

Loving appreciation to my friend Judy Lynne. Her kind initiative in making introductions led me to Douglas & McIntyre.

It was my good fortune to work with Barbara Pulling, an outstanding editor whose ease with language, and appreciation for nuance, made pleasure of the work. She improved the manuscript while protecting the integrity of each story.

Special thanks to Scott McIntyre, who, from the outset, showed keen regard for the value of these women's stories; I appreciated his personal interest in the book's development. I am also grateful to Peter Cocking, Jessica Sullivan and Lisa Hemingway for their beautiful design work. Gratitude extends to Susan Rana, managing editor, and Viola Funk, production assistant.

My deepest thanks go to each of the contributors: Diane, Angelique, Lia, Kathy, Norma, Vicki, Marie, Mattie, Betty, Ann, Christine and Gayle. I value the generous spirit and honesty with which each woman offered her story.

In Chapter 12, women from varied First Nations backgrounds speak as one when they discuss the effects on their communities of forced confinement in residential schools, white foster homes and prisons. I am particularly grateful to Patricia Monture and Lorraine Stick for their assistance and for the constancy of our friendships. Others whose voices are included here are community leaders Mary Gottfriedson, Cherry Joe, Wendy Leonard and Sharon McIvor, and former prisoners Lana Fox and Fran Sugar, who in turn quote other First Nations prisoners. To each, I say thank you.

INTRODUCTION

THESE ARE THE STORIES of women who have been convicted of illegal actions and consequently imprisoned. I met most of them in either California or British Columbia between 1970 and 2001, while involved in prisoner advocacy work.

Prison etiquette does not encourage inquiry into another's crime; it is understood that this is a private and sometimes painful matter. But in time, the stories are shared. Some of the women here served time for conventional crimes such as drug possession, theft and fraud. Others were enmeshed in tragic circumstances resulting in crimes of violence. Still others were political prisoners who purposefully broke the law to effect social change. Most of the women are now out of prison, some for many years. Some of their stories have a happy ending; others do not. Their stories personalize criminal justice and serve as parables of women's lives on the margins.

In my early research at the California Institution for Women (CIW), I taped life history interviews with over one hundred women; a number of chapters are drawn from those interviews. The Canadian chapters were expressly written for this book. Each woman's story is wholly or partly told in her own words, as she wrote it or from transcripts of taped interviews edited for length and continuity.

Chapter 12 is a composite account of First Nations women. Some of the names in various chapters have been changed to assure anonymity. Last names are included only if the woman has been in the public eye. The varied formats reflect the different circumstances in which the stories were offered. Introductions, interjected commentaries and closing reflections serve to clarify, expand on a point or contextualize.

In 1980, with encouragement from women I'd interviewed, I began putting together a collection of their stories, and my friend Anne Near agreed to work on the project with me. We independently transcribed tapes, edited stories to manageable lengths, and wrote introductions and commentaries. We met frequently in her northern California farmhouse kitchen to review our progress, critique each other's work and talk about the women's lives. It was clear that the women's crimes occurred for reasons not always of their own making.

Now eighty-nine, Anne has a long history of social activism, defending human rights, supporting the arts and promoting peace. She brought to the work a keen understanding of political and economic inequities and of the social problems that result in the imprisonment of women. Her twin sister had worked with a childcare program in a women's prison in the eastern U.S.A. Her daughter Holly Near had given concerts in the California women's state prison. On the one hand, for these and other reasons, Anne was aware of women as prisoners. On the other hand, she had not herself spent time inside prisons or with women who had been incarcerated. This benefited our work together; it required that we start with basic questions about who is in prison, for what reasons, for how long and with what effects.

Anne and I also discussed the larger picture, including philosophical questions about personal accountability, the meaning of justice, the state's uses and abuses of power, and feminist perspectives on the challenges women face according to their cultural location. Those for whom the challenges are greatest and the resources fewest are most apt to be imprisoned. Anne brought our discussion of the world of the prison into the wider sphere, viewing the women's everyday lives in broader social contexts. She helped edit four of the stories included in this volume (Angelique, Kathy, Vicki and Mattie). Commentaries written by Anne are denoted by her initials: AN. Anne's humanitarian spirit and her appreciation of the value of a woman telling her story have infused the work as a whole.

MEDIA ATTENTION TO SENSATIONAL cases, Hollywood's demonization of "criminals," and public fears of being physically harmed by strangers (which is uncommon) all reinforce paranoid notions of "criminal types." Women are charged with 10 to 15 per cent of all crimes of violence and between one-third and one-half of minor theft crimes, including shoplifting. Women are more apt than men to be convicted of welfare fraud or breaching prostitution laws. In 1997, seven of ten women in prison were doing time for drug or property crimes; one-third of these were back inside for parole violations not involving a new crime (Reed and Reed, 1997: 154). Although women have less involvement than men with illegal drugs—as users or sellers—women who go to prison are disproportionately drug-dependent, even when drugs are not their criminal charge.

In California in 2005, with over 11,000 women in state prisons, approximately half of all convictions leading to prison were drug-related. Canada, a nation with almost the same population as the state of California (over 30 million), holds just 350 women in federal prison, with relatively moderate sentences for drug-related offences. Nevertheless, the majority of women in Canadian prisons are similarly dependent on alcohol, heroin, cocaine or other stimulants or sedatives. A number of women in the chapters ahead have contended with drug dependency, including a reliance on alcohol, and with the risks of selling illegal drugs. Their stories raise serious questions about the logic of criminalizing drug habits. The U.S. and Canadian governments have both invested heavily in prisons rather than in community resources such as public health, education, vocational training, affordable housing, voluntary substance-abuse programs, childcare and other services that would lower drug-related crime rates.

Some of the stories in this book may arouse compassion for a woman and her children or anger at social injustices that make criminals of victims. Other stories may evoke less sympathy. Some of the women in these pages have spent most of their lives in prisons. For others, prison has been a one-time experience. Some were moved from one prison to another. Others served many years in one cell. Imprisoned women, like anyone, identify cruelties and abuses prevalent in their environment, in this case especially by guards against prisoners. But women in prison seldom challenge their sentences and commonly take punishment for granted. Only rarely does a woman claim innocence, and I find that such claims most often turn out to be accurate.

These women's stories span the three decades, early 1970s to early twenty-first century, that have been the era of the second wave of women's liberation (following the first wave of suffragists at the turn of the last century). Most of these women didn't identify as feminists when they entered prison, but they were receptive to feminist perspectives.

Racism is endemic in criminal justice systems, and some of the women whose stories are told here come from communities that are heavily policed not for their protection but because community residents are seen as de facto suspects. Blacks and Hispanics in the States, even when their crimes are the same in kind and frequency as those committed by whites, and First Nations and blacks in Canada are much more likely than whites to be arrested, convicted, imprisoned, held in solitary, denied parole and rearrested upon release.

It is commonly assumed that people in prison are of lower-than-average intelligence; they did, after all, get caught. However, this is the law of averages at work. Most people in prison have also committed crimes for which they have not been caught, usually the same crime repeatedly, such as using illegal drugs or writing bad cheques. Most crimes are not reported. Less than 10 per cent of all reported crimes result in an arrest; fewer still of those arrested are convicted and imprisoned. For most people who break the law, crime *does* pay. In any case, a lack of intelligence is not generally the reason a woman is in prison, although poor judgement due to a craving for or the influence of drugs, especially alcohol, is often a factor. In the 1970s the average Stanford-Binet IQ score of prisoners at the California Institution for Women was 110, which is the top end of average in the general population (with some prisoners at the genius level and others mentally disabled). This is all the more significant given the cultural biases of tests designed to measure intelligence and the over-representation of political minorities in prisons.

The reality is that all kinds of women go to prison. The women whose stories are told here belie any stereotype of stupid crooks. They also don't conform to stereotypes of prisoners' appearances and personalities. Far from the brutal bull dykes of B-movies, women in prison cover the diverse cultural and age standards of contemporary femininity. And whatever the differences among them, most face the gloom of their situations with humour and ingenuity. Anne Near and I, while listening to their stories, would enjoy what Anne called "the improbable ploys by which some of these women have learned to survive or to keep life interesting."

Poverty is the common denominator among women sent to prison, including a number of the contributors to this book. If a woman isn't poor when she enters prison, she generally will be when she leaves. Other women whose stories are told here are unrepresentative of prisoners, in that they were raised with middle-class values, comforts, choices, expectations and security. Very few middle-class women are sent to prison; when they are, it's most commonly for committing fraud or killing an abusive spouse. However, occasionally a woman is imprisoned for political crime, and such women, particularly white women, often have middle-class or solid working-class backgrounds. Their crimes are not born from personal desperation, nor driven by drugs, material need or violent impulse. Their life experience is generally very different from that of the women with whom they're imprisoned. They're apt to be healthier, better educated and better able to demand their rights as prisoners. They are also more likely to have family and a support system on the outside.

Women who have been involved in social change work are well represented in this collection, disproportionate to the numbers of such women in prison more generally. The politically motivated women whose stories are in this volume—Ann Hansen, Christine Lamont and Betty Krawczyk—broke the law to ameliorate or draw attention to social, political and environmental injustices. Their stories made media headlines, drawing public support (and also wrath), whereas most imprisoned women are anonymous and lack human dimension in the eyes of the public. Gayle Horii did not commit her crime with intent, political or otherwise. However, becoming a prisoner had the effect of politicizing her, and she became a champion of prisoners' rights. Similarly, Mattie's lawbreaking was not motivated by lofty principles of justice. However, she was incarcerated during a period of significant African-American protest and cultural revival; she, too, was politicized by her prison experience. Norma and Lia also became activists within the prison and continued upon their release. First Nations women fought hard to secure the rights to Native ceremonies equivalent to those of other religions in prison. Just as a priest can now perform a ritual, so can a First Nation Elder.

All societies are selective about who is criminalized and sent to prison; the likelihood is not just a matter of who breaks the law, but also of one's position on the social ladder. The following chapters include stories of women who, often as teenagers, fell through the cracks of school, social welfare and criminal justice systems, and, by contrast, women whose crimes directly resisted and challenged the political economy supporting those inequitable systems. The first seven chapters are told as very personal stories, though with perspectives on the politics of punishment; the final six chapters are primarily political stories, told from personal perspectives. All the chapters demonstrate the truth of the old feminist adage that "the personal is political." Most of the stories are encouraging in some way. Collectively they illustrate the amazing resiliency of human beings and the strengths and courage women bring both to recovering from mistakes and tragedies and to acting on their convictions.

For forty years I have been a prisoners' rights advocate while also, for much of that time, teaching, doing research, and publishing about women and justice issues. After a long hiatus from this project, I have returned to *13 Women* as a way of coming full circle. My work with women in prison began with listening to their stories, which they were generous to tell. With their blessing, Anne and I are pleased to pass some of these stories on to you.

Reference

Reed, Diane F. and Edward L. Reed (1997). "Children of Incarcerated Parents." In *Social Justice* 24:3, 152–169.

1

DIANE

PAYING FOR THE PLEASURES OF POT

B Y 1970, MILLIONS OF people in the U.S.A., Canada and elsewhere in the world had organized and mobilized to end the war in Vietnam, liberate women, stem the tides of corporate capitalism, combat racism and defend the human rights of gays and lesbians, migrant farmworkers, homemakers and people with disabilities. Colonized nations across the globe were claiming their independence. Everywhere, people were collectively demanding a voice in the governance of their own lives.

Prisoners also organized during the 1970s, protesting the discriminatory, destructive policies and practices of criminal justice systems, from the point of arrest on through the courts and in the prisons. In 1970 I was teaching at Soledad Prison in California. A number of radical prison authors were incarcerated there, several of whom, including George Jackson, were later killed under dubious circumstances by various arms of law enforcement. Disturbed by the brutalities taking place in that prison, I began attending prisoners' rights conferences, which began with a few dozen people and quickly expanded to hundreds. Former prisoners would speak to their experiences inside, often with an analysis about the state's political uses of prisons. Leftist scholars would speak on the political economy of prisons, and activists would propose actions to promote change in the system. Everyone at those gatherings agreed that prisons as we know them should be abolished from any society claiming to be civilized and democratic.

Prisons were a distinctly blatant measure of the need for radical changes, but it was all about the men. Women volunteered to help with the organizing work of rallies, conferences and other events, but almost all of the speakers were men and all the issues discussed were specific to men's experience—even in the rare instance when a woman was speaking. Whereas many men who had been imprisoned spoke out publicly about the politics of punishment, no woman's voice could be heard.

And then I met Diane Ramsey, who had been released recently from the California Institution for Women; she heard I was researching prisons and sought me out. She wanted people to know what it means to a woman's life to go to prison, and she wanted to share the poetry that came out of her experience. She did, in community halls and churches, as the opener for benefit concerts, on the radio, and at public information meetings. She was transformed from a quiet sixties flower child with an easygoing hippie family to an anxious ex-convict with a wary regard for all the ways one's life can be taken away by people representing the law. Still, she had a healthy ability to speak her mind poetically.

The following interview is presented here just as it was distributed in 1971. We made copies on a mimeograph machine and passed it out at gatherings. To my knowledge, Diane was the first woman in California to speak out so publicly about having been in prison, and the positive public response to her candour gave courage to others to speak out too.

Diane's Story

KARLENE FAITH: *Can you describe the circumstances of your arrest, leading to your conviction and prison sentence?*

DIANE RAMSEY: At the time of my arrest I was living with my husband and our two children in Santa Barbara. My husband was a self-employed janitor. My youngest child was three months old and my daughter was three years old. I was staying home as a house-wife. My husband and I both smoked marijuana, and when asked by a new "friend" if we could get a lid for him, we agreed to do it. He turned out to be a special duty policeman, and shortly the police came to our home and arrested us. They took both of us to the county jail; we were bailed out the next day by my mother-in-law. They took both the children to the County Juvenile Home, and kept them there overnight.

During the next four months, my husband and I were arrested twice again on the same charge, though we were in no way guilty of it. These second and third charges were thrown out of court on the basis of no evidence. It was all simply a case of the police's determination to continue their harassment of us.

For the first charge my husband and I took the advice of the public defender to waive the right of a trial by jury and to accept a trial by judge. The trial was held and the judge sentenced both of us to a prison term of five years to life, with a minimum of three years in the penitentiary.

KF: *How did you cope with this sentence? How did you decide what to do with your children?*

DR: My first reaction was disbelief. I just couldn't believe that I was going to the penitentiary for having sold one lid of weed. My sec-ond reaction was one of shock. I couldn't accept it. For the past five years I've been trying to not let that experience make me bitter or hostile. I try not to think about it. It was really quite an indescrib-able feeling: Wondering what would happen to my relationship with my husband if we both went to prison. Wondering what would happen to my children and to my relationships with them after a three-year separation. Wondering what would happen to the rela-tionship between my son and my daughter, since they couldn't be sent to the same home.

After my husband and I were arrested we had to go to the juve-nile courts so those people could decide where to place our children if we were to be incarcerated. I was more fortunate than many women. Members of my family were able to take the children, so I haven't known the tragedy of those women whose children have been sent to foster homes. My mother-in-law offered to keep my son and my sister took care of my daughter.

During the time between our arrest and the sentencing, my husband and I were forced to move from our home in Santa Barbara because of police harassment. So my children both moved in with family prior to our sentencing. During this time our son had to have major surgery, so while I was being sentenced and awaiting transport to the prison, my baby was in the hospital. I didn't see either of the children again until they came to visit me in the prison eight months later. During the whole time of my incarceration I saw the children only seven times, because of the transportation problem. When they did come to visit we were placed in a small visiting room which was crowded with other prisoners and their families. We were permitted only one hour for each visit. It was helpful to see them and to see that they were all right. But it also increased the pain of the separation when they had to leave at the end of the hour.

KF: *Can you describe your experience of being admitted to the prison?*

DR: As I said before, I was in a state of shock. Especially the day of being transported and being actually locked inside the gates of CIW, in the "Reception Guidance Center" (RGC), an isolated building reserved for new fish. The first thing that happened when I entered was that I was commanded to strip—in the presence of the matron in charge of entries and several other staff members. I was told to get into an open shower. After showering they gave me an anal and pelvic examination to make sure I hadn't concealed any dope on my body. Then I was given uniforms—two pinstriped dresses that came below the knee, two sets of underwear, and a pair of sneakers. All the women in RGC had to wear this identical uniform during the first stage.

KF: *What is the function of the RGC?*

DR: They give you physical and psychological tests so that they can classify you. They then decide which cell unit you'll live in and give you a job assignment. The possible classifications are closed custody (you can leave the unit only to go to your job); medium custody (you can leave the unit to walk around the yard on off-days and hours); and minimum custody (you are allowed to go to the different areas of the compound, such as the library and the movies).

KF: *How did they decide on a classification?*

DR: Damn, I never could figure that out. I was classified as closed custody. My job assignment was to do yard work, pulling weeds. The prison staff called it "Training for Landscape Gardening," and they later gave me a certificate saying I was a qualified landscapist. The prison gets extra money from the state for calling these work assignments "training programs." But it's a farce. Even if I had been able to get a job after release on the strength of the certificate, I would never have been able to hold such a job because I had had no real experience or training.

KF: *Were there any authentic training programs for the women at CIW?*

DR: They had cosmetology, nurses' aide, janitorial service, kitchen and sewing. There were 1,000 women at CIW when I was there, and just 20 of these women were able to get into the cosmetology program. Another 20 were in nurses' aide. The rest of us just worked to keep the institution going and to provide labor for the sewing industry. So hardly anyone gets into any kind of training. CIW is not recognized as one of the better schools in the state! Its single claim to fame is that it was the largest penitentiary for women in the world.

KF: *Going back to when you first entered the Reception Guidance Center, can you describe what your experience was like during those three years at CIW?*

DR: It started out very badly. When I finally came out of shock I became so depressed over the separation from my children and husband that I attempted suicide by cutting my throat. (Once a week we were permitted to check out a razor blade for shaving our legs.) As soon as the hospital released me, I was sent before the Disciplinary Board. It's against the rules to attempt to kill yourself! The board sentenced me to thirty days in solitary detention. That was a long, lonely thirty days. The only human being I saw in that time was the matron who brought the food around. After being released from the "quiet room," as they call it, I discovered that I had become very withdrawn and unable to communicate with other people. Very gradually, I did come out of that depression.

As part of my punishment, my closed custody classification had been extended by six months. (Every six months a prisoner may be reclassified.) During the year of my closed custody I was living in a cell unit with 120 women, with two staff members. The staff alternate in three eight-hour shifts. Their job is to open and close the cells and do the counting. Counting is very important in the prison. Four times a day we had to sit on our bed and face a peephole in our door.

Eight hours a day I pulled weeds in the yard. We took our meals three times a day in the Central Feeding Facility, where we stood in line for half an hour waiting for our trays. In the evening I would play cards or chess. After six months they let me enroll in math and history classes, but they were so boring that I didn't stay with it. The school programs were geared to women who were slow learners. So for three years I wasn't able to get into any program that could have given me a diploma or any kind of mental stimulation. I did make good use of the limited library facilities. And after I was released I was able to go to a school on the streets and take the General Education Diploma test, which is high-school equivalency.

KF: *Were you corresponding with your husband and friends during this time? Did you make friends among the other prisoners?*

DR: My husband and family did write to me. It was hard to form relationships in the prison, because most of the women did less time than I did. I would form a friendship and then I would see that woman leave, knowing that we would never be able to see each other again. One of the conditions of parole is that you can't have contact with other ex-convicts.

It magnified the loneliness to be in such a crowd and not be close to anyone. In fact, it was dangerous to form close friendships. There is so much fear of "homosexuality" in the prison that when two women do become close to one another they are subject to suspicion, harassment and discipline. "Personal Contact" is not allowed. If two prisoners hug or touch one another they are sent directly to the hole, that is, to separate holes.

KF: *In such a stifling and intimidating atmosphere, what did you do to keep from going crazy with fear, boredom and loneliness?*

DR: I spent a lot of time reading and writing poetry. A woman volunteer started coming in once a week to teach a poetry class. We became close friends and I went to her classes faithfully. We still communicate and she helped me get some of my poetry into magazines. To continue her friendship with me she had to quit her job at CIW. One of the CIW rules is that no staff member is allowed to have any communication with any prisoner or former prisoner other than strictly professional contact, and this included volunteers as well as paid staff.

My sister sent me a guitar, and I taught myself to play it and began writing my own songs. I also started going to church on Sunday. I wasn't particularly religious, but it gave me a chance to get close to the chaplain, who was more open to the women than most of the staff. But I did become somewhat mentally ill. When I got out I spent time in a mental hospital, which happens to a lot of people. And then when they get out of the hospital they get sent back to prison for screwing up. I was luckier than most.

KF: *What were the attitudes of the prisoners at CIW toward each other? Do they have the "convict code" that we hear about with men in prison?*

DR: The convict code is a myth, at least with women. A lot of these women will snitch on each other and report rule infractions to the staff, because that makes the way easier. You are rewarded for snitching with good reports on your behavior. This gives the staff more power and control over the prisoners. It keeps the prisoners from becoming close to one another or developing trust among themselves. It increases suspicion and causes a lot of anger. Women will accuse each other of snitching and then get sent to the hole. If a woman wants revenge against somebody she might start a fight close to the woman's parole hearing, and that woman will lose her release date because it's an infraction to be involved in a fight.

Women are also alienated from each other through the job assignments. There is a lot of competition for the better or more desirable jobs. For example, working in the administration building as a clerk, or in the recreation department, or in the staff coffee shop—any job that pays. Wages run from two cents to ten cents an hour. The only way to get one of these high-end jobs is to indulge in high-level ass kissing.

KF: *Are there any examples of solidarity among the women that is anything like what's happening in men's prisons?*

DR: It has been slowly getting started. Just before I left in 1970 I was involved in the first protest demonstration in the history of CIW. It was in support and empathy for the Soledad Brothers, and we decided to demonstrate until they were unlocked—just to show them that we were with them. The prisoners demanded a meeting in the auditorium, and we demanded that the press be there. They weren't admitted, but the men at Soledad heard about it through the prison grapevine.

The warden came to our meeting and told us the men at Soledad had been informed of our support. Then she told us we would be put into closed custody lock-up unless we went back to our units.

This was really a threat of more time in the prison, because if any of us got reported to the board for demonstrating, we would be punished by losing our release date. We went to our cells, but we had made our point. This kind of solidarity movement was just beginning, and maybe it will grow with women coming in because of the way social consciousness is spreading on the outside.

As females we are taught from the time we're children that we shouldn't show aggression. We must behave passively. Women in prison are just like women out of prison. The crimes of most aren't more serious than things women do on the outside who are never apprehended. Most of the women are poor. In all the time I was there I didn't meet one wealthy woman. A large percentage of Black and Chicana women are there. Most of us were defended by the public defenders and couldn't afford good attorneys. We would hear about middle-class crimes on the TV or in the papers but we never saw the women who had committed the offenses come into the prison. They had good attorneys and connections with the judges. Their charges would be dropped or they would pay fines, which they could well afford, or go into rehab, or just get minimum probation sentences.

KF: *You talk about how women have been trained to be passive. What does the prison do, or not do, to make women more independent and better able to make good decisions for themselves?*

DR: They teach you how not to make decisions by making absolutely every decision for you. Every minute of every day you are told what to do, how to do it, when to do it, and who to do it with. They decide what you will wear because only certain kinds of clothing are on the approved clothing list, even though when you leave the Reception Guidance Center, to enter the main prison, you can go back to certain kinds of street clothes. Each woman has four outfits; when I was there we couldn't wear slacks, but that has changed recently.

They decide when you will eat and what you will eat. They decide when you will go to sleep by turning out the lights at

10:00 P.M. They decide when you will wake up; anyone asleep past work hour goes to detention. They do everything they can to strip away your individuality and your ability to think for yourself.

KF: *How does this absolute control over your life affect your ability to function when you finally get a release date?*

DR: It paralyzes you. You leave the penitentiary with a suit of clothing and two other outfits they give you if you don't have clothes of your own. They give you enough money for a one-way ticket to wherever you're going, within the state. I was paroled to my sister's home north of San Francisco. I was very lucky to have my family to go home to. My family had been taking care of my clothes and furniture. I had a home to go to, and people to help me until I could find a job. A lot of women have no place to go at all. They are given less than a pittance to live on until they find a job, but they haven't been trained to do anything.

Psychologically you feel like you have a sign on your forehead saying "Ex-Con." When you walk up the aisle of the supermarket you feel like everyone knows where you've been. Your new neighbors ask you where you're from and when you tell them they withdraw from you. Any time there's an incident involving the police, it is you who is immediately under suspicion and harassment.

The conditions of parole deny you the right to travel without written permission from the parole office. Once a month you have to submit a report to say where you work, how much you earn, how you spend your salary. Normally, parolees are not allowed to be on the radio or TV or to have anything published without censorship. As a poet that's a particular hardship for me, and I haven't followed the rule, without a hassle so far. I'm not being political about it. I'm just saying what the experience was for me. But the women who want to make political statements are censored. Silencing people who have been through it is the most effective way to prevent public knowledge of what goes on in prisons.

Since I was convicted for marijuana, I have to register with the police department in any town I live in. When you first come to a new town, in the hope of making a fresh start, it is really frustrating to have to march straight to the police and let them know you are a bad one.

You want to make a good impression on a prospective employer, but if you admit that you have been in prison you probably won't be hired, and it's against the law to not admit it.

Your children look at you as a stranger. When my son's grandma left him with me he started crying because he didn't know me, and he felt he was being deserted by the only mother he knew. My little girl was older — she was six when I got out. She remembered me a little, but she has never been able to live with me. She and my sister had grown so attached to each other that it would be unfair of me to snatch my daughter up. I do get to see both of my children quite often.

Reflections

It is notable that so many women and men who are sent to prison become poets, or discover their poet selves. To be incarcerated is an intense experience, the effects of which, like others of life's most intense events, cannot be easily described. Poetry takes the matter to an elevated place; it makes art of the pain of it. It gives the experience the respect it deserves.

Following are three of Diane's untitled poems.

> In prison
> time passes slowly
> when surprises are removed,
> when everything expected
> falls in smoothly.
> When every hour is planned
> and all the places manned
> by people who are chosen
> and placed far in advance.
> Ah me, but how the time goes by so slowly.

when it's been a long time
since arms have loved me
and lips,
and tongue
all hot and softly,
when it's been a long time
since arms have pressed me
all tight
and need
and sharing,
when it's been a long time
and the memory gets me
and my eyes get warm
and moist
and trembly
when it's been a long time
since love was mine
i think of you with waiting

      . . .

All those people out there
Who know I've been in prison
For three years,
Who know I'm getting out tomorrow.
They probably think that tomorrow is Christmas, July Fourth,
and Halloween all in one.

I wonder if they think about
the fears, the doubt.
My baby was three months old
Three years ago.
He calls his Grandma, "Mommy."
My daughter just turned six,
She calls Aunt Marilyn
"Mommy."

My children do not know me.
I haven't seen my husband's face
Or heard his voice
In these three years.
I don't know when
I stopped loving him.
I can't love a stranger.
Those people out there,
Do they know?
I doubt it.
I remember elation
I remember singing while I walked
And noticing
The blue of sky and tree green;
    I remember
Like I remember dreams.

The colors and the sounds
seep through the haze
of long ago
And oh so far away.
Clouds grey brightness
Even from the sun,
And memories are not enough for warmth.

The happy ending to Diane's story is that she sustained good relations with her children, she was well integrated and respected within her community, and she never returned to prison. The unhappy ending is that her family was permanently broken apart, for the crime of obtaining an ounce of marijuana as a favour to a new "friend."

2

ANGELIQUE

WHAT'S NORMAL?

O NE WOULDN'T EXPECT A woman who is locked up to be very happy, and certainly many imprisoned women do suffer from anxiety and intense frustration. Yet no matter what problems they face, some women exhibit an irrepressible spirit, even in confinement. Angelique was such a woman.

Angelique was eager to tell her story, and in the telling she was quick, vibrant, serious and entertaining. Until she wrote it out for me, I could never keep track of who was who in the complex chronology of her life. In her thirty-seven years Angelique had been through five legal and two common-law marriages, with six children who were primarily raised by her relatives or the children's fathers.

Mixed-blood, raised in Texas in a black neighbourhood, she left home at thirteen and lived on the street. In our first interview, Angelique told me of how she was born with deformities that gave her the appearance of having horns and a vestigial appendage at the base of her spine that looked like a tail. Those features had been surgically reduced in her infancy, but she grew up with a peculiar facial appearance—which did not, however, deter would-be suitors. She underwent reconstructive surgery in her early adulthood, at the prison, as documented in her official file. Now she was distinctly attractive, in her early thirties, cheerfully striding across the yard in blue jeans and a blue work shirt, her long, dark hair flowing around her face.

When we met in 1972, Angelique was without contact with the "free world" except for occasional messages from or about her children. She had been in jails and prisons off and on for twelve years, and her strength was her attention to Buddhism and her love of solitude. She also received emotional sustenance from the other women, among whom she had developed some rich friendships. Outside prison, her close friendships were with men; she'd known little closeness with women on the outside.

To the authorities, Angelique's attitude was refreshing. She never openly rebelled or fought against the prison regulations. Her resistances were subtle, and she generally attained whatever she wanted for herself and her friends, such as sewing supplies or clean blankets. She took advantage of every opportunity that came to her in the prison. She carved wooden figurines and made pottery and ceramics; the prison staff sold her finished products to visitors, with a percentage going into her account for purchases at the canteen. Her prison job suited her interests: supervising the sewing industry and working as an expert seamstress, teaching others as a night job. With fabrics she mysteriously procured, she had fashioned herself a sophisticated wardrobe, and she relished excuses to dress up. In a prisoner-organized fashion show she modelled a sequined gown she had made, which was complemented by a fancy upswept hairdo. The audience clapped and cheered for a long time when she walked onto the stage.

A natural artist, Angelique filled her 6′ × 9′ cell with art. She created mobiles from twigs, scraps of sparkly cloth, pebbles and pieces of crystal, which cast rainbows on her walls. The volunteer program I worked with sponsored parties with live music, and she was an excellent, energetic dancer. In her poetry she conveyed the dark angst of her mind in difficult times, but in her day-to-day demeanour, she sparkled.

Angelique wanted to be in the academic world, and she was among the first to sign up for the first university course in the prison in 1972. Although she was well liked and had deep friendships with other prisoners, she identified less with prisoners in general than with the professionals in the prison—the psychologists, teachers and medical staff. She longed to be using her own natural abilities in some professional position. She wanted the respect. She also knew that that was not a likely prospect, given her long history with the law.

Angelique's Story

My birth. That's the place to start. As family history has it, I was born at home during an electrical storm. Lightning was knocking over trees. I was born a twin, but my twin brother had been dead over a month. And I was born dead. They put me in hot water, then in cold water, then again in hot, and handed me to my grandmother. I breathed with the touch of her hands. I had a cottle appendage and a little papilloma on each side of my forehead—a tail and horns—and my nose was flattened. My father screamed that I was a child of the devil. In the old days I would have been proof that my mother was a witch. My grandmother and the doctor bundled me up and carted me off to the hospital. They removed the appendages and put me in an oxygen tent. I had pneumonia. It was three months before I went home.

My grandmother named me Angelique. At five I almost died of pneumonia again. They said I was a delicate child. My skin was super-sensitive so I was never the cuddly type. I wouldn't eat and had malnutrition. In pictures I look like a starving orphan. I just didn't want that body. It might have been my father's reaction to it, but I spent most of my childhood trying to get out of it.

I was the first child after seven miscarriages. I was a miracle. And then my sister came, four years younger. My father wanted a boy but my mother drew the line because of the risks. She was one of those women who engaged in sex only to please her husband. My grandmother was a contemporary of Freud, a Victorian.

Between my mother's inheritance and her religious trip, sex became nasty to her.

One summer I came home from the hospital on the 4th of July. We didn't have any money but Pop got one of those pinwheels. He picked me up and put me on the couch and opened the window, and went outside and tacked the pinwheel onto the telephone post, so I could watch it. This was an outstanding episode, one of the few times he did anything for me.

Since I didn't have a brother, I was Pop's son. When he worked on the car, I was the one who brought him the tools. Before I started school I knew the difference between a ⅝″ and a ¾″ wrench, box end or open end, because that was the only way I could stay out there with him.

Pop didn't get past the third grade in school because of a heart murmur. He hung around his uncle's print shop and would read the type upside down and backwards. He always had his nose in a book. When we asked him a question he made us look it up and give him the answer. He had a tremendous head for trivia, like the size of the largest hailstone to hit the state of Texas. He'd know the year and the hour. I'm a lot this way myself. Pop's an angry man, never said anything that he could scream. He also had a tremendous sense of humor. He loved children, except me. He adored my children. He was a good worker, when he could find steady work.

When I was in high school Pop went through ministerial school. I did his English for him or he'd never have made it. I corrected and typed all his papers. And he was ordained into the Baptist ministry. In the end he worked for a Christian printing business, until he retired at sixty-five. Before all that he had worked as a mechanic for seventeen years. The job folded with the Depression. My mother was teaching school part-time, substituting, and my grandmother taught full-time. Pop did jobs like painting the church. We had milk from my rich uncle and chickens in the yard. We had fresh eggs but sold them. When a hen got old we'd stew it. We also had a little Victory Garden, vegetables, and we'd do a lot of canning. We lived on the dirt end of town, and ate a lot of rice and beans.

My mother's mother was Creole French and my father was also part black. His mother was a light-skinned "house nigger," very attractive. My maternal grandmother was the first grandmother to receive a degree from Southern Methodist University, which was quite a distinction at that time. She retired from school teaching when I was six, when she was already seventy-seven. School teaching was in my blood. I loved school and after school I would play school.

My mother and grandmother battled over how I should be raised. My grandmother served wine with all meals, but when my mother got religion there couldn't be any alcohol at home. With my grandmother I drank wine, coffee and Cokes. At home my mother had me praying for the girl next door because she wore slacks, drank Cokes, and was going to Hell. It was as much a sin to go swimming in a pool with boys as it was to steal, because it was a sexual sin. With stealing, you could return what you stole, but thoughts about sex couldn't be unthought.

From age five I lived with my grandmother because my mother got a teaching job in another town. Her neighbor took care of me when my grandmother was at work. Before breakfast I had to give her the multiplication tables with my eyes closed. In the back lot was a stream and palm trees, a rich clay deposit. I would scoop it out and make things—little animals and people, my mother's face, dishes for everyone's dolls. My mother would take them to her school and have them fired; when she brought them home they would hold water, so I had this encouragement. My mother played the piano and she had me playing when I had to stand up on the piano bench. I could hear something on the radio and pick it out. They got me a teacher who taught me chords. My mother said my talent was consecrated to God and I wasn't to use it for anything except praising Him. But I like jazz.

In school I was always the "teacher's pet." I went back to my parents, and when I changed schools they moved me ahead. So I missed some basics, and the older kids I was with thought I was weird. And I was. I was an outsider. My grandmother made all my clothes, Little Orphan Annie outfits. I was pretty ugly. It wasn't until I was grown up and came to prison in California that they reconstructed my flat nose, took the bone from my rib. But in school I was Dishface Annie. Still, I liked school.

When I was eight I got polio, in the hospital until I was ten, then on crutches until I was almost twelve, in the children's ward, kind of a fun thing. My grandmother brought me my lessons and I jumped another grade. When I got out of the hospital I was ready for junior high school. I won the Lens Jewelers Bible Award for two years, memorizing parts of the Bible. I can still quote it for my own purposes, since a lot of people in society are biblically oriented. I can come from the Bible.

I went back to school on crutches. My grandmother's chiropractor friend took me to the swimming pool with eight pounds of braces on my legs and taught me how to swim. He paid for me to study ballet. Just a year later he took me to the chiropractors' convention and showed me off. They made him president of the association, and what I got from it was walking, without limping, rolling from side to side. The next time I had to learn to walk all over again I did the same thing, only then I learned in high heels—but that's another story.

When Angelique was thirteen, in high school, her grandmother became ill with cancer and died. Whereas Angelique felt unloved by her parents, especially the father who thought she was the child of the devil, she knew she was loved by her grandmother, the woman who gave her life and named her. It was her most important relationship.

I didn't cry, not until after the funeral. There was a girl there from Sunday school who I didn't like. I had excluded her from joining a trio I was in; we were singing on the radio. But I looked across my grandmother's grave and there she was. I started crying. Not because my grandmother was dead but because I had treated Caroline so shabbily and here she was, the only one who came to my grandmother's funeral.

My parents and sister moved into my grandmother's house so we all lived together again. But it was a complete turnaround in my life. Everything I'd gone along with because my parents believed in it, I now said, to heck with it. I quit the church, my father's Baptist church. It was distorted and fanatic. There was more emphasis on not wearing makeup or slacks, and not drinking or playing cards, than there was on being truthful and respectful of others.

The first day of speech class in high school the teacher said, "All the girls cross your legs." So we did, and he said, "Now the gates of Hell are closed and we can proceed with class." He also told the girls, "If you advertise you can expect a lot of customers." Still, I learned a lot from him and he was the one who got me interested in acting. For our class play I wrote a parody of *Hamlet*.

I got a locker at the bus station, and before going to school I'd go there and put on makeup and leave my socks. Then on the way home after school I'd go back and take off the makeup and put the socks back on. I had two good friends, brothers, Joe and Bronco, older than me, sixteen and twenty-one. They'd hang around the garage fixing their bicycles. We never had any sex thing going, but I did have sex with someone else when I was fourteen.

Before I started on my life of crime, I was over at Joe's and he was telling Bronco—bragging—about how anybody who wanted to skip class could show me their signature and then when the attendance sheet came around, I could just sign their name for them. So Joe was tripping with Bronco about it and then I showed Bronco how I could do it. "You can do that with anybody's handwriting?"

"Yeah."

"Well, I have an idea. If you went to the bank with me and somebody was at the counter and you could see their handwriting, could you write that same handwriting on a couple of checks?"

"Sure."

"We could make some money." We did it. We'd go downtown as if to school and Bronco would meet us at the bus station. We'd go to a couple of banks. Someone was always standing there writing something. I'd pull a couple of counter checks and write them out with whatever signature I saw available. The next day Joe would take them to the branch banks and cash them, second-party checks which he'd make out to himself or with whatever ID he had. Bronco would meet us the next day. I'd get $30 or $40. We did it two or three times a week. Joe kept my money, because my parents searched me and went through my stuff to make sure I wasn't smoking, and I couldn't spend it or they'd know something was up.

Then Bronco got a border run for weed and asked me to bag it up. So he invested my money in dope and let it build up. If I got a new jacket or something I told my family that Joe gave it to me. They thought I was too young at fifteen to be going steady. At school I'd buy sodas for everyone, and I bought a $75 set of drafting equipment. Anything I could keep at school I could buy. I bought a lot of books and read a lot. This was my introduction to crime. When I was a senior, Bronco got busted and, like a lot of guys, he was given the choice of the U.S. Army or doing time. So he went into the army and the judge dismissed the case. This was 1951.

After Bronco got busted, Joe and I carried on with his customers. Economic expediency. Joe would do the border runs. I did a couple while we were still in school. We lived 800 miles from the border; we'd go on weekends. Joe would be like a tourist visiting Mexico to play around and get drunk, and then he'd go home—with a lot of dope. My end was the dealing back home. That's how I made spare money until I met Rafael, my first husband.

Before I met Rafael I'd been with three guys. The one who took my virginity, I picked him because he was a very pretty guy and if I got pregnant I wanted a pretty baby. He was shocked that I was a virgin and he wanted to marry me, to make an honest woman of me. Finally I had to tell him how old I was and that I only went to bed with him because I wanted to get it over with. This cut his ego. I saw him at the roller rink and he wanted to be with me, but at fourteen I didn't take any of it seriously.

Also, before Rafael, I went to bed a couple of times with a guy named Willie and his buddy Marvin, all together, making everybody feel good. It was just a fun time, a party. Right there I lost any idea that sex was nasty. It was beautiful, these two young men concentrating on making me feel good. Then with Rafael it was also really good, until my folks found out I was pregnant. I'd passed out from a kidney problem and the doctor discovered the pregnancy. So my parents packed us off to a little town in Texas and we had a shotgun wedding in February 1952, a leap year.

Rafael and I were childhood sweethearts, idealistic. They made us quit school although we were both seniors. Rafael finished up at night school and drove a bakery delivery truck to pay the rent. I went to work for the City Planning Department on the master maps of the city of Dallas. When they'd propose a new street I would take the specification and measurement and draw those on the master maps. It was a good job.

When I got too big to work, I quit to have the baby and, because we needed money, I went back to dealing grass, and never did tell Rafael about it. After the baby was born he lost his job and was around the house for a couple of months. I wasn't doing forgery anymore, but I said I did it so he could stop worrying about the rent. He didn't like it and I promised I wouldn't do it anymore, but meanwhile we had the $300 we needed. He then went to work at the post office and never knew the money came from dealing weed, which would have infuriated him.

My first delivery, with Ellen, had been very easy. The next year Sonny was born, also easy. I had a ball, staying home looking after them. I read a lot and made things, knitting, crocheting, sewing. I made Rafael's shirts and my own wardrobe. I was eighteen when I got pregnant for the third time. I bought a piano, a rosewood square grand, paid for it with weed money, $400, but I told Rafael it was $150.

And then I started running around with a fellow named Bob who was courting me, and knew I had children and was pregnant but thought I was divorced. There was never any sex between us, but when Rafael found out about him, he screamed at me that the baby wasn't his, and he kicked me. I passed out and he put a cigarette out on my leg. I miscarried. He had never physically abused me before. The next morning I took the kids to my mother. Joe put me in a car and took me to Oklahoma and left me in a hotel in a little town. I was out of my head. Mixed with all my fear was the thought, "Am I ever glad to now have an excuse to get out of this marriage!"

Angelique called her parents to say that she wouldn't be coming home and she wanted the children to remain in Dallas with Rafael. Her parents drove to Oklahoma and retrieved her, but she stuck to her decision to leave Sonny and Ellen with their father. She considered him a good father. She was overwhelmed.

We didn't want to get married in the first place, and then we tried to make it stick. We weren't happy, either of us. We were both so young, we hadn't done any living, married while still in high school. But now Rafael was more settled than I; my children would be raised right. I didn't want them with my family because I didn't want them raised like me. Rafael was working, I was running. I enjoyed my kids but I wasn't a natural mother. I never played with dolls. I wasn't one of those girls who loves everyone else's babies. I loved my kids. They were mine. They were cute and fun. I was eighteen and diapers didn't bother me. I liked housework, too. But now I was on the move and couldn't travel with them. I felt I did what was right for the kids, just cut it all loose. I was running away.

I got a motorcycle, packed a duffle bag and left for New York with $50 in my pocket. Joe gave me a gun for protection. On the way out of town, sitting at a red light, I see a small park with a public restroom, trees and bushes all along the side. And on the other side of the street was a liquor store and an armored car and four guys carrying money bags, the day they cash payroll checks. It was 9:30 in the morning. I pulled off the road, left the bike in the park, put my waist-length hair up in my white skull cap, and put a black cap on top of it. In the restroom I painted on a moustache and five-o'clock shadow with my eyebrow pencil. Then I put on my butch jacket and stuck the pistol in my waistband. As soon as the armored car left I walked across the street and put it in the clerk's face, say-ing, "Gimme the bags!" He reached out and I said, "No, not the register. The bags." Then I said, "Just the bills," and I stuffed them into my own bags and split. He doesn't play brave. He lets me go. He's insured.

Across the street I pull off my cap and let my hair down. I wipe off my face and stash the money, and sit down on the bench with my hair streaming. I watch the cops come. They stay around for about an hour. Then the cops leave and the armored car comes again. They still have to cash payroll checks, right? So when the armored car leaves I put my hair back up and use the eyebrow pencil on my face and go back in and say, "Let's do that again." The clerk says, "Oh, no, I don't believe it," and I say, "You don't have to believe, just do it, just like before." So I split again with all the bills, go across the street, sit there and wait for the cops. While the cops are still there I get on my bike and split.

I got to Little Rock, Arkansas, that night, took a room in a motel and counted my money, almost $75,000. I couldn't fathom it. The next morning I went out for a paper, and it said there'd been a dar-ing daylight robbery committed by a young man in the same liquor store twice in the same day, and that he had gotten away in a late-model automobile.

The heightened level of excitement in Angelique's life, the power she felt when she successfully pulled off the double robbery and the free-dom represented by the money, was apparently intoxicating. She was breaking through with a wildness she hadn't known she had in her. She went from aspiring to be a conventional wife and mother who sold grass on the side to being an outlaw motorcycle mama who could also dress up and make an impression. Excited about her new life, she covered her tracks and made her way to Washington, D.C., arriving in the spring when the cherry trees were in blossom.

I got me a pad and some clothes and put the money in two differ-ent banks under two different names. All of a sudden I could do anything I wanted. I was free. I was too free. I just played for a while. Now what to do? I wasn't splurging. The $75,000 lasted three years. I had several jobs in D.C. and I worked in real estate long enough to try an embezzlement scam. When the auditors didn't find the fraud I quit the job; I knew I could do it. I applied for a Pentagon job to see if I could get a security clearance; it took four months but I got it, and actually worked there in a boring job for a few months. I'd been a champion amateur roller skater, so I started teaching for amateur competitions. This was the one thing in life that had given me any recognition.

In a bowling alley I met some guys with a little forgery thing going. They all got IDs and I started writing counter checks, just like I had done with Bronco years before. I'd get about 20 percent of their take. Then four of them got busted and two of them snitched on me, according to the guy who bailed. So two hours later I was on my way out of town. In Norfolk I traded my bike for another one, and after a month I went back to D.C., where my money was. And then it happened. My life changed, and almost ended, again. On a trip to Virginia I ran into the back of a tractor-trailer. It was very foggy. I wasn't speeding but I went straight up and came down on the pavement. My backbone twisted like a train of railroad cars derailing. Three days later I wake up with my head shaved, paralyzed from the waist down. They braided my hair before they shaved it and saved it for me. They had to remove my coccyx, at the base of the spine; it had just powdered, severing nerves. I was in traction in the hospital for about four months. Some nerve and muscle loss regenerated but I was in a wheelchair and my roller-skating career was over.

Angelique had never lacked a boyfriend, and after leaving her husband, and before the accident, she had been pursued by various men. There was Jeff, who worked in intelligence at the Pentagon. She confided in him about her robbery and, as with several of the men in her life, he tried to take her out of her life of crime. Another man who had hoped to marry her was Rocky, whom she described as "just

like a kid, a friendly little puppy, boring." Harvey was also a seri-
ous suitor, offering her a three-carat solitaire diamond. But like the
others, "he was the wrong guy." In Harvey's case, it was because "he
wore his pants up too high, and had the personality of someone who
would." It was Jeff she called on for help after the accident.

When I got out of the hospital, I lived with a friend of Jeff's, a groovy
little chick who was a real friend to me. On New Year's Eve she had
gone out and I was at my lowest point, confined to the wheelchair.
I turned on the gas. For some reason Kay and her boyfriend came
back early and found me. They took me to the hospital. Since I had
to live, since I couldn't kill myself, I was damn well not going to live
in a wheelchair, so I got myself together. I got crutches and taught
myself to walk again. Hour after hour, up and down the hallway. In
six months I only needed one crutch, in high heels.

My money was getting low, down to two or three hundred dollars. I went to the old area and found people to do the forgery bit
again. This time I ran some of the paper, cashed some of the checks
myself. I left Washington in a hurry, down through Virginia and
Louisiana and back to Texas, arriving with just $85. It was 1956. My
folks came home from church to find me on the doorstep.

I got a job as a truck-stop waitress and in comes this little French
Cajun guy, doesn't speak much English but a good dude. He tele-
grammed money to his folks. He was good to them, I figured he'd
be good to me. His name was Laurent Killy. I went with Killy in his
truck to California, and back in Dallas we got married. I'd known
him two weeks. I was twenty years old. He taught me to drive the
truck and he got me a job. We'd drive together on a convoy, double
the money. I drove the truck through forty-six states, until I was six
months pregnant with chronic kidney problems.

We lived in a duplex in Dallas, my parents on the other side. Killy
wasn't literate so I taught him how to write. He read comics, but I
think he just looked at the pictures. We were making good money,
so my mom and I would go shopping and have tea at the Neiman
Marcus Tea Room, with the style show and all that crap. And I got

ready for the baby. I made a hand-stitched lace christening dress because I'd promised his parents in Louisiana that I'd have the baby baptized Catholic.

The night I came home with baby Jacques, Killy forced me to bed with him. I was begging, "No, you can't do this." He didn't understand, and he got angry. I was fighting with him and he bopped me with a lamp and proceeded. When it was over, he sees all this blood, post-natal hemorrhage. It scared him so he called Pop from next door. Pop came and called the doctor and ordered Killy out of the house. My father knew what had happened.

When I got out of the hospital again, Killy had gone on another run, and I made sure I wasn't home when he came back. I went fishing with my parents and the baby. I left the door locked with his suitcase on the front step. The restraining order was in an envelope on top of the suitcase, and I right away started divorce proceedings. I didn't see him again. Jacques was home with me. When I found work at a laundry in Dallas, my mother would watch him during the day.

By age twenty-one Angelique had had two marriages and three children plus one miscarriage. She was unable to stick with the minimum-wage jobs that were available to her, but she tried. Apart from her double robbery, her crimes had not been lucrative. She played it safe when she forged cheques, never taking the risk of large amounts. Selling marijuana was for the most part a low-key operation. Ever the optimist, and despite her independence, she continued to watch for the white knight who would rescue her from a life unsuited to her age or creative intelligence.

I met Guy at the roller rink, and we were together all summer. He was stationed at the Abilene air force base and had a girlfriend there, but I didn't know that. When my divorce from Killy was final I married Guy. It was 1958. I was twenty-three and getting married for the third time. He was nine years older, seventeen years in the service, really stable. Here was security for me and Jacques, I thought. We moved onto the base, and for a while I just kicked back and played with the baby. On weekends we'd go fishing with Guy's buddies. Every night we'd have pinochle games at our house. His friends would even come over during the day when he was on duty, and he wasn't jealous. He didn't need to be, because he was making out with his girlfriend, Rosa. But I didn't know that.

I got pregnant again and came down with phlebitis, a blood clot in my leg, and I was hospitalized. They kept me in the hospital until delivery. While I was there, Guy went off with Rosa. When the baby was born he still didn't show up. I had complications, and when he finally came back I was still in the hospital. Kathleen looked just like Guy, square jaw, and he was tickled. He told me he ran off because he felt so guilty and couldn't handle it because I'd almost died.

Guy said he'd been cashing bum checks all the way to Salt Lake City. He got put in the brig for going AWOL and was threatened with dishonorable discharge. I went to the commander with Kathleen in my arms and Jacques by the hand. Guy had three children by a previous marriage, and his former wife was strict about child support. I told the commander, "I'm leaving this man. I'm not going to be with him anymore but he has this child to support and these other three children. I can work. But his first wife is going to bug him. Don't give him a dishonorable discharge." So Guy was discharged with an honorable with conditions, and I left the air force base behind.

Repeating her pattern, Angelique returned to Dallas where, again at the skating rink, she ran into an old school friend, Tom, who invited her to go and live with him in San Diego. So she did, leaving Jacques and Kathleen with her mother while she got resettled. Arriving in San Diego on New Year's Eve, Angelique right away slipped into her habits of petty crime.

This was the drug culture scene—the beginning of the hippies, all weed and pills. I started writing checks and somebody turned me in. That was my first bust, for forgery, first time in jail. It wasn't a frightening experience, just new. They had twenty-one counts on me and gave me three years' probation.

I didn't do that probation square and straight. I was smuggling most of the time. I'd gotten involved with the set that was selling weed. Butch was my partner, my connection, and I was doing some of his runs. I started getting hassled by the vice cop, who knew I was on probation, so I moved to Los Angeles. Butch had a connection with a dude whose legal front was managing apartments. In a bar I met a sax player who lived in one of them, and he said I could stay with him. I was accepted as a big dealer from San Diego, which I wasn't. I was a smuggler, which is bigger than a dealer. After a while I got pregnant by Greg, the sax player, and when I told him he said, "Out, out, out! None of this!" So I got my own apartment.

One day when I was about five months pregnant I stopped by a coffee house where this guy came over and said, "I know you," and I felt I knew him, too. But it must have been in another life. His name was Dave. He worked at the shipyards and lived with his folks. We spent the whole night talking, and the next day I picked him up after his shift. He wanted me to live with him, and I said, "What about the pregnancy?" He said he couldn't have children and "I want this one to be mine." I told him about the sax player, Greg, and how I got kicked out but wasn't heartbroken. Here I was, with another kid coming and no visible means of support, and here's this guy who wants a kid. So we got a pad in San Pedro close to the shipyards where he worked, and just moved in as having been married. It was his kid. Nobody knew different.

Birth control was not commonly available or legal during the 1950s and early 1960s. Given her active sex life and obvious fertility, it is not surprising that Angelique got pregnant so often. What surprised me was her cavalier separation from her children. They were cared for, she saw to that, but they weren't often with her, and yet they kept coming. I contemplated the harm that could come to them given her unstable and insecure life. However, this mad-scramble life was the only way Angelique knew how to live. In discussion about how the post-war ethos of the 1950s and 1960s severely constrained high-energy women, Anne Near raised

the question: "What is there in our morality, our religious institu-
tions and our culture that challenges someone to break with them
in order to be a creative, honest, vibrant, original, independent
woman, a woman who will not commit herself to poverty when
money can be had so easily another way?"

I met some people in L.A. who wanted to open a bookstore. They
had the capital but needed help getting started. I did a lot of
research, studying stock. I was also thinking about pottery. Since
childhood, off and on, I had worked with clay. In high school the
teacher taught me how to fire the kiln. From my weed thing I
had $220 to buy a kiln and some clay. I worked in the back room
of the bookstore.

My mother died in 1961, just before Melinda was born, my fifth
baby. I went to Dallas and brought Jacques and Kathleen home
with me. Dave quit his job at the shipyard and went full-time into
the ceramics thing with me. He was good, and I taught him the
whole business. He knew I didn't love him. I knew he loved me.
The whole thing was that he wanted kids and I needed help. It was
a healthy relationship. He wasn't jealous of other men who came
around. They were my dope partners, but he didn't know that.

I went out and bought a hearse, took out the track that the cof-
fin runs on and put in a floorboard, a 4' × 8' piece of plywood, three-
quarters of an inch thick. Underneath was a deep, hollow space.
I covered this with white velvet to match the white velvet curtains,
and then a heavy tarp. My connection in Mexico had a relative who
owned a clay pit. So I wrote a letter to him asking what he'd charge
for a ton of firebrick clay if I drove down and picked it up. Then I
got a bid for this clay for a local brick company at three times what
I'd have to pay for it. I took the quote and the bid to the probation
department, and they were happy to have made a businesswoman
out of me. I arranged for weekly trips to bring clay back to the
brick company.

Dave would keep the kids and I'd drive to Mexico, with all my
papers in order. In Tecate I gave my connection dry clay bags, which

he stuffed with weed and kegs of pills. I packed them in the bottom
compartment of the hearse, replaced the floor with its white velvet
carpet and the tarp. Then I drove to the Mexican cousin's place
and he put one ton of clay in bags on top of it all. Every week. All
the bags went to the ceramic shop in San Pedro. For a while we
lived upstairs, overlooking the harbor. Artists set up in our living
room, painting the view. Dave ran the ceramics business while I
and my partner, Stew, worked the weed. Dave never knew what
I was doing. He was a square, but we were friends, companions,
good buddies.

After my mother died, my father retired and came out to
California for a week. We were wide-open beatniks, but it worked
nicely. He stayed with the people who had the bookstore because
it was more respectable. A year later, 1962, he started losing interest in life, just going to my mother's grave every day. So I packed
up the three kids and Dave and a little dude named Ace, who had
just done a year at a prison ranch and now I was teaching him the
ceramics business. We all loaded up the hearse, pulled a trailer
behind us and headed for Texas. In Dallas we moved into the
duplex beside Pop. I had brought along twenty-five kilos of weed,
and I had a connection there. No one questioned me about where
I got the money. Dave was a carpenter and union man, so he got a
tract housing job.

*Both Ace and Dave decided to go back to California, leaving
Angelique with Jacques, Kathleen and Melinda. Meanwhile Guy,
Kathleen's father, reappeared. He was married but would visit
his daughter, and soon Kathleen wanted to live with her daddy.
Angelique took Melinda and Jacques back to San Pedro and got
an apartment with Dave and a drag queen who was their govern-
ess. She then lived for a time on the beach with other people in the
street drug trade, leading her to a serious narcotics habit. She also
got involved in a scam, using different post office box addresses to
order the free books and records offered to new members of book and
record clubs.*

I got strung out on opium. A friend had asked me to pick up a drop, a nice hefty package. The guy gave me $500. I didn't know what was in it, but a few days later he gave me a quarter pound of Hong Kong opium. It got so I'd get sick if I didn't smoke it every day. Then I came down with hepatitis, and for the first time I had to have my children placed with welfare. I explained everything to the children, and when welfare came to pick them up they were clean and well mannered. This was the summer of 1964. I was in isolation for two months. And meanwhile I'd been charged with twenty-one counts of intent to defraud the book and record companies, which was a federal case.

While I was waiting for the case to end, Dave divorced me and married someone else, so I moved in with a friend who'd been visiting, Harmony. I'd kicked the opium in the hospital. I would never use it again. It's too good, so it's addictive. The mail fraud case kept getting postponed. Finally I was sentenced to Terminal Island, federal women's prison in northern California, at first for a ninety-day observation period.

After several years of illegal activity, Angelique finally went to prison, where she spent 18 months in federal custody. Like many women in prison, she had a long rap sheet, and it was the frequency of her offences, not their seriousness, that sent her to prison. She thrived there.

Terminal Island wasn't horrifying. I smoked weed when I could get it, and worked, and acted like a society club woman. I was an officer in AA, even though I have no experience as an alcoholic. I was president of the Bible Study class, which was a social function. I would bring Kahlil Gibran and read that. I sang in both choirs, first with the Catholics, then I'd go out and smoke a joint if anybody had any weed and come back and sing with the Protestants. It wasn't hard time for me at all.

Harmony kept coming to visit me in prison, but I made the decision to cut him loose and not mess up his life. Now I would be an

ex-con, and I felt he deserved better than that. He never did anything wrong in the world. He worked at the hospital, in a good position. It blows my mind to find people who are square but who are
really with it. They're not square, not really. We need another category. When I let Harmony go I did something worthwhile, one of
the few times in my life. That was my last experience with anyone
with any semblance of squareness.

*Angelique was released in 1965, after eighteen months, and she went
back south to L.A. and the Venice beach. For several months she
lived with a new boyfriend, Renaldo, until she was arrested for possession of marijuana.*

It was just half a joint, and it was under the floor mat of the car. But
the police were gaming for me. I was on parole. Renaldo and I had
been burglarizing office machines. In fact, I had bought the car
with two IBM typewriters and an Olivetti adding machine. I had
the pink slip in my name, a red Thunderbird. Renaldo is very black.
The police pulled us over and asked me, "What are you doing with
that nigger?" I said, "That nigger happens to be my husband." They
didn't like that, so they tore up the car and came up with somebody
else's old half joint. Here I go again, losing in somebody else's game.
But if I ever got busted for all the things I actually do, I would never
be out to get busted for the things I don't do.

This time I did a year in Sybil Brand, L.A., county jail, for
possession. It was really ugly. But again I was lucky. I ran the kilns
in the ceramic shop, lead girl out there. I made more money for them
than they had made in any four-month period since the ceramic shop
had opened. I knew the business. I'm good. At ceramics, I'm good.

*Released in late 1966, Angelique went to live with Renaldo's friend
Redfearn. Renaldo was now in prison for armed robbery of a Safeway store. Redfearn was a mason, and on the side sold marijuana
and pills. Undeterred by her prison experience, Angelique was
by then thoroughly enmeshed in "the life," and she took over the*

"weed business." For lack of apparent alternatives, she had become a confirmed outlaw, her illegal activities supporting her creative endeavours.

Mostly I stayed home and played with clay. I was like "Mrs. Redfearn." He was in the process of getting a divorce. I made him a gorgeous chess set with knights on motorcycles, queens in miniskirts, and pawns in the lotus position holding a joint. I also learned to play bass guitar, and I had dubs made of Redfearn singing with a band.

The police had been watching the traffic on our street. They got the places mixed up and kicked down the door across the hall from us; it turned out to be a bookie. Close call. So Redfearn kept his place but I moved to a little apartment in a well-off part of town. Traffic was heavy there, too. I was making $400 on weekdays, $1,000 a day on the weekends.

No surprise, I found out I was pregnant. Redfearn was really pleased, but what he said was, "I can't marry you yet; my divorce isn't final." I say, "So who in the hell wants to get married?"

For many months into her pregnancy, Angelique continued to sell drugs and to leap into new relationships. As she recited the catastrophes, one after another, and the endless hustle to feed the purse, I marvelled at her nonchalance about a lifestyle that law-abiding people abhor but was perfectly normal for her circle of high-energy people who couldn't be contained in a routine life. One of her pill customers, Phil, who she said was a "big shot, a fancy dude," had a place close to Beverly Hills, and when he invited her to move there she did, platonically. She and Redfearn meanwhile continued their relationship.

Phil and I stole a car and it turned out it was already stolen. I was on my way to the laundromat. Busted! A stolen car, and a hypodermic outfit in the glove compartment. It was Phil's, and he had the prescription for it, some legitimate problem. Of course the L.A. police were already angry at me. They wanted Redfearn and told me that if I didn't tell them where he was they'd testify that the syringe was in my purse. I wouldn't tell so they took me in.

In court they got me on grand theft for the auto and meanwhile sent me to Sybil Brand for ninety days for possession of an outfit. It was hard, because I wasn't well, skinny and really pregnant. Again I worked in the ceramics shop, through the Christmas rush, and it was very hard. They knew from before that I wasn't a troublemaker. I just went along with them and then did what I wanted to do.

I was released after the ninety days, near the holiday, and went to Redfearn's place, but he was now in prison so I went back to Phil's. I began writing prescriptions for methadrine and speed. Other people would cash them. I had four different doctors' prescription pads, and eight drugstores. All these doctors were writing for jugs of speed for addicts, so they weren't going to blow it.

I went to see Redfearn in prison on Christmas Day. After being locked up I had nothing, pregnant with not a diaper for my baby and no money to buy one. In the next seven days I pulled seven burglaries, one in a doctor's office. I was busted again in a week, but not for the burglaries. I was in a bank cashing a bad check. I bailed out, came to Phil's, and started labor. Buffy was born on the morning I was supposed to go to court. They gave me a month's postponement. Buffy had lots of problems and was taken immediately to Children's Hospital, to the intensive care unit. I could only see him ten minutes every hour.

Usually, when Angelique spoke of her children, she was brief and self-controlled, avoiding becoming emotional or saying anything that would betray her vulnerability to others' judgement. Starting at age sixteen, by age thirty-one she had given birth to six living children: Ellen, Sonny, Jacques, Kathleen, Melinda and Buffy. She suffered one miscarriage. She was officially married to three of the five fathers of her children, Rafael, Killy and Guy, and she married

Dave, who raised Greg's baby. All of her children except the baby now lived either with their fathers or with other family members. Redfearn was also prepared to marry her, but he was in prison. Just as she had taken up with Redfearn when his friend (her then-boyfriend) went to prison, so did she now, with Redfearn's blessing, take up with his good friend Prentice.

In 1967, following her release from Sybil Brand on the syringe charge and the birth of Buffy, Angelique was still out on bail on the cheque-cashing charge. She was a good forger. Even when the police caught up with her, with eyewitnesses, they knew from experience that the handwriting experts in the state capital, Sacramento, would not issue a positive ID on the signature. This irritated the police, so they were digging for other potential charges against her. She pleaded guilty to one count of mail fraud, for the book and record club scam, hoping to placate the police.

But then I got a second count of receiving stolen property, and there was no way out of that because the check was in my possession. Prentice was busy trying to take care of Redfearn's business, and I taught him everything so he could take care of it when I went back to prison. When he asked me to be his old lady, I knew I needed someone for moral support and I said okay. Didn't last long.

Buffy came home with me for a while and then was back in the hospital, back with me, then back in. He had two operations before he was fifteen days old, ruptured intestines. When I told the doctors I was going to the penitentiary, social services had me sign papers. I gave the foster home legal guardianship so they wouldn't have to contact me in an emergency—they could sign for it.

Buffy's still with that family. They're good people and have a beautiful home with eight children in it. Every one has come from parole or probation from juvenile hall, or from parents in prison. All the kids have pictures of their parents. It's a healthy situation, and I'm really pleased about it. They have a good social worker.

It's been just over four years since I first arrived here at CIW [California Institution for Women]. No matter what, I don't do hard time. We were allowed two or three of our own outfits but I didn't have any clothes so I wore state issue. My old boyfriend Renaldo and I had been writing for a few years, he from the joint after his armed robbery. So I listed him as my common-law husband. I didn't have a runner [an outsider who helps with supplies] or a visitor. All my mail came from Renaldo, nothing from outside. We wrote constantly and planned to get married. Those were my parole plans and they'd been approved by my parole agent. But when I went before the parole board for a date they said a condition for release on parole would be that Renaldo and I could not associate with each other.

The board also said I couldn't see my children for two years. The board chairperson, a woman, told me that she didn't think criminals ought to have children, they were just populating the jails of the future. They gave me a parole date after saying all this. I got out with very conflicted feelings. I wrote checks, five of them, and bought a car. I quit writing checks. I got a job in a ceramics shop. I got an apartment.

Renaldo's appeal came through, and I testified that he was under the influence of LSD when he did the armed robbery and that I had turned him on to it and it was all my fault. Renaldo's ex-wife was in the courtroom. When the lawyer brought him to the rail, he told me that when the board said we couldn't associate with each other, he told them he was going back to Janet, his ex-wife. I felt desolate, very hurt, depressed. The bottom had dropped out. I couldn't see my kids, my boyfriend was out of the picture. I went to see Sam, an old friend, and fixed. Heroin. I moved in with him. I didn't have anybody else in the world. He was dealing. I got righteously hooked but maintained my job. Every time the parole agent would call and tell me to go for a naline test, I'd go straight to the coke man's house, get me some cocaine, fix it, go in for my naline test, pass it, come back out, and fix heroin again. Cocaine cleans out your system. I passed naline for three months that way.

Then one afternoon I was with my friend Carlos, who's black. He's driving. I had on a dark natural wig, and Carlos, almost as light as I am, also had a natural. The pigs pulled up. "What are you niggers doin' in this neighborhood?" "We came to see a friend." "Who?" We sure weren't about to tell them, so they ran us in for suspicion of burglary.

The second day in jail I'm kicking, a dealer's habit. The detective came in and said, "Your partner's kicking. How are you feeling?" I was so sick I couldn't act like I wasn't. So I got charged with being under the influence of heroin, to which I pled guilty and got ninety days in Sybil Brand. My agent came to tell me I'd be released for the holiday, as usual, and that on Christmas Eve I'd be going to a half-way house. The twenty-fourth arrived, and they hand me a bag and put me on the bus. Merry fucking Christmas, Angelique! I'm back in state prison on a straight parole violation.

When Angelique recovered from a difficult period of withdrawal from heroin, she was demoralized. The absence of her children from her life was hitting her. She told a guard in her unit that she didn't want to go to her parole hearing and listen to the board members express their contempt for her.

They couldn't talk to me any worse than I was talking to myself. But I did have to go before the board to answer for my violation. That was when a board member started in on me about my IQ. The prison tested everybody when they were admitted, IQ and other tests, personality questionnaires and such. I asked him why that was important, and he said, "Because your IQ is higher than mine and I'm sitting here in judgment on your freedom." He said he thought I had the makings of a good citizen and that, despite everything everyone said, I could fit into society out there. It blew my mind.

They gave me a job in the Psychiatric Treatment Unit, where I found a good counselor. Physical restrictions in the prison had loosened up. You could wear your own clothes, but no pants were allowed. No telephone privileges. The most amazing thing was when the whole cast of *Hair* came in. My counselor's interest in me helped me change my self-image, so I could think of going to college. He worked with me for three months. Before that I didn't have that image of myself. I hadn't been to school for many years. He saw that I didn't think I was worthy. Thanks to him, when I got out I completed almost two semesters of college.

I also really respected the MD psychiatrist. Because of him they did the surgery to remove my deformities. They fixed my nose, too. It was a major turn-around in my life. I always knew that with proper makeup I could be attractive. But I also knew it didn't matter, because I had a personality. I only worried about my appearance when I was interested in a guy, but I hadn't had trouble attracting men. After the surgery I was more appearance-conscious, not liking being flat-chested or not as pretty as other girls, but knowing I looked better than a lot of them. Physical changes were icing on the cake, but not necessary. It was what happened in my head. I left prison with a positive self-image, first time ever.

The counselor told me about an education clearinghouse in East L.A., so as soon as I got out I went there. They talked to me and then called someone at Pasadena College. I got a minority grant. When they asked me what minority I represented I said "female ex-con," and they did everything they could to get me that grant.

School was the best. I went through that semester with a 3.5 grade point average. One of my psychology professors hired me, at about $2 an hour. I started recording grades for her and whatever would help. She introduced me as her teaching assistant, which made them figure I was a graduate student. She took me with her to a professional meeting at a big hotel. I feared that if these people knew who I was they wouldn't let me be there. But they accepted me. Have you ever seen a bunch of psychs? They're nuts. I felt right at home.

While Angelique's life was changing in very positive ways, she ran into an old friend, Pike. They moved into a room together, then an apartment. It was not romantic, just "a very caring situation." While studying at Pasadena she also spent time in Venice, with her friends there.

Well, I made it as a college student for nearly two semesters. Then I got busted in Venice by my personal pig, he said for being under the influence. It was bogus. It was two weeks before final exams, spring 1971. I was brought back to prison for violation of my parole. This was a wrong done to me, in an ugly manner, and it messed up my education.

The parole board said they didn't want to hear anything more about education, so that summer I went to work in the sewing industry. I took the Vocational Rehabilitation program, which was a farce because I already had the skills. But I got the piece of paper that says I can do what I've been doing since I was twelve, which is sew.

I got out of prison just before the start of the fall semester. My professor couldn't work with me anymore. She felt I'd let her down and that she'd let me down, which she hadn't. But I started school again, with no job, no grant, no place to live, $68 in my pocket. I got the idea to be square, but it didn't last long. I got a little apartment, some groceries, and went to school. When it came time for rent I didn't have it. A dude I knew offered me these credit cards, and I got an ounce of speed to sell. All my busts have to do with needing money. This time it didn't work and I'm back in prison, doing county time for the credit cards to run concurrently with my parole violation for the dope.

I still hope to go to college and study design pattern drafting. What I really want is to study psychology. I want to be stable enough to get my gold seal [that is, no longer accountable to the board of parole]. I want to be stable enough to have my kids with me.

Just this month, I was so tired, teaching pattern design two nights a week, going to your class two nights a week, plus working all day. My father is dying, and I was pressured into signing away rights to my kids, but they promise it's just until I'm out. There's a lot of trouble here, a lot of tension. I don't get off on anyone else's business. Occasionally I sit out on the lawn with my few really close friends before we eat, but mostly, when I'm not working, I do my time in my room. I enjoy my own company. I don't get bored with me. I have a runner and she's good to me. She sent me the striped pants, maroon shirt and tank tops I wear. She sent me yarn and I made a poncho for her and a sweater for her roommate. I have a good job in pattern designing and helping with the teaching, so I make about $30 a month.

Where you're headed is more or less predictable from where you've been, unless you go off on a tangent. In the early beatnik days I ran into Zen and the Book of Changes, the I Ching. I've adopted it as my bible. In my room I write or make something. I read a lot and study Buddhist philosophy. It helps with the problems, and I have a lot of them. I believe in peace and love. I believe in the influences and changes that happen in a given moment, the decisions you make from day to day, through which you direct your life. I'll be here another year. I wonder if I'll ever have a normal life. What's normal?

Reflections

For all her cheerfulness, Angelique suffered. Many people behind bars do hard time, suffering with each slowly passing moment of confinement. Angelique's winning card was her resilience. Her life on the outside was a steady chase, a chaotic scenario of squares versus outlaws. Circumstance and impulse led her to the side of the rebels. She was resourceful. She rolled with the punches and only rarely got the blues. She did feel guilt about her children, but she avoided self-pity by helping other people. The following story told me a lot about her generosity.

The youngest woman then in the state prison was a seventeen-year-old girl, Laura, who had been convicted of killing two children while they were in her care. The parents arrived home to find them suffocated, with the babysitter crouched in a closet in a catatonic state. Laura was assigned to the same housing unit as Angelique, who expressed considerable concern about her. In the year Laura had been imprisoned she had never spoken to anyone, and she seemed uncomprehending when anyone tried to engage her in conversation. When I asked the administration why she wasn't receiving some kind of treatment, they acknowledged that she was withdrawn but said that they weren't set up to help with her problem. Since Laura had shown no further inclination toward violence, they just left her alone. Normally, women convicted of harming children were not welcomed by the others. But Laura was very young, obviously ill, and she had to live with having committed a heinous deed. She aroused the other women's maternal and compassionate impulses, even though she didn't respond to them. The one person to whom she did respond was Angelique, who was very protective of her.

It was Angelique's idea to take Laura to occupational therapy, which became a ritual. One day Laura drew a picture of a tiny, semi-human figure. Angelique asked her who it was, and for the first time Laura spoke; she said his name was "Marty." Angelique asked Laura, "Does he speak to you?" "Yeah," said Laura, "I talk to him, too." At which Laura went back into her shell, sad-faced.

Angelique drew Marty's image on a piece of wood and carved a figure of him, using coloured stone for his eyes and pieces of wire for his antennae. She wore him around her neck and explained to everyone that he was Laura's friend. They understood, and as the months passed, Marty became a fixed character in the life of the cell unit. Gradually Laura began to speak, and then she began to make sense. She never did speak to anyone of her crime, and may not have had any memory of it. But thanks to Angelique's ingenuity, she regained her ability to relate to other human beings.

I WAS AT PEACE sitting with Angelique in her 6′ × 9′ cell, rainbows from her crystals dancing across the wall, across the shadows of the bars on her windows. It created the illusion that her space was larger than it was. When I sat with her in that life-affirming little place, I could almost forget that we were in a prison, that she could not leave. Almost. On that subject, she wrote the following poem.

ALLEGORY

Having tried all night to write the poem
I felt was in my fingertips
I cut off my hand and gave it a pen
To write psalms of its own independence.

But severed from that which had given it life
It wrote only of sorrow and sadness.
For alone and cut off from all that it loves
Even freedom was empty and pointless.
It implored its return to that which it needs
To give meaning to its own existence.

. . .

Realizing the pain I unintentionally caused
I restored it at once to the wrist whence it came.
And it gratefully picked up the pen and wrote songs
Of sailing ships and strange new lands and sunshine
and flowers and things.

3

L I A

WHEN WELFARE ISN'T ENOUGH

A TALL, STATELY AFRICAN-AMERICAN woman, the mother of two daughters, Lia had been convicted of welfare fraud. She was self-educated and intellectually oriented, but, like most prisoners, she was formally undereducated. On average, imprisoned women have completed just over grade eight, with 20 per cent having completed high school. Most have worked at minimum-wage jobs. Single mothers choose between the degradation of a demeaning and poorly paid job and the degradation of the welfare system, which likewise does not provide a livable income.

The first part of Lia's story is transcribed from a taped interview with her in prison in 1973.

Lia's Story

My earliest remembrance is from about 1955, when I was about five years old, in a house with my father and the person I thought was my mother but found out later was my stepmother. Her name was Alice. There were no other black people in our neighborhood. My father was the manager of a Safeway and Alice was a registered nurse. In those days, Daddy used to buy a Cadillac every year, so I guess I was a middle-class child for a while. The house we lived in was a corner property, and Daddy had a fence put up around it, a big, wood-frame, two-story house, yellow shutters, four bedrooms, a basement apartment, a lot of property around it and a great big pine tree. I played under the tree with my dolls and made believe I was a princess.

My father and Alice quarreled quite a bit, and one of these quarrels resulted in me and my dad moving to live with my grandmother, her three brothers, two [of their] wives, and their eight children, including baby twins, in Jamaica, Queens, two stories and an attic. Periodically Daddy would change girlfriends, and, at one time, Jessie was staying with us with her six kids. So we almost always had a pretty full house. I would hear my people quarreling. Like my uncle and my grandma would be fighting about something, and they'd be saying bad things about my father. I'd always stick up for my father. I didn't know what was going on. I had a dog, a black cocker spaniel. I was always a misunderstood child, and I could always talk to my dog if I couldn't talk to anyone else.

I was unhappy living with all the people in Queens, over in Jamaica with my grandmother. When I lived with my dad and Alice we had a beautiful house and everything was clean. I was an only child, the center of attention, and Alice called me her Precious. I remember how good it made me feel, when I thought she was my mother. I was secure, going to a Catholic school, where the local cop on the beat helped us cross the street. I went to Sunday school at a majestic church. It was all good.

When I moved to Jamaica with my grandmother, it was me versus all those kids, in a predominantly black neighborhood. The kids were rough and they picked on me because I talked funny, and they said I was white because of it, and they called me "slanty-eyed Chinese." I was just a child. I constantly tried to run away. Once I managed to catch the bus and get all the way back to where Alice was living. I loved Alice, and I thought everything would be all right if I could just get back home to her, because she's my mama. And I got there. I was only about six or seven years old and the trip involved a couple of changes of buses, but I got there.

And so I was there, and I told Alice how unhappy I was, and that I wanted to stay with her, and we could get back together with Daddy. She told me to stay downstairs while she went upstairs to do something. I got bored so I did walk upstairs, quietly, and I heard her on the phone telling my dad to "come get this brat. This fucking kid has no business in this house." I couldn't understand. I went back downstairs. I didn't understand it at all. Not at all. When I was returned home, Daddy finally told me, "Hey," you know, "Alice ain't your mother." Later, one day Alice called and asked to talk to me, and Daddy says, "That ain't your mother." And I said, "Mommy, Daddy says I can't talk to you anymore, because you're not my mama." Daddy used me against her, and I didn't understand any of this.

Most of the time during those years Daddy was out working, so I never saw him. All the disciplining came from my Auntie Virginia and especially my Uncle Herman, who was really, really mean to me. I felt that he hated me. One time he kicked my dog down the stairs and I screamed at him to stop and I started hitting him. I got a good ass-cutting for that. My cousin took me under her wing, kind of, but she still gave me hell. Everybody would give me hell and I didn't even get along with the other kids. The next-door neighbors would pick on me and call me a crybaby and wouldn't let me play their games. So I said, "Fuck it," and just like that I started reading. I got into being a real bookworm.

And then we had a fire. The kids started the fire in the attic. The twin girls were up there, and they died, just two years old at the time. I just really fell apart. I couldn't understand it. First my Aunt Sarah had died giving birth to the twins, two years before that. Now the twins were gone. And it was only the week after that that my uncle was found murdered in the back of his car. I just couldn't understand any of it.

The neighbors were wonderful, one or another took all of us kids, and took good care of us until the house was kind of rebuilt and we moved back in for a while. Then we moved to the Bedford-Stuyvesant area in Brooklyn, a pretty rough area at the time but we found this great big brownstone. There were three stories, and we had the first two, with three bathrooms, and there was room for everybody for a change.

I was going to junior high school but I didn't get along very well there, either. There were a lot of tensions and frictions. One time in particular I knew Daddy had to come up to school, and I was really scared about that. What happened was that I was sitting in class, bent out of shape in the desk, because I've always been tall for my age. I was just sitting there minding my own business, as always. This girl took my book and threw it at a boy and he threw it back at her. I said, "Okay, that's enough. Let me have my book back," and she threw it in my face. When we got out of class, somebody pushed me into her, and all the frustration I felt I took out on her. I had one friend, and it was just me and her against everybody. I had a big bite on my face but I know I won the fight. My father was upset. That was Brooklyn.

When I was thirteen, I left home and stayed with different people in Greenwich Village. My Puerto Rican friend was a groupie, and we went to all the clubs and got to know a lot of musicians. We knew the Lovin' Spoonful when they just started out. At the same time, I started going round to NYU and talking to college students. They accepted me, taught me how to play chess, and we'd sit around and have intellectual discussions. I felt very grown-up. I wasn't living anywhere in particular, and looking back it's difficult to understand how I survived. I was still a virgin until I was sixteen, trying to be Daddy's girl, a good girl. I wasn't screwing, because good girls don't do that. And I wouldn't smoke dope, because good girls don't do that.

Periodically Daddy would have a new girlfriend. There was Sylvia; I really liked her. Sylvia and Daddy for some reason couldn't make it, and it was the same way with Ethel. I really liked her; she had a lot of style. And then Anna; I didn't like Anna at all. She kept the filthiest house, and she was ... she just seemed stupid to me. But it turned out that her baby sons, they were about four years old at the time, were Daddy's kids. So somewhere, aside from the five brothers and/or sisters recorded on my birth certificate that my mother had before me, I've got a pair of twin baby brothers, half-brothers running around somewhere out there. I already said how I thought Alice was my mother, but that it didn't work. Then there was Janie, me and her kids didn't get along, we fought. When we were living in Queens, Daddy owned his own cab service. Sometimes it went well, sometimes it didn't. For a time I lived right around the corner with Janie. I had a fight with her son, and he broke the TV, and I busted him in the face or something. I was upset, and I went to my father crying, and I says, "Well, Daddy, look, I tried to come home, I really tried to come home but I know you don't want me." And I turned around and left. And Daddy let me leave.

And so I went back to the Village, just hanging out and waitressing at little coffee houses, storefront-type places where we'd put rum or brandy flavoring in the coffee, and they'd have dancers. I would sit on a stool, they'd play the records, and I would dance while I was sitting down. And that was the entertainment. Sometimes they would have a poetry reading, or someone who could play an instrument. But most of the time it was just me dancing. And I got paid $3 a night for that plus tips. My hotel room, what I got most of the time, was $3.15. I was friends with the guy who was the night clerk and he'd give me a room for free if I didn't have the money, or give me a reduced rate so I could stay there. I met all kinds of people, like Bob Dylan. And then I started hanging out at Hullabaloo. I knew Jimmy James and the Blue Flames, who was later to be Jimi Hendrix, and Richard Pryor, before he was famous. I was coming into the Village at the beginning of the end of the beatnik era, with LSD to transmit the beatniks into hippies. A couple of months earlier I'd started smoking weed, and I had a good LSD trip.

I had friends who squatted in buildings that were condemned. There were not even doors on some of the apartments. We'd stay there anyway, a place to crash. We'd take our blankets and go up on the roof at night when it was really hot, a lot of really laid-back people. But in the midst of all that good feeling, I got raped. I insulted a man and he raped me, a fork at my throat. That's the only time I've ever been raped and I was very sick from it.

Then I got mixed up with a guy involved in drug deals. He protected me. I stayed with him two months, partying. We listened to the Who and Pink Floyd, and smoked hash chunks with this monstrous water pipe. I cooked for us sometimes, but then it was time for me to move on and do something different. So I did. I moved on to alcohol. It was about getting drunk. I'd get a thirty-nine-cent bottle of Ripple and chug it. I had this white friend, blond-haired woman. I didn't know she was a prostitute. We had fun. Like one night we were partying and at four in the morning we caught up with the guy who delivers the milk. We went on the rounds with him and helped him deliver the milk to all the apartments in his area of the Village in New York. It was really fun.

I loved being a hippie, so open and free. People were really trying to communicate. The drugs were flowing, the vibes were flowing, and Nina Simone was playing on the jukebox. I'd go over to the East Side to this disco where they had beer for twenty-five cents. We'd dance all night, bodies against bodies. New Yorkers dance very deeply and intensely, nobody stepping on toes, 'cause we were all cool and knew how to move. It was a beautiful time in my life, even though it was stressful trying to survive and have a place to sleep.

I was fifteen now. I still kept in touch with my family and called my father once in a while to let him know what was happening. By that time Daddy was living with Bernice, and she and I damn sure didn't get along, but he's still together with her today. And then finally I went home and was there for at least a month when I met a friend of a friend of a friend who was driving his van to California. I told Bernice I was going and she told me, "You ain't goin' nowhere till you ask your dad." Daddy happened to call, so I got on the phone and told him what was happening, and how much I wanted to go. He just said, "Well, listen, you take care of yourself and keep in touch." I felt like he really understood. So when Steve came in his van the next day to pick me up, I just grabbed my stuff and left. I had $5 and a suitcase. It was 1966, and I was California-bound.

California was a major turning point for me. By that time I was overweight and I had a natural [Afro]. I'd been burned out disco-ing, and burned out from hanging out. I wanted something different. We stopped first in San Francisco, in the heart of the Haight-Ashbury. We dropped acid with some people we met, and I had the most intense, incredibly spiritual trip of my life. Then we headed for Los Angeles, where we stayed with people Steve knew on the Sunset Strip, which was still the place of drugs and street people. And I was hardcore street people.

Once again I started following musicians and I started singing, got to do some background vocals with Buddy Miles and other people. I was a regular at the Whisky a Go-Go. I got to attend recording sessions, like with Buffalo Springfield. I joined "Vito's Freaks," a little show he took around. I knew Frank Zappa, Joe Crocker and James Cotton, and toured with each of them for a quick minute. I met Leon Russell. Those were exciting years, being part of that culture, with the "in" crowd. At the time, Jimmy Messina was a sound engineer and he and I were friends. Same with Stephen Stills before Crosby Stills Nash & Young. I'd go with people to Peter Tork's house. I'd met him years before, but now he was successful with the Monkees. We'd go in his sauna and his swimming pool, eat health food and lie naked in the sun, a good way to spend youth. I was flowing, but I never had an anchor.

Of course I had all kinds of problems, and I always blamed myself. I didn't understand racism, how it acts on people. I felt that things that were happening to me were personal rejection. I thought people who snubbed me just needed to get to know me. I thought maybe they had some kind of hang-up. But they just didn't want blacks around. In retrospect it's real clear. People would seem to accept me for the most part, but then if someone had a wedding or something, I wouldn't be invited. It was painful.

I started changing, getting older, and I moved up north to Marin County. There I got pregnant, had the baby by myself. I had been going to Lamaze classes with my friend Leo, who was play-acting as the daddy to help me through it. But by the time he got to the hospital I had already had Columbine. I did have a lot of supportive people around me right at that period. It was really beautiful. My girlfriend gave me a shower. I felt so warm, so good, so positive. The people I lived with moved away, which led me to Sonoma County. Columbine and I lived in Glen Ellen for about six months with an older woman from Rotterdam and her five children. They looked like the Dutch Masters' paintings, skin so white and clear, with roses in their cheeks.

Then we moved to Mendocino County and lived in a cabin in the woods. We had to hitchhike into town, but a lot of people did that. There was no indoor plumbing, or heat except in a pot-bellied stove. I ground my coffee fresh every morning and hauled water from the creek in the back. And used the outhouse. We were there through the winter months, hitchhiking from San Francisco with groceries. It was another beautiful time in my life. I'd wake up in the morning, and there'd be rainbows around the room from the crystals hanging in my window where we slept in the loft. There'd be deer in the woods, and it was quiet all around, very peaceful. I would sometimes just look out the window, crochet and knit, and feel very content.

Soon I had a boyfriend, Steve, and we got married. This was the beginning of me trying to "square up," getting more conservative and bourgeois in my tastes. Columbine was maybe a year old. Steve and I didn't get along very well, but we decided to have a baby, thinking maybe that would help. I knew it was time for me to straighten up. I had dropped out of city life and living in the country was really beautiful, but it was time to drop back in, and it was important to have enough money. We had a really beautiful two-bedroom apartment with a terrace and a panoramic view. We rented furniture and my father-in-law co-signed for a car for us. Our apartment complex had two swimming pools and a game room with a billiard parlor.

We had it so good, but we were fighting pretty regular. I was enrolled in Chabot Junior College, so I could advance myself and we could get ahead. He wanted me to bring in more money, but he couldn't keep a job himself. And he goes off on this whole trip about women's work, and exactly how he wants the house to look. It was a huge fight. Also, the welfare people were hassling us and we were going to have to move anyway. It was the beginning of the end. I was pregnant. My husband would get feisty with me, and he's about six foot two and strapping. His fist is like one and a half of mine. I was thinking about leaving, and thinking about not having the baby.

My family disintegrated mainly because of our financial situation. Steve tried many jobs but he could never manage to bring home enough money to take care of us, and he depended on me. We'd fight about why he didn't make more money, or why I couldn't make it stretch further. Finally he just deserted us.

At first I felt lucky to be getting welfare—just to know there would be a regular amount coming in. But nothing had really changed. Columbine needed new shoes, one thing or another, and they raised my rent but didn't raise my allotment, and I was desperate. And I really wanted to go to school, to gain a marketable skill. I went to another county and signed up for welfare using a friend's address, now collecting two checks. I knew it was against the law and I didn't care. For the first time since Columbine was born we still had some food in the cupboards at the end of the month.

My husband came back, and I was glad to see him. He was still having the same old hassle finding jobs, and mostly we just lived on my welfare scam, which with two checks brought in over $500 a month. And then I went to a third county. We got away with it for almost eighteen months, but when they caught me they came down hard. They didn't ask why it happened. They indicted my husband on the same charge, but for his punishment they sent him off to join the army. As far as I'm concerned we were both guilty, but he got the military and I got state prison. Now the army is supporting our kids. From one government check—well, three—to another.

In the spring of 1980 I was assigned to teach a course at the University of California at Santa Cruz on "Feminism in the '70s," and there in my class was Lia. The following is excerpted from a letter I wrote on April 6, 1980, to Anne Near:

> It was a wonderful surprise to walk into the classroom and find Lia sitting in the front row. She was in our class at the California Institution for Women in 1972. Now she's a junior at UCSC, living on campus with her two little girls. She's now twenty-nine, very tall, elegant, feeling slightly displaced as a black woman who never before lived away from her own people, including in prison, and now she's smack dab in the middle of young white kids from Beverly Hills.

I told Lia about the interviews Anne and I were putting together, and she wanted her story to be included. In particular she wanted to speak with candour about her experiences with "the system." She wrote the following account in 1981.

In 1972 I became a prisoner. It was in a prison that my second child was born. I was arrested during my third month of pregnancy, when I still believed in the "Just Us" system. It was my first offense, and I expected leniency and understanding from the courts. I believed that if I were truthful everything would work out all right. My experience was about being female in the most fundamental sense, about being Black and poor, and about the conflict between my expectations and what happens in the real world.

Although I committed welfare fraud, I didn't see the commonality I shared with other poor women of color until much later in my life. I was poor but I didn't see myself that way. I humiliated myself with welfare people and a psychiatrist to get Aid to the

Totally Disabled. I hated the groveling and tears required to earn my aid and transcend bureaucratic indifference and intransigence; however, inside I felt I was striking a blow against the system. For everybody on crutches, or despondent, or old and ill, my fraud was the little people winning—a minor atonement for what we all had to submit to. Because I was cheating, if one of my checks were late, my life would only be disturbed, not completely disrupted like the others.

We all stayed in sweaty, filthy offices all day as they processed us. We stood in one line after another, taking insults and condescension, carrying babies, hungry and tired while the media and politicians portrayed us as indolent and parasitic. We raised our families on pittances—$280 a month for a family of three at that time, when our rents were three-quarters of our checks. We were uneducated, inarticulate, Black, Brown, White or Asian, spiritually decimated and broken. We had no political or any other kind of power.

I made the decision to fraud when I decided that I wanted to go to school and learn a skill. We couldn't live on the one welfare check, and I needed extra money for school, babysitters and transportation. Two checks didn't make it, so I went for a third. I was pretty much the sole support of the family. I had planned to continue the fraud only until I graduated from the college, after which I expected to qualify for a good job. I had never even attended high school, because I had run away when I was thirteen. However, I was self-educated because I loved to read.

Going to college was my dream, and my ticket to legitimacy and the good life. I recognized that I was living on the margins of society, but I never did consider myself a criminal. My definition of criminal required a human victim, and the state was not that. I knew that taxpayers would never get a reduction in taxes on the basis of the state not meeting human needs, because the connection is political, not economic. Minimal tax funds are allocated for human services.

I was twenty-two when I was busted in Marin County for welfare fraud. It was like in the movies, the way I was captured. The welfare department called me in to discuss some papers as a ruse to facilitate my arrest. The all-afternoon wait in the welfare office had me there past closing time, so I was the last "client" to leave. When I walked through the door, a woman came up to me and asked if I was me. I tried to tell them I was someone else and they were making a mistake. My husband was asleep in the car with the baby, waiting for me. The baby was standing at the window watching what happened. She started screaming when the police came over and woke up my husband to let him know where they were taking me. He got out of the car looking bewildered and disheveled, the baby screaming. It would be more than four years from that day before Columbine and I were reunited, but I didn't know that then.

At the time, I was more embarrassed than afraid, because I didn't believe anything bad would happen to me. But those first days were monstrous. I'd never been incarcerated before, and the conditions in the jail were horrible. They gave me a complete body search, which was mortifying, then put me in a cell with five other women. We ate together, slept together, and there was no shower curtain or door for the privy. We were together twenty-four hours a day, from October 1972 until March 1973. For fresh air we were let out to the yard once weekly for an hour.

The yard was like a concrete box, four concrete walls with a net across the top between us and the sky. During the winter months we weren't allowed even that; the county wouldn't provide coats. The cells were constrictive, six bunks in each, four on one wall and two on the other. The beds were attached to the walls, which were concrete, as were the ceiling and floor. One wall was just bars. One woman wouldn't bathe, so even the air was foul.

I was confused and depressed with nowhere to turn. There were confrontations with the jailers every day over the petty rules. Surprisingly, and most comforting to me, I got along fine with the other prisoners, but I couldn't understand the police [guards]. I expected them to be human in spite of the circumstances. This was a bad time. There I was in jail and my husband, who had the same charge, made the "choice" of enlisting in the army.

I was still with child throughout this period, not knowing what it would come to or how it would end. Before I was arrested, having trouble with my husband, I considered abortion, although I was against it on principle. Now it really became an issue. I did not know if I would be convicted or what the future held. My husband had pretty much abandoned me already. My oldest daughter was not yet two, and if the family was to be separated I would have to deal with it alone, with no vocation or education. How was I to provide? I wanted to go to school. Who would watch them? I knew I wouldn't get welfare after the bust, and I didn't want to raise my children on welfare anyway. I had so many thoughts running through my mind. So many questions. No answers.

The decision was never mine. To get an abortion a prisoner had to have a psychiatric evaluation, and that took time. There were long bureaucratic details to go through prior to seeing the psychiatrist, and I was already into my twelfth week. It was clear the matrons disapproved of abortion, and they supplied a few more obstacles for me. The initial appointment wasn't set up until six weeks after I requested the abortion. Another appointment was required two weeks after that. I could still terminate but it would be more than a simple D&C. If I wanted to abort I would have to go through labor. To induce it, a needle would be inserted in my womb, painful to say the least. Meanwhile I changed my mind. Looking back I felt it was all encouragement to me to keep the child, and I am happy to say it was the correct decision for my life.

I was loving the child I was carrying more every day, while wondering at our future. I couldn't count on my family for assistance. My father wouldn't make bail for me, or write to me. Columbine was in New York with my cousin that I grew up with, so she was okay for now, but I wasn't. I didn't know who would be able to keep the new baby while I was in prison. And I got a letter from my husband telling me he was having a wonderful affair. The letters are censored, and the guards had a good laugh. I was bitter as I felt my world crumbling around me. I was no protection for my children and he was none for me.

There were immediate problems to deal with at the jail. I was health-conscious with a respect for nutrition, particularly during pregnancy. The jail food was starchy, with few vegetables. Breakfast was cereal, toast, coffee and fruit juice. Fresh fruit and vegetables were rare. Lunch was ravioli or cold sandwiches. We had a salad just once a week. Dinner was noodles or rice, toast and coffee. The rare time we had meat or poultry it was processed and pressed, tasted like rubber. The inadequate protein and vitamins affected our energy and appearance. I had deep circles under my eyes. Being in the jail was threatening my health and my unborn child's.

Then came more bad news. I might have to spend time in jail in one of the other counties where I committed fraud. My public defender in Marin County said he obtained a reduced sentence through plea bargaining. I would spend nine months in the Marin jail with two years' probation. But this was just one county. I was afraid of going to court in the other counties, where the jails were reputed to be even worse.

I met many women from the state prison, the California Institution for Women, through this time. Their description of fresh country air, real meat and a school seemed a more constructive way to do time. Also, I learned that the law held out the possibility of keeping my baby with me for up to two years. For these reasons I agreed to go to CIW rather than do all the jail time and probation. I thought I would extend the time in prison by just three months beyond the original sentence, because it was my first charge. Also, I was attending school when I was arrested, and I hoped that would show my non-criminal nature.

When I went to court for voluntary sentencing to state prison, they reneged and said I still had to answer to Alameda County for fraud. I cried all the way to the jail in Santa Rita. I'd heard it was a hellhole, but it was worse. I felt like a leaf in the wind, being tossed around, powerless. I was subjected to another degrading internal and external body search. They used a stick to separate my buttocks for examination. And it was another fingerprinting and mugshot before they took me to lock-up.

The women there weren't cared for well at all. Two women had serious medical problems. One was kicking cold turkey and the other had migraines which were known to make her violent. The only medical attention was a morning visit by a male "nurse," but they weren't nurses. These men would hand out medication in the morning, intended to last all day. No one supervised, and women had their medications stolen by other prisoners, never replaced. If they complained they were ignored at best, but often taunted by the guards. One night the woman with the migraines was in very serious pain, and all night she paced. We kept calling for help, and no one came. Months later I found out that this woman had to have surgery for a brain tumor after her release, but that she was required to finish her sentence before she could have the surgery. She was subjected to an extra month of suffering and wasn't cared for in the interim.

The night before my initial court appearance I was put in a holding cell at the Alameda County courthouse, another horror. The cells are similar to barren public bathrooms, all tile, cold, under constant camera surveillance. I was alone until I was finally called to appear, but then my case was rescheduled for two months later. I was taken back to Santa Rita, then back to the Marin jail, and two weeks later they took me to the state prison. On my departure morning, I had an argument with the matron. I had given my breakfast to another prisoner and wanted to go back to sleep. But according to the rules, I had to personally get up to give it to her, otherwise she couldn't have it. I was tired, half asleep, so I refused, but when the matron started to take the tray away I was infuriated, and knocked it over. She left and came back with the male jailers, telling them that I was inciting a riot, even though by then I was again half asleep, as were the others. But the men dragged me out of bed. I was huge with child and threatened to sue if they hurt me. The matron laughed and said, "Just try and sue from prison." They put me in the hole, a small dark room. I tried to explain to the next deputy on shift, but she wouldn't listen. It didn't matter. I was to be transported by plane that day, cuffed and shackled, to CIW in Corona.

At CIW I was kept at the intake unit for about six weeks and then had to return to the Alameda court. Again my case was rescheduled, and after another day in the holding cell I was upset. They could have rescheduled without an appearance. However, the judge was a woman and she was kind to me. She said that I should be returned to CIW to await the next appearance, but it wasn't to be that simple.

Back at the Santa Rita jail I was informed that I would not be returned to CIW until my case was completed. The judge had told me that if I encountered any difficulty I should inform her. I asked the deputy to call the judge, but the deputy said that judges would be angry if disturbed. I was hysterical.

One of the other prisoners, a young girl, had fallen down a flight of stairs while being arrested. She was kicked in the back by the police before she could get up. She couldn't move without extreme pain. It's as if people cease to be human when they are incarcerated. The nurses (male guards) said she couldn't have anything stronger than aspirin, which didn't help at all. It took more than two weeks for her to see a doctor. The x-rays showed three dislocated discs in her spine. There were many such incidents.

I'd been at Alameda for a week when I was called to court unexpectedly. The charges were dropped, and I expected to be returned to CIW for the Marin sentence. But there was another confusion. The deputy got the mistaken idea that I had a second charge in Alameda. It got straightened out, but I still wasn't scheduled for the transfer to CIW. And then the deputy said my case wasn't finished, and the sergeant wouldn't check when I begged him, and the deputy who had figured out I was finished was off work for a while, and it was the last straw. My nerves were shot. I asked the nurse for a tranquilizer but he just smirked. I felt resentful and angry, and I tore up the dorm and broke whatever was breakable. I was seven months pregnant, and I brought on false labor pains. Everyone was shocked at my behavior, which wasn't my way. They put me in the hole, of course, and when the contractions came and I called for help I was ignored. The next day the deputy who had helped me returned, and personally carried the message through channels until it was finally rectified. Later the sergeant apologized to me, but I was beyond that. I almost lost my baby because of the stress.

Back at ciw I was in the intake unit for another two weeks before transfer to the prison compound. After what I'd been through in the jails, I knew I could cope with anything. At ciw there were real doctors and nurses. And I had a counselor, I thought. In the penitentiary words take on different meanings, I soon found out. The penitentiary was quite different from the jails. It looks like a college campus, but the façade provided little relief. On my first day whatever remained of my belief in the system and fair play was destroyed.

I went to meet my counselor immediately after I arrived, to introduce myself and discuss my case, because I expected to go to the board [board of terms and parole] the upcoming week. We started to talk but there was an interruption, so he told me he would speak to me at one o'clock that afternoon. At one sharp I was waiting in front of his office. He didn't return until 3:30, and he called in another woman who was waiting to see him. When they finished he started to leave, so I stopped him to remind him of our appointment. He started screaming at me, extremely hostile, and said he didn't have time for me. Was it an emergency, he asked? I said it was important to my future. And he started again, screaming, "Who do you think you are? You'll do some time, I'll make sure of that." I later found out that this man was known for going off on women, pimp-style. He said he was going to rehabilitate me and make me wish I'd never been assigned to his unit. I never expected to be yelled at by someone who was supposed to help me. Nice "counselor." All my hopes disappeared.

After that I kept mostly to myself, because it was difficult for me to adjust. I couldn't relate to anyone, and the counselor refused to see me. Soon it was time for my parole hearing with the board. I wanted to present as honest a picture of my circumstance as possible, believing that honesty would gain my release. I had made plans to continue my education, and I had letters of recommendation, an acceptance letter from Cabrillo College, and hope, although I worried about the counselor's threat.

I received a seven-month review, that is, an appointment to return to the board in seven months for a reconsideration. But if they wanted to, they could keep me up to ten years. I was depressed, but it got worse that evening at our mandatory group "therapy," which we called "attack therapy." The so-called counselor would pick out one woman and criticize her, and everyone else was supposed to join in and attack her. The idea was to break down a woman's ego so she could rebuild her character, but it was just a cruel attack. That night the counselor told the group that I had talked about them like dogs to the board, and that I thought I was superior to them. What I actually said was that I couldn't relate to prison and that it was difficult for me to make friends. But the women followed his lead and made me feel miserable. He had made enemies for me. I had seen it happen to others and felt sympathy for them. Now I needed sympathy for myself. Now I was more isolated than ever.

The baby was due any day, and I'd experienced false labor quite often so I knew I would deliver soon. It was Mother's Day, May 24, 1973, when I started true labor, in the morning. I was taken to the so-called hospital section of the prison, prepped and left alone. It would be a natural birth, I decided, like I had had with my first child. I knew I could anticipate a difficult time because of the stress I was under and the poor condition of my body. Also, I knew the baby would be huge. I could feel it. I labored eighteen hours before Alexii was born. She weighed in at ten pounds, eight ounces. The army paid for her to be taken to New York with my cousin, so she didn't have to go to a foster home. My baby was gone from my life for four years. That was the hardest part.

No one would choose prison, but I learned a lot. I especially learned a lot about the sisterhood, the commonality of women who have been oppressed because of their race or sex. Over the years I came to know women very well, and because we shared so much experience it was easier for us to struggle together against every force that would hold us down. I was lucky. Others' stories ended tragically. Mine did not.

Afterword

Gradually Lia became integrated into the life of the prison, getting to know others with whom she shared life experience, making friends, taking classes and becoming active in the African-American Sisterhood. Highly articulate, by her second year she had become a leader, and other women sought out her judgement.

The administration created a behaviour modification unit with the intention of isolating prisoners like Lia who did not succumb to every attempt to rob them of their personal identity. Any woman who stood up for herself, such as Lia, was admired by the other prisoners, and the administration worked actively to discourage their influence. The behaviour modification unit was specifically designed to squelch potential leaders. Lia helped initiate what became a state-wide protest campaign that resulted in the closure of the unit.

Lia was released in 1977 and reunited with her daughters in California. She attended college and then university, where she was able to live on campus in family housing with on-campus daycare. Her girls were beautiful and well behaved, happy to be with their mother.

She had completed a number of accredited university courses at the prison, and her life-long love of reading served her well as a student. She eventually completed her degree. When her life settled down, Lia also participated actively in advocacy work for women in prison, helping to educate the public about prison practices that are indeed cruel but not unusual. She was a key speaker at a rally at the state capital in Sacramento where a thousand people gathered to protest human rights abuses against women in prison. Now that she was free, she was able to publicly articulate the frustration and humiliation experienced by women inside. She admonished politicians to devote more funds to education and less to punishment of people who are victims of poverty and discrimination. Clearly the politicians weren't listening, but others were, and Lia was an early voice in what is now a broad-based movement challenging the cruel conventions of imprisonment.

Reflections

Women who steal commonly assert moral justifications for their thefts, especially when they steal or commit fraud, as in Lia's case, to support their families, usually very modestly. There is, however, a convict code that says a thief must not steal from those who are themselves in need. Not atypical is the woman who said, "I always stole from the rich. I'm proud I never took from the poor." Lia's victim was the state, the taxpayers, but her actions were a protest against a state that coddles the rich while abandoning those who lose their bearings or have no means of uplifting themselves. The Robin Hood imagery romantically exaggerates the motives behind most small-time thievery, but most thieves subscribe to the spirit of an old British verse:

> The law chastises the man or woman
> Who from the common pasture steals the goose,
> But leaves at liberty the greater knave
> Who steals the common pasture from the goose.

Over a third of women in prison are serving time for money crimes. Thefts for the purpose of supporting drug use weren't respected at CIW, but if the motive was to rake in a haul, there was a certain admiration. Crimes were ranked according to status: safecracking, counterfeiting, embezzlement and clever fraud or forgery got top rating; all of these were money crimes involving more than a few hundred dollars, achieved without violence. Many enthusiastic prison conversations have to do with inventing schemes, often based on successful experience, for getting money. For fun-loving outlaws, half the fun is conning those who would be quick to condemn them. But for most women, theft wasn't any fun. Welfare fraud was borderline pathetic, but too common to be remarked on one way or another.

Whatever the nature of their theft, few convicted women will repent in prison for their sins and transgressions. Their problem is not that they are wayward souls, but that they don't have the resources to meet their needs and responsibilities. The word "penitentiary" stems from the Quaker idea of penitence, doing penance, which is what prisoners are supposed to be seeking. But guilt is not a commonly expressed emotion where money crimes are concerned. Lia overcame the odds when she successfully completed university and made a good life for herself and her girls legitimately, but she did not apologize for her previous fall from grace. People steal that which they feel is their due.

4

KATHY

JUST AN AVERAGE AMERICAN GIRL

Introduction: Anne Near

THE STORIES OF WOMEN in prison are the parables of a society that is deeply flawed. Kathy's story is so common in its ingredients. It blends elements of tragedy with mere unlucky coincidence. It exhorts us to examine the social fabric from which a life springs. Kathy's story pleads eloquently for more creative ways of preventing human tragedy. Who are the women in prison? Who are the women whom we have removed from our midst, away from contact with their neighbours, from their natural families and their street, from their children? Walled away.

Kathy wanted to tell her story, however painful. Searching to understand what happened, her memories flow back and forth as memories will, however much our minds try to find explanation in sequence. As Kathy says, "I've forgotten a lot back there in the cobwebs. I backtrack because something I remember reminds me of something else."

With candour, Kathy reveals that she is a young mother accused of killing her stepchild, and she explores the crime without defensiveness. As a parent of four children I can hear truth in her story. Two of a very young woman's deepest life experiences—love with a sexual partner and motherhood—appear at times to follow nature's best design, and at other times to be in hurtful conflict, one role with the other. For parents, a very real danger derives from an unidentified draining away of energy at the workplace and at home. When energy is not available to tend to children's needs for attention, a mother or a father may fall back on the irrational idea that an adult has to spank a child. ("Spare the rod and spoil the child.") And "spank" is a euphemism for "strike." In Kathy's story we see two young people who were victims of a conspiracy of serious proportions, whereby they were taught to substitute personal violence for the energy they lacked to respond to or cope with their children's needs.

In telling her story, Kathy gives important clues as to how the resources of her personality were being drained away and exhaustion was occurring at a hazardous level. In her own modest self-image, Kathy is "just an average American girl." In her own original perception, her husband and co-defendant was an above-average mate. Her story sets off a warning alarm: among other needs for social services, we need community childcare and parent assistance programs to reduce child abuse by isolated, harried, sleep-deprived parents who lose control.

Comments: KF

At the time of my interviews with Kathy, she was twenty-five and looked sixteen, olive complexion with some Cherokee heritage, with a strong, slender body and a sweetly shy manner. We were asked by other prisoners if we were related because, they said, we looked alike, so we called ourselves sisters. Kathy was always pleasant, but her eyes revealed pain. She was a quiet prisoner, in her second year of a five-years-to-life indeterminate sentence. Because of the nature of her crime, she was a solitary figure, though cheerful in conversation. She kept her mind and hands busy, doing her best to cope with the shame and stigma of her crime, the agony of missing her children, and the monotony of prison. Our first interview session took place in a nearly empty office in the highly secured prison administration building, where we sat on hard-backed chairs.

Kathy's Story

I guess my life's been pretty ordinary. Nothing too exciting has happened. Just having my kids. I'm just average. Just went to school and tried to stay good. I'm just an average American girl, I guess.

When I first came in here to prison I was petrified. It took me about four months to get myself straightened out where I wasn't afraid I was doing this or that wrong—afraid of getting a write-up that would keep me here longer, or of going to rack [solitary confinement]. You have to feel it out, get to know the guards, figure out what you can get away with, how you can talk to them, the routine of things. I don't have any hang-ups here now. I've adjusted pretty well. Accepting.

A lot of women have been here for years and they are still fighting it. They can't have anyone telling them what to do or they go off on them. Two, three, four years, and they still don't belong. And maybe they don't belong here. But they have to accept the fact that they are here and they can't change it. Just look at it as your home away from home, whether you like it or not.

A common theme in the prison is parole plans, and this was one of the things Kathy focused on in our first interview, even though she wasn't close to release. She considered training for work as a dental assistant, or for office work. In Oakland she had worked at the courthouse in data processing, and she liked it. She was also comfortable in traditionally male work environments.

I'd like to work in an auto-parts place—I like being around machinery. Here I have a new job in utility maintenance. Every Friday I get to drive the fire truck and wash it. For a while I was on a paint crew. There are a lot of bosses out there, but I know my job and I do my job and they don't hassle me.

I don't know my real dad. He and my mom were divorced when I was young. He spent thirteen years in the navy. When I was three my mom married my first stepdad. I thought he was my daddy. I didn't know any different until I was about nine years old and she was in the process of divorcing him. I told her she was crazy.

Both my parents worked, so we had pretty much everything we wanted. I can only remember one time when my stepdad spanked me, and I deserved it. I was maybe four. I locked all the doors so he couldn't get in when he came home from work. He banged and hollered but I wouldn't let him in. I thought it was funny, and then I got scared because he sounded mad. I split out the back and didn't go home for a long time.

My parents never did fight or argue. But then my mom got infatuated with this new character. She just knew she was madly in love with him. So my parents got a divorce. Called it "sexual incompatibility." My mom's real attractive. She knew when she got married that my stepdad was fourteen years older than she, a time when a man slows down. So my mom married this nineteen-year-old kid—this character. She was thirty-five and two months pregnant with my brother.

My impression of my second stepfather was that he thought he was God's gift to women. When my mom told me they were married and he was my new dad, I cried for two hours, locked myself in the bathroom. He said, "You either show me respect and call me daddy or get a spankin' every day." He spanked me all the time. Like, instead of saying, "Please pass this or that," I said, "Please please please pass pass pass… " and he told me to knock it off and smacked me real hard on the chin. He spanked my brother with a belt, left a buckle imprint on him. I really didn't like that man.

My mother had to accept it or she'd get knocked down too. She always had a bruise or a black eye. When we went to the south once for a while, to where his family was, we'd go out to chop wood for the fireplace and he'd make the baby carry a big log. I'd get switched with a peach tree branch, cut pretty deep, bled. This was almost every day, getting beat or hit or cussed at.

My mom and I were really protective of my little brother. I'd tell this stepfather, "He didn't do it. I did." I can't figure my mom letting this guy keep beating her. I guess she was afraid. She did finally divorce him after six or seven years. She didn't get married again until I left home to get married, when I was eighteen. Then she married her fourth husband, seven years younger, a man with a bunch of kids for her to raise. She couldn't handle it after a while; they were getting into trouble and getting sent to juvenile hall. But they all became my good friends. My mom and her husband are good people, satisfied, content, overweight. They now have the kind of life I'd like to have. I'd like to have a nice house. Comfortable furniture.

Whenever permission was given, I conducted interviews with Kathy in her cell. Her space was tidy and comfortable, enlivened by bright colours. The cells in her unit were 7' × 10', larger than the usual 6' × 9', but hers seemed even larger, decorated with yellow curtains over the bars, photographs and poems taped to the wall, and stacks of books and letters on the shelf. Relaxed in her own space, with music from her radio mediating the noises outside her cell, she spoke freely. I asked her what or who had been the major influence on her. "Men," she said, "have been a big thing. Almost everything." And so she began a chronology of her romantic life.

There was the little boy down the street, he was in the fifth grade, older than me, like a big brother. I invited him to my birthday party and he bought me one of those storybook dolls. He had a bad home life. When I was nine my mom got her divorce, and we lived with my aunt and cousin. Seventh grade was a good year. I was a cheerleader, and I knew everybody in the whole school from first grade up. In eighth grade I had a crush on a boy who wouldn't dance with me at graduation, but he danced with my girlfriend. Made me mad. Another girlfriend had a brother in high school and I liked him, but he called me a kid and hurt my ego. There were lots of boys I liked, and I didn't get too serious with anybody then.

Then there was Mike. We'd go to the show, and he'd call every morning before school and every day as soon as we'd get home. His people were well off. I thought we'd get married. My first time for sex was with Mike. That's why I thought we'd get married. I don't know why I never got pregnant. Then he got in trouble, a hit and run, and left town, sent to youth camp. I didn't see anybody for a while after he left, but there were lots of other boys around. When I was with Mike they were all like big brothers to me, and when he went away they thought they'd take care of me, in Mike's interest, you know? It was the wrong way.

My mom talked to me about the consequences of messing around, and did I know how to take care of things. She probably thought it was her fault that Mike and I got so involved. After she divorced my second stepfather she was super-lenient with me. But she liked Mike and I guess she had hoped we'd get married. After Mike, I went out with a lot of dudes just to be going out. Sex? I liked it.

What Kathy didn't like was being coerced into having sex, or guys who took it for granted that she would be sexually available to them. She wanted me to understand that she wasn't an "easy lay."

I went to the drive-in with a guy, and as soon as we got there he started unbuttoning my blouse. I told him to take me home. It made me furious. I thought, is this all guys think about, you know? I just shined him on at school. It burned me up.

By the time she was seventeen, Kathy had dropped out of high school, and she had a steady boyfriend, Ellis. They shared an apartment with another couple. In a common 1950s-'60s scenario, teenaged Kathy became pregnant after a few months, and she and Ellis got married.

I was almost three months pregnant when I found out, and we got married about two months later. Ellis and I didn't really belong to each other when we were going together, but we got along better then than after we got married. We weren't financially able to take care of a baby. First thing that came to my mind was, "Oh my god, how am I going to tell my mom?" Well, Mom cried and fumed and ranted and raved. But after she got over the shock she was cool.

I wanted the baby but I wasn't sure about the marriage. Ellis started messing around with other women, coming in late.

I could never sleep because the baby moved around so much. When Timmy was born I think that's the first time he slept! [When I was overdue] the doctor induced labor, but I didn't have a bad time of it. Ellis's mom was a nurse, and she taught me how to breathe. She helped me a lot.

Marriage is supposed to be pretty final, and I wanted to make it work, but there wasn't anything stable with Ellis even after Timmy was born. He would leave and not come back for days. Then he'd come home and cry on my shoulder and I'd let him, and in one of those times I got pregnant again.

Kathy talked about suffering jealousy, resenting Ellis's affairs with other women. Their conflicts accelerated until Kathy said that she did "some pretty hateful things." She would go to the bar where he worked and confront women he was seeing. And she threw all his personal belongings onto the street.

We had a big fight. He shoved me onto the floor and broke my tailbone. I began to have some problems, but I thought they might be normal.

Then I started having premature labor pains. It was Ellis's birthday, but he wasn't around. A girlfriend took me to the county hospital and my mom came over for Timmy. I was in emergency for twenty minutes and the nurses delivered the baby, tiny, less than three pounds. He only lived six hours. Ellis came to see me. His face was white. He asked how I was, but I was really bitter, because when he shoved me it ruptured the water sac. I told him, "Happy birthday!" It was ugly.

While I was in the hospital, the landlord had taken all the stuff out of my house and a lot of things were missing, like Corningware. I went to Legal Aid and got my rent money back and $160 for my missing stuff.

Ellis and I separated. When I got back [from the hospital], Timmy, who was just over two years old, didn't want to have anything to do with me. We'd been so close. I'd never been away from him, but I was gone suddenly for four days and he didn't understand. He'd run from me and start screaming. So Ellis took him for a few days, and would bring him over and we'd all go for a drive. But Timmy didn't want to be with Ellis, either. He locked himself in a room and Ellis spanked him, the wrong thing to do.

Then it was the other way around. If I left Timmy, like with my mom, if I had to go downtown on business, he'd just stand at the window and cry. He was so afraid. So I had to take him to the doctor, who hugged Timmy and calmed him down. The doctor said I had to stop being constantly close to Timmy, so I started going with him to my mom's and his other grandmother, and staying there with him until he got used to being there. My mom bought him a little bike and a little car to keep at her house so he'd feel more at home. He finally came out of it real good and was able to go to preschool when he was four.

Ellis and I talked during this time, but not about ourselves. I still wanted to be with him, but there had been a lot of bad times. I didn't feel like I'd be doing him justice to go back to him. I knew I could be hurtful and hateful. I knew he still cared, because he came to the hospital. But then he started going with someone else. I was working at the courthouse and going to night school. We weren't legally separated but we were both seeing other people. Soon I met Ed.

My dad and Ed were both working at the munitions plant. The company had a big family day picnic for everyone who worked there, big party by the pond in the park. Ed and his old lady were ready to split up. That day Ed and I fooled around, threw each other in the water, poured beer on each other—having a good time, playing like brother and sister. He was gone for a few weeks. When he came back he called my mom, wanting to talk to me, and it just so happened that I was over at my mom's that evening. I was shocked that he called. I knew he was an all-right guy and that he was a good worker. Nice-looking. Came from a big family. His mom is Blackfoot and Arapaho, and my mom was part Cherokee (my great-grandfather was full blood). So he came over, and from then on it was me and Ed and Timmy. And it didn't take long for me to get pregnant with Brenda.

I don't think Ed ever went out on me. But still there wasn't the closeness. He was always wanting to be going out somewhere, but it was a hard pregnancy for me. Ed and I weren't married yet. I had to quit work and go back on welfare. I was getting some support from Ellis and trying to keep that from the welfare department. And here was Ed living with me, both of us legally married to other people. And here I was—going crazy.

Kathy talked about how she was pregnant three times from ages seventeen to twenty, and said she attended night school because she wanted more choices in the work force. She talked about having minimum-wage jobs, being dependent on a man, and sometimes having to rely on welfare. To further complicate her life, Ed's wife, Andrea, still wanted him.

Andrea called the welfare department and told them I had a man living with me—her husband. And she told them I left my little boy at home by himself. That made me hot, really burned me up. This lady came out to talk to me, and I told her, "Yeah, Ed's living with me, but I don't leave my little boy, and you can ask anyone. If I leave him, I leave him with my mom. Nobody else!"

Ed had to move. He went to stay with my mom and stepdad. They were nuts about him. But Ed's wife kept on harassing us. She was also pregnant. She watched my house, followed me in the car, made phone calls. And she called Ed at work and told him she was going to put the baby up for adoption. She didn't mean it, but she had a friend in welfare fix up the papers. Two days later there was a warrant out for his arrest, charging him with ransacking her house and stealing $170, which he didn't do.

Even when Brenda was only a few days old after I'd just come home from the hospital, I got an ugly call from Andrea, and it really upset me. I was having the baby blues anyway, and then to be bad-mouthed. And she was bothering my people, who had nothing to do with it. Being with me was Ed's choice. Ed didn't know if her child was his and he didn't want any part of it. They divorced, but she went to court and he had to pay child support. She moved north and we followed, because Ed wanted visitation, since he was being held responsible. She didn't want the visiting, and when it was arranged she wasn't there. We were trying to comply with her. She kept calling Ed at work, reversing the charges. He began to have some ugly thoughts. She upset him so much he'd take it out on me.

To make matters worse, our baby Brenda had a bad heart. She was born on the eclipse, a month and ten days premature. [The day she was born] I woke up at seven with a backache. By nine I couldn't stand it. I knew it was a girl, and I didn't want her to be born in the seventh month. I knew that was too early. Ed got up and was running around the house like a chicken with its head cut off. I made some coffee. He called the doctor. The doctor told me to come in and they'd have my bed waiting. I went into delivery fifteen minutes before I had her. I had no drugs with her. They were wheeling me out with Brenda beside me when Ed came out of the elevator after checking me in. When we were in my room, Ed was looking at Brenda and he turned around and was crying. Mom came and told me that Timmy, who was not yet four, said, "I guess my mama is never coming back again." So they brought him to see me. He was so happy I was all right. He wanted to see Brenda, and then he looked at the nurse and said, "That's my sister. Ain't she purty?" The nurse looked at the two of them and threw up her hands. He's so blond and fair, and Brenda has dark hair, eyes and complexion.

The day I got the ugly call from Ed's ex-wife, Andrea, he came home and found me crying my eyes out. The following day a girl-friend came over with a friend and the friend's four kids, to see the baby. I was cooking lunch, and Ed came home. With all these people coming in and out all the time, I was really getting exhausted. When Brenda was ten days old we took her in for her check-up, and they found out about her heart. I was freaking out, could hardly say anything. I was coming unglued, ready to break down. The doctor said there was nothing to worry about; by the time she was four she'd grow out of it. But every three months I had to take her in for x-rays, and they found a hole in her heart the size of a quarter. When she was nine months old, she was seen by a bunch of specialists. She was beautiful, just delightful. She'd touch the doctor's moustache and pull on his tie. They said if she didn't improve by the time she was four, she'd need heart surgery. All this was driving me insane.

No one could believe there was anything wrong with Brenda. She never looked sick, always bright-eyed. She never cried, for four months. I'd go in to feed her and she'd be lookin' around. She was so tiny, but she was happy and gaining weight. Eight months old she gave up baby food and wanted to do everything for herself. An unusual baby. Timmy thought the sun rose and fell on Brenda, but Ed lost interest. We'd gotten married just two and a half months before Brenda was born. Now, if I wanted to go to the store, he didn't want to sit with the babies. I got the feeling he was feeling trapped. He'd get super-strict with Timmy, and I'd tell him, "Hey, let up, let him be. Now we have the baby Timmy is going to feel left out." So Ed would seem to get it, but it would only last a few days. Timmy was always showing Brenda his cars and trucks. He'd sit down with her and her books. Teach her about horses, dogs, cats. After a while it was just me, Timmy and Brenda.

In every interview with Kathy, she talked most of all about her children. They clearly occupied her thoughts. At first it seemed that she felt compelled to speak a lot about her children because she wanted

*me to understand that she was a good and loving mother despite
her crime. But it was easy to imagine her as a good mother. She had
stores of memories of her kids' first steps and all the clever things
they said and did in the six years she was a mother and home-
maker. She also reiterated her appreciation for how both her own
and Ed's mother adored Brenda, although she explained how she
had to win over Ed's mother, because Kathy got pregnant while Ed
was still married to another woman.*

As Brenda started filling out, you could see her mouth is shaped like
Ed's and the shape of her head is identical, and soon Brenda was
accepted into the family. Ed and I were doing pretty well together.
He had good intentions, but he didn't let me share in the decisions.
It was, "You clean the house and you do this and you do that. What
I say goes." He worked overtime at the plant so he could catch up
on our bills. He put the truck and car in my name so his ex-wife
couldn't take everything from him. He tried to build on our house,
sawing and pounding. He was a good provider, but he controlled
the money. If there was any extra for something special, he spent
the money on himself instead of on the family. Like, he took off for
Reno with his friend. Mom was nearby, and he left money for us,
but it isn't the same. I'd get up and fix his breakfast, make his lunch,
and ask him if he was coming home from work at five so I'd know to
have dinner ready. And he'd say, "Yeah." But I'd know at 5:15 that he
wouldn't be home for a while. So I'd feed the kids and I'd be too irritated to eat. Sometimes I'd get in the car and we'd go see Mom or
whatever. Sometimes I'd go looking and find him sitting in the bar.

With sex I'd been on the decline since having the baby. I guess
it put Ed on a bummer, because he couldn't understand it. I'd try to
explain and he'd say, "I understand, it's cool." But I knew he didn't.
And it wasn't that I didn't love him. I always had this inadequate
feeling. I couldn't satisfy his needs. I felt responsible.

*As Kathy talked, and heard herself, she realized that she didn't
accept all the responsibility for the problems in her marriage. She*

became increasingly resentful of the ways she'd felt short-changed in her marriage, especially because of the events that led her to prison. Then one day she came to the session visibly excited. The previous night she had for the first time heard Helen Reddy's song "I Am Woman" on the radio. She had written down the lyrics and brought them to me because, she said, since I was "into women's lib" I would appreciate it. It seemed that the song had given Kathy a new and stronger feeling about herself.

I really spoiled Ed. I'd be taking him hot lunches. If he worked overtime sometimes I'd take dinner to him. Then I'd know he'd come home, because I'd stay and we'd come home together. When he didn't come home, he'd have cashed his check at the liquor store. I'd have all the envelopes made out to pay our bills and he'd be minus $50. I'd ask, "What happened?" and he'd say, "I've been drinking." "Not fifty bucks' worth!" "Well, I gave this girl a twenty and bought two shirts but lost one." Another time we were packing up to go camping. Ed got ugly and was shoving and pushing, then his friend came by and they went out drinking, didn't come home all night. It was like I didn't exist. No phone call or anything. He could have been in jail or in a wreck somewhere. He said they just drove north for the hell of it. For a week we were cold to each other. He said if I didn't want to go to bed with him he'd find someone who would. I don't know if he ever did.

And then Andrea was killed in a car accident. She and a friend had gone to the air force base and picked up a couple of guys, and the accident happened. We went up to pick up her son, Steven, to take care of him. Everyone was acknowledging Steven as Ed's boy, even though Ed hadn't wanted to accept it. Now he wanted the responsibility. The problem was that his ex-wife had left a will saying her son should go to her sister, and this sister went to court. We got an attorney, and a caseworker checked out our house.

We did get custody of Steven, and at first it was beautiful. Steven and Brenda were almost twins, just two months and three days difference in their ages. Steven had been an only baby with lots of grown-ups, but when we got him his bottom was just raw. I couldn't understand. And his little face was all red and chapped. They were told he couldn't drink regular homogenized milk so they had him on soybean milk, and that's what we had to get for him. He whined a lot, an awful lot.

I got his skin cleared up with ointment. At first the kids all got along really well. During the day when one or another was sleeping I'd have special time alone with the other one. Still, Steven whined, real fussy. I started giving him extra-rich milk and vitamins.

For about the first six weeks, Ed was interested in Steven and pulled his attention away from the other kids. This made Brenda feel left out, because she'd always been the center of his attention. Steven was walking and she wasn't yet. The kids started being jealous of each other and hateful with the neighbor kids, crying constantly, day in and day out. I'd love Steven, hug him, play with him, give him what he asked for, and he'd just whine. I felt like I was battering my head against a stone wall. I thought about talking to a psychiatrist.

I never liked to holler at the kids, but sometimes it was something I had to do. You can't let them do things they're not supposed to do. I guess a lot of times when I was hollering at them, the neighbors thought I was killing them, because I'd be cussing and they'd be screaming and crying, and I wouldn't even be touching them. I didn't holler every day. I thought things were bound to get better.

Ed did a turnaround and starting giving all his attention to Brenda. But poor Timmy. Ed had no time for him. So I started letting Timmy go visit his dad, Ellis, about twice a month for a weekend, and on holidays. We were having a lot of family communication, Ellis's mom and me, and all the kids. Ellis started popping in unexpectedly and Timmy would want to go off with him. But Ellis had to go to work, so Timmy would be upset and I'd have to make it up to him, do something extra. We set up a little swimming pool in the yard. I'd leave Brenda with Ed and take the boys for ice cream cones.

A trip to Monterey was my Mother's Day present. I stayed up half the night fixing chicken and making potato salad. We had to get up at 4:00 A.M. to leave, and when we got there it was so cold I had to stay in the car with the little kids, who were fighting and spilling milk all over each other, the two of them still in diapers, and I'm wondering, "What did I do to deserve all of this?!" The next day we had a picnic on the beach. I had to carry Brenda on one hip and Steven on the other. What a Mother's Day!

On the day that Kathy described her ordeal we both laughed a lot. In retrospect it was a pretty funny story. I could easily imagine two fat little babies with sand all over them, in wet, drooping diapers and grimy T-shirts, bawling while Kathy struggled to hitch one onto her left hip and the other onto her right, and then trudge with them through the sand and back to the car for the long haul home in the night. Just an average American girl.

By now Kathy and I had been meeting for almost two months, building a friendship as I travelled with her through her life. Sometimes we would bring each other a thought-for-the-day. For example, one day she had written out: "The worst sin toward our fellow creatures is not to hate them but to be indifferent. This is the essence of inhumanity." We met in staff offices, classrooms, her cell, the "feeding unit," and on the grass outside when the prison regimen permitted. After many hours of speaking about herself, Kathy had carefully evaded (and acknowledged her evasion of) the crime that brought her to prison.

Our next interview would be our last, and I reminded her of that. She looked at me and said, "The time has come," and I nodded yes. We both stared at the glass of ice tea she brought to our meeting. It was a very hot day. Her empty glass was still covered with tiny droplets of moisture. When I looked up, I saw tears running down her cheeks, and then she wept. When we ran out of tissues, I fetched the key to the bathroom and got some paper towels. Kathy calmed down and said she'd never told the whole story, but she was ready. Several days later I sat in the classroom facing Kathy, our chairs

angled at a corner of the table. She was silent, as if meditating, and
then she got tearful again.

I don't know if this was something... something very... that was
building up. A lot of things I just couldn't handle. I was trying so
hard. I had a lot of responsibility but I thought I could handle it. I'd
holler at the kids and once in a while I'd spank them. Except I never
did spank Brenda, because of her heart condition. She'd get a swat
now and then, like a slap on the hand. But once in a while I'd have
to give a spanking to one of the boys. I did not like to holler at them
or spank them, but sometimes there wasn't anything else I could do.
You can't reason with an eighteen-month-old child and you can't let
them do things they're not supposed to do.

In the 1960s, many children were abused, just as they are today,
by parents who lost control of themselves. But even more children
were abused by parents who thought that spanking was necessary
to good parenting. Kathy's intuitive resistance to using violence as
discipline was countered by the dominant culture's acceptance of
violence by the strong against the weak. Kathy had witnessed her
own mother's victimization as a battered wife, and Kathy and her
brother had also been abused by their stepfather. His violence was
cruel, not civilized like a normal "spanking."

When Steven first came he was just a baby and didn't have to be
disciplined. But later on he would get indignant if you'd tell him
to do anything. You'd tell him "no" and he'd fall apart and start
screaming. He would deliberately fall. One day when I told him
"no" he got so mad he ran headlong into the wall. I spanked him
for doing it. It was like he was trying to destroy himself. I tried
to solve it myself, instead of taking the baby to a psychiatrist and
getting him a tranquilizer or getting myself on tranquilizers. I
knew from watching my neighbor how that was. She had older
kids and could afford to be knocked out for three or four hours. I
couldn't. I was fighting pneumonia. I also started having migraine

headaches again, after two years without them, and I'd get violently sick. Timmy was getting into trouble and didn't want anything to do with the little ones, who were always tearing up his toys. All this was driving me insane.

At this point she stopped talking. I could see her reflecting, preparing to tell the story, to say everything. I was trying to stay detached from the anxiety I could see building in her, to avoid emotional risk. I worried now about the ethics of what I was doing, expecting this young woman to talk about something so painful to her. She had volunteered, but she was in a prison, accustomed to having to do things that caused her pain and suffering the stigma of her crime even in the world of the stigmatized. For a split second, I felt myself colluding with the correctional system, subjecting an individual to the prodding and poking of an "expert" who will then have something to say about it. But when she started talking again I knew from her determined voice that it was important to her to be able to talk about it, to an outsider who was not in a position to punish her. After a pause, she continued.

It was a bad day. It's hot. Ed and I aren't talking. The kids are being monsters. My head... I had these pills but didn't take them because I knew I'd be knocked out for hours, and then what will happen? Timmy got into the paint. He denied it. He had never lied to me before. With evidence all over the place, I spanked him for lying to me.

Things got progressively worse on this day, and my head just couldn't handle it. I'd been helping Ed in his job by making ceramic orifices for him, for a welding unit, and he needed them. Timmy had missed his bus so I had to take him to school. The little ones were still sleeping. I only had until noon to finish these orifices. Plus I had to make Ed's lunch and take it to him. So I was just running crazy. But I did manage to get everything done.

That afternoon the kids and I came back from taking the things to the ceramic shop to get them fired and glazed. We had lunch out. The kids are tired and cranky, and me too. So we're all going in to take a nap, including me. But Steven won't stay down. Fighting all the way. I put him in his bed, and he knocked over a glass of juice, all over the wall, and the floor I'd just mopped and waxed the night before. I'm almost in tears. I want a vacation. Even all by myself. Two weeks before I had said, "I really need to get away, even for a day or two." And Ed kept saying, "Oh yeah, yeah, we'll get it together, just me and you, we'll take off."

Timmy went in and lay down on his bed, and Brenda lay down beside him. Steven tried to climb out of the crib and fell; his mouth was bleeding. I tried to calm him down, and then I just blew it and started spanking him. I didn't realize how bad I had hurt him. I used my sandal. He lay down after I spanked him. I bruised his leg really bad. I smacked him on the head a couple of times, too.

When Ed came home I told him I had spanked Steven, and he said, "Well, he probably deserved it." And I told him, "I bruised him really bad." And Ed said, "Well, the bruises will go away." I was feeling scared. But Steven wasn't unconscious. He heard me talking and woke up. I fixed dinner and then I left, and Ed stayed there to take care of the kids. But he didn't take Steven out to feed him.

I went over to Mom's. She had to go to a meeting and I'd promised to take her. I was gone almost two hours. When I came back Ed told me he had spanked Steven again, that Steven started acting up. I knew I had already spanked him really bad, but he hadn't appeared to be really hurt. When Steven woke up he had just been mad, screaming and crying. So when Ed told me he had spanked him again, I went in and checked on Steven, and I knew when I touched him that something was wrong. I was freaked. I couldn't tell Ed. He had told me that he'd used his belt on him. I was almost positive Steven was dead. There wasn't any heartbeat, none at all. So I told Ed before he went to bed, "You'd better check on him," so he did. He turned him over. But he said, "He's all right, he's still breathing." I had known before when I touched Steven there wasn't any breath, there wasn't anything, no pulse, nothing. But I thought, well, maybe I was just too upset.

The next morning when I woke up Steven was cold. What were we going to do? We... Ed... hid his body in the storeroom and I called the police... oh god... oh damn... and told them Steven was missing.

It was ugly. We had Explorer Scouts out looking for him. We knew we had done wrong.

The whole thing was terrible.

Steven was dead.

They took me in for questioning. My people were there. The neighbors, everyone. I still wasn't telling them anything. I'm still telling them that Steven is missing. Then they gave me a lie detector test and I told them I spanked the baby really bad, but I didn't think he was that badly hurt. Ed told them that I had told him I'd spanked Steven bad, but he didn't think that the baby was that badly hurt either. And he told them he had spanked the baby too.

They booked both of us, for first-degree murder. I didn't care. Just send me off and let me do my time. I pled guilty to the whole charge of first-degree, and the judge broke it down to a stipulated degree of second. Ed got involuntary manslaughter.

We had different attorneys. Ed's was the public defender and mine was from an attorneys' firm. When Ed testified, he pled innocent. He denied he had spanked Steven with his belt. He said he didn't have anything to do with it. I got five years to life, and he got one to fifteen.

I worry about getting out. A lot of people have bad feelings about child abuse. They say I ought to be on Death Row.

Through the telling, Kathy watched her crime unfold, the horror of it, perhaps seeing it through my eyes, watching for my response. Nobody wants to be judged, or treated with contempt, but people sent to prison are no less likely than others to be prejudiced. Women who have harmed children are the most vulnerable to judgement, contempt and exclusion within the prison community, as elsewhere. The isolation exacerbates the suffering of a woman who is already tormented by guilt, remorse and the irreparable loss of a child, by her own hand or neglect.

It was less difficult for me to comprehend Kathy's violent out-burst against little Steven in his crib than it was for me to com-prehend her consistent disregard of Ed's former wife, Andrea, and Andrea's needs to have her child's father's attentions. That Ed's first family is dead is a horror that Kathy has to live with, but she seldom expressed empathy for what Andrea was suffering. The terrible irony that Ed and Kathy fought in the court to have Ste-ven with them, against Steven's mother's final wishes, balloons the already unfathomable injustices, and physical and emotional torments, that were suffered by that infant child. It's righteous to be angry about that. That anger, however, does not translate for me into wanting revenge against Kathy. She is one of many moth-ers who have lost their temper with their children, failed to pro-tect the child from attack by someone else, or lost their senses from sheer exhaustion.

What I want is not more punishment for Kathy or others who have harmed their children, but for there to be genuine zero toler-ance of abuse toward children, not from fear of incarceration but from having learned the skills to prevent that abuse, with commu-nity support systems. The end of child abuse means diverting more funds and intelligence into safety nets for adults at risk of abusing and for children at risk of being abused.

In 1972, when Kathy had been at the prison for over two years, a former prisoner who had herself been an abused child and who had served time for child abuse returned to the prison as an orga-nizer. With the encouragement of her parole officer, she established a prison self-help group called Mothers Anonymous, tailored after Parents Anonymous, an outside organization of parents who have been, or who fear they are becoming, abusive to their children. Kathy became involved with this group.

In the Mothers Anonymous group, I'm learning a lot about child abuse. I've learned there are different forms of abuse. Physical abuse, at least until death, is final and permanent. But there's also the abuse of neglect or of indifference. And there are a lot of people who kill their children out of exhaustion. A lot of violence comes out of mental and physical strain.

Another organization the convicts started up in here is WHIP— it stands for Wives and Husbands in Prison—for women who have husbands in other state prisons. I went to the first three meetings. I've been writing to Ed off and on since we've been in prison. But he doesn't answer letters or make any kind of contact with me or with my family. He doesn't even write to his own family. He should be telling us what's happening. We have no way to find out. I used to think, "I can't live without this man," but I can. I've signed my divorce papers. I blame myself and I blame him too.

It's very hard, but I'll make it. I feel better talking about it, and trying to reason things through. But maybe I'll never understand why it happened.

Reflections: KF and AN

Of the 600 women in state prison in 1972, four of them, including Kathy, had been convicted of participating in the death of a child. None of the women intentionally murdered a child. In two of the cases, the child had been killed by the woman's husband, but she was held equally responsible for having failed to protect her child.

Kathy snapped and targeted her rage at a little boy whose crying prevented her from resting when she was exhausted beyond her limits, although in all likelihood it was Ed's blows, not hers, that killed the child. She didn't hesitate to embrace Steven as part of her family when his mother died. Yet, although she treated Steven as if he were her own child, and was affectionate and in many respects patient, she never conveyed the same pure love for him that she expressed for her biological children. Andrea, Steven's mother and Ed's former wife, had been a steady source of grief to Kathy. It is easy to conjecture that resentment toward Andrea contaminated Kathy's relationship with Steven, even though she thought not.

Perhaps Kathy's momentary fury against Steven was weighted with her disappointment and fury against his wayward father. The men in Kathy's life repeatedly failed to fulfill the roles women were taught to expect from them—monogamous sexual partner, full-time provider, companion, friend, protector. What if Kathy and Ed had found a wise counsellor? What if there had been high-quality, low-cost childcare available, allowing Kathy to establish her own poise, get some respite, find time for her own creativity and to be with Ed when both were not burdened and drained? Why did Kathy, and perhaps Ed, have to pass the breaking point before anyone took a caring interest? These are some of the questions that arise from this tragic story of an "average American girl."

It is understandable why, after "spanking" Steven, Kathy didn't take him to the hospital. In the late 1960s, child abuse was not yet on the public agenda, people didn't talk about it, spankings weren't considered abusive. She didn't believe she had seriously hurt him, but she was afraid, bewildered, shocked at herself, ashamed and incoherent. She herself had been the victim of violence. She was out of control. When she learned Ed had whipped the already abused child, she did not question his actions; he was the head of the household, and she was too tired and troubled to protest.

Today, corporal punishment by parents against children is illegal in Sweden, Finland, Denmark, Norway, Austria, Cyprus, Latvia, Croatia and Germany (Fattah, 2001: 18). In North America since the 1970s, increasing numbers of people have turned to non-violent ways to discipline their children, such as taking away privileges or having a child take a "time out." But many parents still use corporal punishment. People who "spank" their children may well be abusing them, particularly if they use a weapon—a shoe, stick, belt or hairbrush. Although Parents Anonymous is an important organization for those who participate, most child abusers don't recognize themselves as such, or aren't willing to come forward and bear the stigma. In public opinion, child abuse is the worst of all possible crimes. Yet there are still few social services designed to assist parents who struggle with using physical or emotional violence against their children. Not incidentally, prisoners, whatever their crime, have a high rate of having been abused as children.

In Kathy's second year in prison she experienced two more tragedies. Her son, Timmy, lived with his father, and the courts ruled that she could no longer have contact with him. Her daughter, Brenda, was with a foster family who failed to bring Brenda for visits and didn't give her the letters and gifts that Kathy mailed to her. One day Kathy came to our session in tears because she'd received notice of a custody hearing for Brenda. The foster parents had petitioned to adopt her, and the hearing was set. Kathy applied for an "escorted absence" to attend the hearing, but the prison did not accommodate her. Because she was unable to appear at the hearing, the court ruled that she had "abandoned" her daughter, and Brenda was adopted by strangers, with all of Kathy's rights stripped away.

Kathy was a very good prisoner, and she was released from prison in 1974, after having served her minimum five-year sentence for second-degree murder. She returned to her hometown and found work in a factory. In time she fell in love with a man, became pregnant by him and then called off their plans to get married. Her brother shared an apartment with her and her new son. Her mother and stepfather later moved to a distant state, and Kathy was then on her own.

With old and new friends, all of whom knew the tragedy she had suffered, Kathy organized a mothers' group when her son was young. When any of the women in her circle started getting anxious or overstressed, they called each other for help. She became active in her community, took good care of her health, found order in her life. Losing Brenda and Timmy, with whom she was never reunited, caused her permanent pain. But she didn't succumb to sorrow, and she gave her whole attention to raising her new son with quiet gratitude.

Reference

Fattah, Ezzat A. (2001). "Victimizing the Helpless, Assaulting Children as a Corrective Measure." In *Victim Policies and Criminal Justice on the Road to Restorative Justice*. Leuven (Belgium): Leuven University Press.

5

NORMA

SEX IS ALWAYS THE HEADLINER

I N 1972, NORMA STAFFORD was enrolled in the women's studies class I co-taught, with Jean Gallick, in a university pilot program at the California Institution for Women. Although only in her forties, Norma was one of the eldest of the prisoners. Both Jean and I were moved by her writing, a talent Norma was just discovering. With Norma's permission, the quotes that follow are excerpted from writings she submitted to the class, letters, transcribed interviews and her unpublished autobiography.

Outside the prison, a lesbian-feminist political and cultural community was building across North America and beyond. Young women who were newly self-identifying as women who love women had respectful regard for lesbians of previous generations. Their foremothers' achievements and courage, in the face of rejection and outcast status, lent inspiration to the younger women to come out en masse and to stake their claim as a civic entitlement. Until the 1970s, bars were one of the few places where working-class gays and lesbians could safely meet one another; thus, these older lesbians were sometimes generalized as "old bar dykes." Norma was one of these women.

Relatively few lesbians go to prison, and those who do have been generally advised to conceal their sexual identity, to avoid stigma among the women and extra punishment by the staff. At CIW, women who had "an H on their jacket," that is, whose prison files correctly or incorrectly identified them as "homosexual," were marked for difficulties. However, even heterosexual women in prison frequently come to love other women. One of the few positive outcomes of incarceration is that women who formerly regarded other women primarily as rivals for men often learn to appreciate and trust one another. They also sometimes experience physical or platonic passion with another woman, although physical intimacy is infrequent given the pervasive surveillance and the punitive consequences if caught. At the beginning of the twenty-first century, many women's prisons have relaxed their scrutiny of "inappropriate" touching between women (such as hand-holding), but many others are still punitive over the slightest display of affection. Norma wrote in 1973:

> The institutional policy at CIW is "Don't Get Caught." Otherwise you get a write-up and disciplinary action, including segregation. They can't officially condone it, even though it's no longer against the law on the outside. There's no such thing as rape in here, the way they play it up in books and movies. "Homosexuality in Prison!" They make it sound like prison invented it. If a woman cuts her hair, they figure she's turned gay. Sex is always the headliner.
>
> I walk carefully. The fact that I'm a "butch" requires that I think twice on every word and action that could possibly have any significance regarding another woman. I can't talk to the same woman too often. I cannot use the word "love" lest it is overheard: in here, love equals sex equals hanky-panky. At the same time I need to have regular friends who shield me against other fools chasing after me. This place makes homosexuality something ugly, and they try to give you the feeling that you are base and degraded. I am neither.

It's a minute percentage of prisoners who are sure enough homosexual. And I do not need sex, per se. It is hard to find someone to hit it off with in order to have a happy relationship, like it is anywhere when you're new or alone. I've found that there are lots of things to do with energy, and sex is just one of them.

Norma sometimes expressed impatience with young, first-time prisoners who were "Jailhouse Turn-outs," meaning their first (and often only) sexual experience with a woman was inside the prison. She objected to the way they "flaunted" their new sexuality and indiscriminately came on to other women, with no idea of the challenges lesbians faced in the real world. Norma was open about her sexuality, but she never postured in the way of the young converts. As she said, from the perspective of age, "If you know who you are you don't need to signify."

The last of ten children, Norma was born to a family of Tennessee hill-country dirt farmers. They lived about fifty miles from Nashville, but her parents had never been there. Norma was the only one of her siblings to complete high school. In the 1950s, at age nineteen, she left the "severe rigid hard existence" of Tennessee for nursing school in Alabama. There she suffered discrimination, and she was expelled when her lesbian identity was exposed just before graduation. Having shamed her family and community, she was briefly married in an attempt to be "normal." Her marriage ended soon after both her parents died, her father by suicide. At a time when homosexuality was illegal, and considered both sinful and a disease, she was virtually chased out of town.

Running from the court of public opinion, Norma began her life of crime. She and her girlfriend drove around the country, with Norma financing their journeys and rented homes with forged cheques. She told me that up to the time of her first arrest she had a stereotype of a "criminal," and she never thought of herself or her girlfriend that way. For ten years they enjoyed adventures on the road, chasing their fortune and being chased by the law.

For her crimes of fraud Norma intermittently served five and a half years in Alabama and California state prisons, and weeks or months in a series of county jails in several states. Routinely, the arresting police wanted Norma to name the man they assumed she was working for. They had trouble accepting that a woman might travel around committing fraud on her own, or with another woman. On one occasion in a jail in northern California, when the police kept drilling her to name her connection and wouldn't let her sleep, she finally

> copped to a mythical Allen Goldberg, 40 years old, medium height, dark, 165 pounds, driving a new red Chevrolet Impala with a Florida license plate. The police were so pleased with themselves!! I got to go to sleep and they got to put out an APB [all points bulletin]!

Norma, having never thought of herself as a criminal type, was shocked to find herself at the Julia Tutwiler Prison for Women in Alabama in 1965. She describes the shock of being in a place where women tried to commit suicide as "the only way to eternal freedom." And she speaks of

> those who freaked out only to be locked in a strip cell or carted off to the state mental institution. Sometimes the pressures grew too heavy and we fought with each other. We prostituted our bodies for $16.00 per month as human guinea pigs. We swallowed diet pills, heavy tranquilizers, and even birth control pills. Each month the doctors did cervical biopsies on us. We were hungry. We used the $16.00 per month from the drug experiments on our bodies to buy food from the prison commissary to supplement our unhealthy prison diet. The food was the same in California. We were tired, hungry and overweight.

Norma was again subjected to medical experimentation in the California prison, where she and others were deliberately infected for clinical trials of the drug Flagyl.

Norma's key criticism of both the California and Alabama prisons was the lack of vocational programs. Instead of education and training that would help women become self-supporting upon release, they were (and are still) assigned to the drudge tasks of running a prison: washing dishes, cooking, mopping, hoeing weeds, picking up garbage, sweeping floors, painting buildings, digging ditches, doing laundry and sewing (making uniforms for men in prison). The more fortunate women are assigned to maintenance of state cars, driving a tractor, clerical duties and cosmetology training or work as nurses' aides, doctors' assistants, lab technicians, medical librarians or x-ray technicians. Only a few of these activities could potentially lead to employment, a situation that hasn't improved in thirty years. Even if someone acquires a skill, the equipment is always outdated, and many employers refuse to hire anyone with a prison record. When applying for work, it is a breach of parole to fail to acknowledge having been in prison.

When on parole from her first sentence in the California prison, Norma was unable to find stable employment. She was sinking into alcoholism, so she committed a string of conspicuous forgeries with the intention of getting caught, and she was. Then in her forties, she didn't know what to do except go back to prison.

Prisoners maintain the prison as a place of employment for the guards, administrators and other staff. In this new century, as serious crime rates continue to drop, prison populations continue to rise; then as now, as Norma observes, this increase is a political decision. More prisoners means a greater share of the state budget and more jobs for guards, even while education budgets are cut back.

In her second prison term at CIW, Norma worked for eighteen months on the yard crew and was then trained as the x-ray technician's assistant. Grade eight was the average school level achieved by women in the prison, which made Norma better educated than most. Most women's lives had been dictated by efforts to simply survive, and Norma's life of crime too was driven by economic need. She recalls:

> My mother and dad were born into poverty, hardships and heartbreaks. Few people where we lived attained a higher level than what birth gave them. "We may be poor but we're honest" was the battle cry, to overcome the sight of empty corncribs and smokehouses. My mother and father were hard-working, honest, God-fearing people, clearly attested to by the enormous crowds that attended their funerals. The funeral was a way of making up for those years of toil that bowed their backs and gnarled their hands.

Despite the poverty of her background, and compared with many other women's lives on the street, Norma had lived well during her decade of writing bad cheques at the expense of large businesses, banks and insurers. For a time, she and her partner even rented a pleasant suburban home, where they stayed for over a year until they could feel the law approaching and moved on again. Norma recalls the joy of those times when they were nestled into domestic bliss:

> When I remember my love, I think of intimate conversations; two heads bent together studying a small seashell; lying in bed late on Sundays with the coffee pot, TV and Sunday paper; dressing up together and stepping out now and then, knowing we made a striking pair and laughing at befuddled males; walking in the house and feeling contentment flooding over the tension and the tiredness; not being able to afford a whole dozen red roses, so I bought just one, and she cried.

At CIW, Norma and the few other over-forty prisoners hung out together, black and white, for which they received disapproval from younger women, black and white. Norma said simply, in regard to racial integration:

> We mix ourselves in the good company of each other. Too bad the young ones don't know what us older ones know. We're all in this messed-up world together.

As a twentieth-century southerner, Norma was unusual in her anti-racism, although she too had grown up assuming that segregation and white dominance were the natural order.

> Some of my earliest memories are of the good ole white brother so-and-so standing in the pulpit of our white Southern Baptist church praising the virtues of white Christians and damning the ways of sinners. I keep hearing the message: "So steeped was he in the evil of his sins his heart was black as the grave. Once purified of his sins he became as white as the pure driven snow." Thus my young mind conjured up visions of beauty = white = good: ugly = black = bad.
>
> I was taught: "Colored folks ain't got the same kind of feelings white folks do." If a white woman felt the need to make a verbal comment about a colored man's good looks, she'd say, "Well, you know for a nigger he looks alright." No one questioned that since we were white, we were superior to these people. I was never taught to hate colored folks, just to stay away from them. Most people had an air of amusement toward colored folks, and an attitude of condescension.
>
> I'd never heard of colored people working in medicine until I entered nurses' training, and learned that they hired colored women to take care of colored patients. Colored doctors were barred from hospital staffs. I was a student nurse in the emergency room of a hospital in Birmingham, and even that was segregated, one side for whites, one for colored. This was where all the poor people came with their tragedies and injustices. Here I became a woman and a nurse.

Her respect for black culture grew when Norma was first imprisoned at CIW. In the Alabama women's prison where she had previ-
ously done time, black and white women were strictly segregated,
with separate cell units and work assignments. It was assumed that
close association with blacks would contaminate whites, even if
the whites were already criminals by law. In California, the women
were generally segregated by choice socially and at meals, but cellblocks were integrated and there was no law against intermingling,
as Norma did with her friends.

Norma recalled being surprised the first time she saw black and
white women engaged in the same activity:

> ...like typing. And in the crafts shop I watched talented black
> hands mold clay into creative, fantastic shapes. I started hear-
> ing educated, sophisticated voices in the cellblock, the voices of
> black women who were articulate and strong. To Helen Terry,
> wherever you are, my humble "thank you," and may you always
> walk with God. You were the first black woman to become my
> friend here. Our talks made me hate segregation, and the laws
> of a hypocritical government that calls itself democratic yet
> walks on those whose skin is not white.

Our women's studies class was made to order for Norma, with
discussion of stereotypes about women, cross-cultural differences,
race and class, female sexuality, the role of the family, and the uses
of autobiography in self-study. It was exciting to Norma to learn
about the second-wave women's movement that was raging by the
early 1970s, and affirming to her to realize the importance of the
lesbian experience to that movement. In remembering, reflecting
on and writing her own story, Norma found her voice, which gave
her emotional strength. She became a bridge between the few other
"old dykes" in the prison, who were all very dignified, and the young
"whuppersnapper butches" who strutted around the prison grounds
with sexual vanity.

Norma writes of how, for lack of alternatives, while in prison in Alabama she killed time with canasta and embroidery. At CIW she took up knitting and handicrafts. She had no interest in any of these activities, so she spiced up her life by getting reinvolved in crime, right there in the prison:

Eventually I got off into peddling contraband. My contraband business became so profitable and interesting I devoted all my energies to it, supplying everything from chewing gum to clothes. I had a foolproof method of getting my wares into the prison. One of my best customers loved nice clothes, perfume and makeup, which were denied us, things that help make a woman feel and look like a woman.

Once I had my business together, I lived as comfortably as one can live locked up. There were only two other of my sisters who knew what I was doing. They worked for me. My personal conduct was flawless, so no one would have suspected.

One Saturday, just before Easter in 1970, I was coming from the administration building to my unit. It was an unbelievably beautiful day. Suddenly I was aware of the panoramic view that was laid out before my eyes. On the large circular concrete area, the Protestant chaplain and some of his congregation were working. They struggled against a stiff easterly breeze to set up their things for the Easter sunrise services. To my left sat six Indian women. One of them beat out a haunting rhythm on a tom-tom. They were chanting in their native language. In front of me, approaching the circle from the opposite direction, were three heroin addicts. The impact of that scene inside a state prison has stayed with me for years.

In 1971 I simply grew tired of my business and gave it up. The person who took it over did not do so well. She cheated her sisters and stayed in trouble on the dark side of prison life. Her pick-up spot was busted not too long after she started. Maybe I was lucky that I quit when I did. I could have had a new case.

Norma was an avid reader, which compensated for her isolation from the world; she didn't have visitors or correspond with anyone. She had a high-school education and almost four years of college and nurses' training, but she had no sense of direction for her future.

> The thing I have always feared most is getting to be like so many of my sisters in here, that is, to lose interest in life, in myself, and just stagnate. For almost a year I just drifted through my time. At night, alone in my cell, I saw myself as a robot. I functioned only when a guard pushed a lever that indicated I should move so many paces in a certain direction. When they pushed another lever, I would stand, sit, eat or lie down and sleep. I had quit questioning anything. I succumbed to mental lethargy, and physical lethargy overwhelmed me.

What Norma is describing is being a "good prisoner," also known as "cooperative." Independent women do not do well in prison. Compliant women do very well. At the point that Norma had almost given up on her life, the university program started up, and Norma was one of the first in line to enrol. Her enthusiasm never abated for the year and a half she was enrolled in courses prior to her release on parole. She describes what it meant to her:

> That women's studies class was a first. Never before had a college or university been here. They brought us books. They gave each of us our very own books. Dear God! What excitement, what energy flowed through those classes. Fifty of us started and fifty of us graduated. We shoved a three-month academic quarter into six weeks. We tripped with Margaret Mead, growled over *The Female Eunuch,* and cheered and applauded *Sisterhood Is Powerful.* Time flew by too swiftly.
>
> I could hardly wait from one class until the next. We had been able to hold our classes without the supervision of a guard. Once their curiosity was aroused, some of them wanted to sit in. Karlene put their request before us and our answer was a unanimous

no. The "no police allowed" policy continued when the program expanded that fall. The doors to the prison swung open to allow our new teachers to bring us new knowledge. They arrive in the wee morning hours after driving 500 miles from Santa Cruz. By 9:30 Saturday morning they are set up in their classrooms. They teach all day Saturday, then return to teach a half day on Sunday. I am unable to express the pleasure of associating with these positive-thinking individuals. I always come from class feeling renewed in my inner life.

It was in this class where I discovered I can write something other than bad checks, and where I first felt accepted by free-world people, instead of looked upon as a menace to society. Here I could talk openly about being a lesbian and not feel intimidated. I found my voice as an individual, my power and the power of other women. A unity was forged among us, a bond I'd never felt before. Unity among women is not tolerated in prison. The women's movement is a threat when it seeps through the barricades of a women's prison.

Through her studies Norma was able to focus and channel her creative energy. She was a dedicated student, and her age, experience and ease in the classroom gave her leadership status with her classmates. All volunteer groups that came to the prison were periodically shut out due to some actual or contrived crisis. This included the Santa Cruz Women's Prison Project, which coordinated the university program. When classes were cancelled by the prison administration, it was Norma who organized a protest.

When I read in the Daily Bulletin that the classes were canceled, I flashed on how much we needed, wanted and looked forward to those classes. My pain gave way to anger. I went searching for more of my sisters who might be feeling the same way. They were not hard to find. We were of one accord. Those beautiful people who came here to teach us were shut off from us. Our education was stopped. All communications were blocked.

It is illegal for prisoners to hold a meeting without a guard present. We held ourselves an illegal meeting, a short and quiet gathering. The unity among us was powerful. That was the first time that I saw Chicanas, Blacks and whites organize together. We wanted our college classes, we wanted our teachers back, whatever it took. We elected five of the strongest among us to carry out our wishes. Our group was offered meetings with everyone but the warden, but she was the one we wanted to see. And soon it was announced that she and Karlene, representing the Santa Cruz workshops, were to have a private conference. After their meeting the warden would meet with our committee. The powers that be tried to slip Karlene into the institution without our knowing it, but we knew when her plane landed at the airport! After their meeting the word came, "Karlene is come and gone, everything's okay, our classes start up again next week." The staff thanked us for keeping everything under control until the warden could solve the problem. Out on the prison grounds I kept meeting faces with big grins. Our people were coming back.

That was the first of a number of times that the Santa Cruz Women's Prison Project was temporarily barred from the prison during the four-year program. On another occasion, Norma and her classmates, and their supporters, conducted a sit-in on the lawn in front of the warden's office, declaring a work strike until the university program was back. They effectively impaired the functioning of the prison until, again, we were reinstated. Norma had a strong spine, but she was also sensitive and intuitively oriented to fairness and justice. She proved to be a prolific writer, including in correspondence in which she mused about the state of the world. For example:

I understand why poor people go to war. It is good to have an enemy to direct all our frustrations and hate toward. Uniforms, speeches, excitement, the attentions never before shown a boy, and amidst hugs, kisses and tears he is sent off to war.

Women should join hands with thousands more sisters to cordon off their sons. Women must stop furnishing soldiers for the money-holding rulers, stop the flow of sons who are sent off to die.

It has always been demanded that we, the women, be weak and submissive to the rule of man and never raise our voices in protest. The sons of the rich are protected from wars, while the sons of the poor are taken for target practice at home and abroad. The time has come—it is now—when we, the women, must realize the responsibilities we have toward ourselves, our children and the world.

Norma was specifically opposed to the war in Vietnam, and she wrote poems about it, including the following:

to an unnamed guerilla in vietnam

rumpled hair, bloodstained face
that was you in the stillness of
a photograph that won't quit my senses.
young man, without a name, you
stood thick in muscle and loving someone.
with nostrils distended, eyes blazing defiance
you stood as strong as I now stand, deep in shame
for your tortured body and lost young life.
they said you wouldn't talk, so
my government killed you.

my brother,
there is no requiem for you here
except this:
i love you and I love your defiance.
at the foot of your hate for me and mine
i do obedience to the fire passed on by your death.
your seeds have not been wasted
nor has your blood run in futile streams.

> i kiss the earth, squeeze the soil between my toes,
> yell at rivers and hug trees.
> because I know in these simple things of life
> a peasant, even like me, can touch
> your still form letting you know
> that you do not lie in the dark alone.
> i love you, young brother.

Norma also mused on what it was to be imprisoned, in the following two poems acknowledging vulnerabilities that other women sought to hide:

> [UNTITLED]
> tonight loneliness is my bed partner.
> he has been every night for five years,
> as steel bars wrapped in blackness
> take over my life at ten o'clock
> when the guard turns out my light.
>
> . . .
>
> [UNTITLED]
> nothing ever changes in a prison.
> the convicts are as old as time.
> their agelessness is offset only
> by the embalmed air of the keepers.

Fear underlies every negative dynamic within any prison, and Norma wrote about its effects:

> Today I walked as one always walks in here, a short distance. I felt the fear that prevails here as in no other place. Fear puts us to sleep at night and covers us with nightmares. Fear drags us from sleep each morning and pushes us toward a dull state assignment which we fearfully complete for fear that the powers that control our lives will keep us here longer otherwise.
>
> It is fear of losing her child that makes a laughing young

mother shrivel. And we all have the fear that our families and friends will give up on us. Fear rides above us like an overseer. Fear's whip lashes our heart.

Fear of me will keep an employer from reaping the benefits of my skills when I get out and ask him for work. Fear of hunger because I can't get a job will cause me to start lying on job applications. The fear of being caught will make me run, because I am afraid to come back here to live in this fear.

Fear merges with excitement when someone attempts an escape, providing an uncommon break in the monotony of prison life. Paradoxically, the woman who attempts to escape is often "short-timing," that is, she is very close to a release date after years of incarceration. As the date approaches she is obsessed, overwhelmed by anticipation, and can't wait. Also, there is often a fear that something will go wrong at the last minute and she won't get out after all.

Like most prisons, CIW boasts an abundance of security hardware—double chain-link fences topped with coiled razor wire, armed guards in watchtowers, cameras, laser detectors and so on. Anyone with the ingenuity to get past all that surveillance is much admired. Additionally, the prison attempts to prevent escapes by having regular locked counts of the prisoners. Each woman must go to her individual cell (sixty in each unit), sit on her cot, and face the narrow wicket in her door. This ritual occurs four times a day and begins with the guard walking up the corridor between rows of cells and calling out "Count Time! Count Time!" If the guard finds that someone has gone missing, she calls out "Frozen Count! Frozen Count!"—which means that no one will be able to leave her cell until the escapee is located. Following is Norma's poem about one woman's successful escape:

THE GONE ONE
"Count Time! Count Time!"

One hundred twenty feet
scuttling toward respective cells,

outlined with goodnight embraces and kisses
(called "queer actions" by our keepers).
Instant silence as the whole shuts it mouth.

No voices now.

In crepe-soled hush puppy oxfords
the Guard clomps ninety-seven steps
peeking in cells along the way
making a mark for each head she sees.
Totaling her marks she seeks a count
of sixty marks to equal sixty heads.

Furious pencil frightened guard
Her count refuses to be but fifty-nine.

"Frozen Count."

Fifty-nine hearts speed up to jolt
Fifty-nine bodies erect listening in the dark.

"Frozen Count."

The whole freezes.

Count again you female St. Peter!

Face red, steps angry
Pencil still furious unable to make sixty
Out of the true total fifty-nine.

A Sister Is Gone.

Gritty bitch, traitor to us cowards
Run, gone one, run, while I sleep
with a smile just for you.

Norma nurtured and gave encouragement to other imprisoned
women. She witnessed the valour of women in painful circumstances and made heroes of them in verse.

WOMAN SOLDIER
Lying in your captive labor bed
womb straining sweat pouring
you deliver your child
within these concrete walls and steel bars
because your infant is born of you/in here
she is labeled numbered and her mug-shot is taken
before she has breathed before the cord is cut
she has a number and she is called criminal
but you and I know you have delivered to us
another awesome female warrior.

I hear your deep woman's laughter
ring out through every cell block
and my heart is strengthened
my courage renewed because you are here just as
you are everywhere noble warrior
goddess of Death to the Power
giver of life, sweet sweet woman soldier.

As Norma's parole date came near, she felt the uneasy tensions of her own rebirthing:

[UNTITLED]
the contractions are coming harder now
all my efforts are more concentrated
i feel the wall thinning
more endeavor goes into my efforts
the pushing the straining the pain
bearing down from everywhere
will end
blessed relief the emergence of me
when I finally walk out those gates.

Upon release, in 1973, Norma felt she had "entered a new world, a women's world where I was accepted as a sister." Indeed, she was among friends from all over California who, in the previous year, had volunteered in the prison program and had become acquainted with her. We all wanted to see her succeed and did whatever we could to ease her adjustment, but our expectations only added to the pressures Norma felt in facing the practical realities of making a living. Before long she was again fighting her addiction to alcohol. This time, however, she quickly got involved in Alcoholics Anonymous and completed a thirty-day recovery program at a Los Angeles women's rehab centre. There her life underwent a pivotal change, and her self-identity shifted from "ex-convict" to "poet."

Through her readings, Norma quickly gained a following, and she was frequently invited to do radio and press interviews, as well as to speak at public events and in schools, churches and prisons. Invariably, she had a powerful effect on audiences. The cadence of her speech and the passion in her voice recalled the sermons of the Southern Baptist preachers of her childhood. Always generous with her time, whether or not she was being paid, Norma gave presentations across California at many community fund-raisers in support of the university courses at the prison. Her reputation spread, and soon she was doing tours in other states. She said of those experiences:

> I have been honored many times as a guest speaker in college and university classrooms, in California, New Mexico, Iowa, Kansas and Indiana. Each occasion has filled me with humble pride. And I have found myself in the unbelievable position of standing at the pulpits of churches. But nothing affects me so deeply as when I am allowed to enter a jail or a prison and share my poetry with my sisters there.

Whenever she gave readings for prisoners, they shouted out affirmations, black, white and brown alike: "You're telling it like it is, girl." "You got that right!" "Amen!" She had to hold back tears when saying goodbye to women who couldn't leave, including old friends with whom she had once been incarcerated.

Norma's poetry was published in various periodicals, including *Ms.*, *The Realist* and *Crime and Social Justice*. In 1975 her work was compiled and published with the title *Dear Somebody*, financed and distributed with support from the Unitarian Fellowship in San Francisco and the Santa Cruz Women's Prison Project. In time she also wrote short stories and essays for a number of anthologies. She was gratified that her work was published and that she was now reaping some of the rewards of "an educated woman," having nearly finished her nursing degree before her formal schooling was aborted by lesbophobes.

> "Git yerself a good education and then you'll have somethin' that ain't never nobody gonna be able to take away from ya." I heard that from my Mama from as long as I can remember. I can still see her grim determination as she urged me to acquire that which "ain't never nobody gonna be able to take away." And now here I was speaking in universities, reading my poetry and prose, which started in my final year of incarceration. For me those are times of honor. The classroom holds a sacred place in my life.

One of the classrooms where Norma honoured students with a talk was in a course on prisons that I was teaching at Sonoma State College (now University) in early spring, 1978. When she arrived, with her partner, Jan, it was a happy reunion for us after some time without a visit. However, what started as an eloquent guest lecture ended as a fiasco over their tiny dog, Shelsie, a Yorkshire terrier. Following is Norma's account of what happened:

> I take Shelsie everywhere. Walking across campus I turned her loose on the grounds and she ran and romped. Then I carried her to the Stevenson building and proceeded, with Jan and Shelsie, to the third floor. No signs indicated that no dogs were permitted in the building. The talk went well, and there were a lot of

questions from the students. Shelsie stayed on Jan's lap the whole time. At about 9 P.M., during a break, Jan went outside so Shelsie could get some exercise and water. When Jan returned with her, in the hallway she encountered two men, one elderly, and he told her dogs weren't allowed. Jan told the men that she and Shelsie would have to return to the classroom to get me, but that they'd be gone in less than an hour, when the class would be over.

Jan came back, Shelsie was on her lap, and the 40+ students were in the process of forming small discussion groups, when suddenly the door opened and in burst an armed, uniformed police officer and behind him the small elderly man she'd seen before, now wearing green work clothes. The policeman was irate. Shelsie's so small he didn't see her at first, but when he did he marched over, leaned across the desk, and shook his finger in Jan's face, telling her that bringing the dog in the room was illegal. Jan stayed calm, agreeing to leave with Shelsie, but the policeman became even angrier and blocked her, shaking his yellow pad in her face. I went over and picked up Shelsie, and told the policeman that I was unaware that we had broken a rule, that we were sorry, and if he would just give us time to gather our belongings we would leave. But he was furious and continued to badger us. Everyone was bewildered.

He got more and more agitated and soon the classroom was in an uproar. Karlene asked him if we could all just please leave now, and offered to accompany the policeman in retracing our steps to and within the building, so he could see that there were no signs prohibiting dogs. But by then he was out of control, in a rage, and I began to feel fear rising up in me. Here before me was a very angry man with a gun and a badge. I am on parole. Some of the students started leaving the classroom, and he attempted to block their exit. The students pushed by him, and then a group of students encircled Karlene, Jan, Shelsie and me and practically carried us out of the room, where the rest of the students were lined up on both sides of the hallway to let us pass, then closing up to block the policeman chasing us. When we got outside he did reach us and grabbed Karlene but she pulled away and students got between them. During the tussle I put Shelsie in Jan's arms and she ran off with him.

All the time this was going on, my mind was filled with fear, a fear borne from witnessing irate policemen pull their guns on unarmed people. The policeman was out of control, his face was red. It was a power trip for him. He was shoving students and threatening to arrest everyone. When he used his walkie-talkie to call for backup, everyone instantly dispersed, and Karlene and I ran together and found Jan behind bushes, holding Shelsie close to her chest. In the parking lot we met up with a bunch of students. Everyone was still frightened and shaking, and relieved that no one got shot. The beauty of that night was the spontaneous unity of the students, which sprang up in the face of an armed adversary. The students understood the sanctity of the classroom, where the search for knowledge and understanding must not be desecrated by uniforms and guns.

The next day I went to the administration to complain and learned that the campus police wanted me to be arrested for "harbouring a dog." The college authorities called in students and others as witnesses. Everyone had experienced what Norma described, resulting in an apology and a reprimand of the officer. In our defence, the absence of signs prohibiting dogs was significant. Also, when the college created the no-dogs rule, they didn't have in mind a dog that could fit in a purse. Everyone agreed it was a case of outrageous overkill, a silly farce and kind of exciting for the students, though frightening. For Norma it was a nightmare.

This incident occurred in 1978, and it was easy to speculate that the elderly groundskeeper and the officer he summoned were hostile to feminists on their campus. And it didn't take much "gaydar" to identify Jan and Norma as a lesbian couple. Moreover, the two men could have known that Norma was a former prisoner. The two men had behaved irrationally, in the way people do when their actions are based on prejudice.

IN ALL HER PUBLIC talks, Norma effectively described the tragedies that beset women who go to prison. For example, when she worked in the prison hospital she often witnessed atrocities, and she was especially affected by the anguish of women who gave birth there.

> Sometimes if a woman gets pregnant when she's on parole she is sent back to the penitentiary, a "get tough" policy. I saw twenty-six big-bellied women come in for violating their parole by getting pregnant. One woman, who was brought back right away, delivered two babies in the prison within a year. Her new baby was taken away from her within seventy-two hours. If the family can't afford to get down there and pick them up, the welfare people come and get them.
>
> One of the worst things I ever saw was in the prison hospital where a large black woman had given birth to her son. The baby was born, they took him, and didn't let him nurse. There she sat on the side of her bed crying from the pain of engorged breasts dripping milk for a baby that wasn't there to nurse.

Resolved to make a living without resorting to illegal activity, Norma worked at various jobs along with doing volunteer advocacy work and readings. While living in Santa Cruz, she worked at a halfway house, assisting other former prisoners who were making the transition from prison to the "free" world. In another counselling job she found she could work effectively with men. Some years later she worked with young mothers who were drug-dependent. In her personal life she fell in love with several women before settling in with a nurturing partner in a mountain home in northern California. There she had a menagerie of farm animals, including a pot-bellied pig and peacocks, and she raised and developed special breeds of goats.

Over the years Norma continued to write and to stay active in support of imprisoned women. She had done readings in various other prisons, but she didn't return to CIW until 1995, twenty-two years after her release. It was demoralizing.

More than three times more women than the 600 when I was
there. The guards are even meaner and crueler to the women.
Medical services have deteriorated. All pain medication was
taken from the AIDS victims. They told me about a woman
who died in handcuffs, crying for medicine that they wouldn't
give her.

In the mid-1990s Norma became an advocate for Daisy Bensen,
a prisoner at CIW who has never had a fair trial. Charged with murder, though her guilt is in question, Daisy had been heavily, forcibly drugged by the jail staff, and she had slept through most of her
trial, unable to participate in her own defence. Norma wrote a play,
She Stands, about Daisy's experience. Following are excerpts.

> He Is the Doctor!
> The doctor keeps prescribing
> pills to give our Daisy.
> He has never even seen her
> but he keeps prescribing.
> Do not argue with the doctor!
> It is your sleep time, Daisy
> the courtroom is your cradle
> your lullaby sung by the prosecutor
> backed up by the jury
> directed by the judge.
> Do not argue with the doctor.
>
> VERDICT
> Guilty! Guilty! Wake up, Daisy
> You have been found Guilty
> By a jury of your peers
> Here are your pills, Daisy
> Take your pills, Daisy
> They will calm you down.
> Seventeen Years to Life, Daisy.

In 1996 Daisy filed for a new trial, but at the court hearing her request was denied. Norma attended Daisy's hearing and sent out a newsletter about the case. Her mission was not only to defend Daisy, but to expose more generally the practice of forced drugging that has been prevalent in many jails. She gathered medical records and court documents from men and women who had been excessively drugged against their will. Norma says of them:

A few of the men suffered terrible brain damage from the drugs that were forced on them while they were detained in a county jail awaiting trial. One man lost his eyesight due to brain damage caused by psychotropic drugs administered to him by the jail staff. Another guy is in a wheelchair for life, due to the forced drugging he endured while in a county jail in Idaho. This fellow was hale and hearty at the time he was arrested. He was a truck driver. Never again will he walk, doing his time in a wheelchair. Another man has to have help feeding himself, due to brain damage from forced drugging while awaiting trial. He is now a "spastic" forever. People who are fortunate enough to have a private attorney do not have to worry about being drugged by force.

She Stands was produced in Philadelphia in 1996, and Norma was there. Her experience of that city pulled at her desire to be focused on her poetry. In a letter she wrote:

Opening night I hadn't slept for forty-eight hours. It was really happening, Daisy's story at last before the public. And the city is intoxicating. Music, art galleries, buildings standing sturdy and proud after 200 years. Out of the residential sections there are theaters and playhouses on each block, some regal, some raggedy, actors, musicians, dancers working hard, putting their energies into this night. Walk past coffee houses, faces intense, pouring out the poet spirit. I am hungry to be in that atmosphere, charged with creative energy.

Ever conscious of the injustice of incarceration for those without the resources for a defence, in a 1972 conversation Norma imagined a world where, instead of prison, communities offer services to help people learn how to take care of themselves.

> I like the idea of "Do your time where you commit your crime." Counseling and education on the streets would work for the majority of incarcerated people. Prison is a total waste of human life and taxpayers' money. Everyone here needs a decent paying job out there, instead of being stuck in here, worthless to society. Being in prison is like being dead.

Norma often used the image of death to describe how she felt as a prisoner until she was awakened to herself through her writing. In 1973, she wrote in a letter, "I used to think that I was dead in here. That isn't true anymore. I am alive." She surely was, and still is today, marking more than thirty-two years of freedom.

For all the years I've known her, Norma has lived with gusto for all that life offers, without complaint for that which she lacks. She is a success story, a woman who finally left prison never to return. These were her parting words as she was leaving the prison in 1973:

> I think I will
> put in my false teeth
> go forth
> and attack the world.

And attack it she did, with a fierce embrace. She has made a life for herself, a poet of consequence. Now in her seventies, still living in the mountains, Norma has suffered serious physical problems. Like most people, she has suffered personal disappointments. But she has also been blessed, and she is grateful. She retains her love of life. Her mind is still at work, her heart is still open, her spirit still shines brightly, and she is well loved and cared for.

6

VICKI

THE LOW-DOWN HIGH LIFE

Introduction: AN

VICKI PRESENTS A FORTHRIGHT accounting of her young days on the road to freedom lost, and she marks the milestones in sometimes unforgettable language. The former Baby Queen of Hollywood seemed bound to become a Prisoner of the State.

Vicki's was not a childhood of deep poverty, yet it was burdened by a heavy share of adults' work, when through play she should have been fashioning talents to define her own future. It is symbolic that Vicki's first theft was from her mother's house—to furnish a rented room far from the responsibilities of home. Then, as a teenager, she married a man whose mother supported them in style.

The culture in which Vicki lived lacked a credible exchange of information between generations. She perceived her mother as preferring a lie to the truth. She did not want to hear her father tell her how smart she was, sensing a trap. Vicki was a chronic truant, untouched by schooling she identified as coercion rather than opportunity. Her bright, inventive mind was on the loose.

Drugs are central to Vicki's story, and it was her mother who gave her her first "dexie," from a home medicine cabinet bursting with prescription drugs. Frequently left in charge of a large family of children, while the parents went out to play, Vicki developed a peer loyalty, a sense of "us" against "them." In this same spirit she got attached to the drug culture, which swept into middle-class communities, terrifying adults but enchanting the young with exotic code names for secret highs that could be pirated from behind the local drugstore counter. Alas, Vicki's play became her work, and for that she was sent to prison.

Comments: KF

Vicki's story is the parable of a woman who embraces life, takes risks and lets herself be seduced by pleasures that then end in disaster. We met in the women's studies class at the California Institution for Women. Short, dark, strikingly pretty and womanly, Vicki was outgoing, intelligent and kind. In our interview sessions, she was animated and funny, at the same time remembering situations that couldn't be construed as fun.

Vicki's Story

My father was born in Krakow and grew up with four siblings in a Polish neighborhood in Pittsburg, where he maintained equipment for the city. His mother never spoke English. He came to California around 1940 and met my mother here. She was born in Midland, Texas, on the fourth of July, one of thirteen children, her father an evangelical minister. She grew up during the Depression, very poor. Her family moved between Texas and California several times before settling in Inglewood, California.

When my parents were married, he was thirty-two and she was twenty, he European Catholic and she Southern Baptist. They had nothing in common except they both liked to party a lot and both liked sex. They were married in the bird sanctuary at Griffith Park [in Los Angeles] by my mother's father. The marriage was for the birds from start to finish.

I grew up in a racially integrated community in the San Fernando Valley, mostly Chicano, some black, a few white. I never heard racism at home. I was aware of prejudice, but it wasn't close to me. The whole school was pretty delinquent, and our hostility was directed toward the authorities, not each other.

During the war both my parents worked at a defense plant. When my mother got pregnant my father was very upset; he didn't want children. I was born on September 30, 1943, in Los Angeles. My father changed his mind, and from that day on I was Daddy's girl. I was more a toy than a child to my mother. She had pictures taken at every studio in Hollywood and entered me in all kinds of contests. I won some for being a smart baby and others for being a good baby. I was Baby Queen of Burbank and Baby Queen of Hollywood and Little Miss America.

My dad went into real estate, and we bought a house in Redondo Beach. My mom still worked at the plant, and my grandma took care of me. She was a Sunday school teacher, cooked a lot, was very kind and soft-spoken. My grandpa was a preacher all day every day and yelled a lot about hell and damnation. He scared me.

My sister Sissy was born when I was two and a half. I hated her, really jealous. I liked going to nursery school and parties. My family all liked parties for any reason, and we always had birthday parties.

My mom decided she wanted us to go to Catholic school, so she became a Catholic. Until then we had been attending the Baptist church. I had to take a bus to and from school and go to mass every morning. We also had religious training during school and had to pray almost constantly, it seemed.

My sister Dolly was born when I was six, and Mom said she could be my baby. I named her. I really loved her, and she's still my closest sister.

My mother never did cook or do housework. She had jobs, and I resented doing the work at home. I had to stand on a chair to do the dishes, and it took me hours. I used to plot how to kill my mom, and usually poisoned or stabbed her. But the best time of day was when my dad came home from work. We would run and jump on him. He'd take us on picnics, to the beach, movies. He was the good guy around the house.

When my mother became a Catholic she didn't believe in birth control anymore, and the babies started coming like hotcakes. Bibby was born fifteen months after Dolly.

My dad loved to gamble and also drank a lot. He eventually became alcoholic, but he was never mean—always laughing and cheerful with us. My mom and dad fought a lot, violently, and made up passionately. She usually started it. She threw boiling water on him, and stabbed him, and she screamed a lot, at everyone. Also, she was fooling around with other men, and it seemed to us that she did everything she could to make his life miserable. All he did was love her.

My mother was pregnant again and wanted to move to a better neighborhood. Instead, my dad bought two lots on the same block, for us and our uncle. I was nine in September and Marty was born in November. I liked her, too; I liked all of them except Sissy. Sissy was constantly lecturing me when we were kids, threatening to tell Mommy. But she wouldn't. All us five kids would get mad at each other, but we'd never tell on each other, no matter what happened. It was us against them. When one of us got a whipping, we'd all cry.

When I was nine I learned to cook, and from then on I did most of the cooking. My dad cooked some; my mom never learned how. She didn't eat with us, either. She took her meals in bed on a tray. I was responsible for all the housework, but all of us kids did it. My mother was a tyrant. My father worked long hours and went out with his customers, always pretty well lit by the time he got home.

One of our favorite games was knocking on the neighbors' doors at night and then running away. When my mom went to the hospital we'd all dress up in her clothes and have parades. And we liked to undress and look at each other with all the kids in the neighborhood.

Susie was born when I was ten, my youngest sister and the prettiest of the six of us, very dark and sort of oriental-looking. We nicknamed her the Queen of the Jungle.

When I was eleven, I went to live for a few months with my bachelor uncle in his big house across the street. He was bald and told me the Chicago wind blew his hair off. He told me a lot of stories about his travels with the merchant marines. We had a lot of fun together. I would cook and we would eat and gossip about my mom and the neighbors.

When I was eleven, Teddy was born. It was kind of a novelty, having a brother. When he was about two months old my parents would go out and leave me with all the kids. I'd sleep with a broom by the bed to beat away the kidnappers. My mother told us a lot about strange men and little girls. I still don't speak to strangers much. Some of my sisters hitchhike all around, but I'd be afraid to.

The next year we got another brother, Ricky. Our mother did give us a good sex education. She bought books and read them to us on where babies came from, and how nice it was, but only for married people. For others it was a sin. The nuns used to tell us about virgin martyrs. Sex was an open subject around the house, and our parents spent a lot of time in bed. They'd even come home at noon when they both worked in the real estate office. They were either making love or trying to kill each other all the time.

When I was fourteen Andy was born, ninth child, third son. My mom was all messed up inside and had to go to the hospital for a hysterectomy, so a big fat woman named Flo came to live with us, a real nice lady.

Mother was a hypochondriac, spent a fortune on doctors. She took so many pills she put in an extra medicine cabinet in her bathroom: stimulants, tranquilizers, sleeping pills. When there was a lot of work to do for a party or something, she'd give me one of her dexies. I liked them.

Vicki's casual mention of her mother throwing hot water at her dad and stabbing him, and of her father's reciprocal violence, is troubling. She also told me about living briefly with an adored aunt whose life was threatened by her husband. Violence seemed rampant in Vicki's life, but she treated it lightly, with a cavalier acceptance of it as a regular part of life. Yet violence was in no way a factor in her crime. As a child Vicki was the most grown-up, stable member of a chaotic-sounding family. But that changed when she entered adolescence.

I ran away when I was fifteen, with my boyfriend, to the house of a girl I knew in Hollywood. The next day my parents arrived with the police, and our boyfriends were booked for statutory rape. But I was still a virgin, and they got out a few days later. The police said I'd go to juvenile hall if I didn't go home and that I'd get raped there. But I said I'd rather get raped than go home with my mother and be her slave. A probation officer investigated, and she said she didn't blame me; she wouldn't go home either if she were me.

I stayed at juvenile hall four and a half months, during which time they tried to place me in a foster home. I refused. The psychiatrists decided I was not delinquent, and finally they put me in a place for girls from broken homes. I refused to go to the Catholic school, and then got kicked out of public school. I like to read and got in trouble for reading when I should have been doing other things. I went to live with my aunt and stayed out of trouble. [She and my uncle] had just bought a drive-in restaurant, so I went to work for them.

At the end of the summer Mom conned me into going back home because Flo, the nanny, had quit. I skipped school all the time. My girlfriends and I drove around to schools in the valley and stole hubcaps to sell. I hung out with a car club. At this point, my mother was playing the concerned parent role to the hilt. So I'd just sneak out. I'd lie to her. She'd rather hear a lie than the truth any time. Except for the hubcaps, I wasn't doing anything wrong. I didn't even smoke cigarettes. Most of my friends drank and smoked weed, but I didn't.

My parents went away for the weekend a lot, and every time they went I had a party. I would start on Friday night and throw everyone out on Sunday in time to clean up before they got back. My uncle across the street and grandparents at the corner must have known, but they never said anything. All the kids liked the parties and would run in and out and play with people, and they'd help me clean up. Then Rosa came to live with us and stopped the parties. She was from Mexico, didn't speak English. My parents spoke Spanish, but we didn't. She was a fun-loving girl, would dance around the house, play the guitar and her Mexican records. On days off she would play in bars.

I was fifteen when I decided to quit school. My dad was disappointed, because he wanted me to go to college. He was always telling me how smart I was.

Vicki quit school to party. She didn't drink but her friends did, and they'd crash other people's parties or have their own in the street, at the beach, on a cliff outside town, or at the home of someone whose parents were out of town. Sometimes the parties lasted as long as two weeks. Her parents were protesting her absence from home, so at age sixteen she moved out altogether.

I'd been working for my aunt and uncle and had saved a little money, so I rented an apartment with my friend Dolores. She was fifteen and I was sixteen, but I had ID for eighteen. It was a rooming house, with the bathroom down the hall. Our "apartment" cost $14 a week and we loved it. I stole a couple of credit cards and a few linens from my mother, then we went shoplifting to get more things. We lived only three blocks from town, and "town" was only one street. Dolores had a car so we could trip around. When the rent was due again I went home and took an air conditioner and a stereo and hocked them to pay the rent.

Vicki's mother had introduced her to prescription pills to pep her up when her assistance was needed. At age sixteen, for the first time on her own recreationally, Vicki took an amphetamine someone gave her at a party. After everyone else was gone or asleep, she stayed up most of the night speedily cleaning the entire house, including the patio and the porch. She continued to socialize with her friends all the next day, which turned out to be a memorable day for another reason. When she went home to her apartment that night, her room-mate's boyfriend was visiting, along with his brother Dan.

As soon as they were gone, Dolores told me, "Stay away from Dan, Vicki. He's no good. He just got out of jail. He'll only hurt you. He doesn't care anything about anyone and he sells marijuana." Of course, I was fascinated. The next day Dan came over. I still hadn't been to sleep from that pill. We drove around and he gave me two more pills, bennies. I took one and dropped the other in my purse and forgot about it. That night we [Vicki, Dan, Dolores, and Dan's brother Gene] were talking in the car in the parking lot of Howdy's Drive-In, where we hung out. I had a lid of weed in my bra that I was carrying for them. It worried me, and I was feeling sort of dazed because I hadn't slept in three days. I saw a famil-iar-looking woman coming across the parking lot, and I couldn't place her until she walked right up to the car, stuck her head in the window, and said, "Victoria!" Oh my god, it was my mother! She said to get out of the car, because she was taking me to the police department.

Dolores knew I had that weed, and she told my mom to leave me alone, to distract her so I could get rid of it. I handed it to Dan without her seeing, before she dragged me off to the police station. She told the police I ran away from home, stole her credit cards and other things, and was hanging with a bunch of hoods. All true. They put me in a little glassed-in booth. She dumped my purse out on the desk for the sergeant to see. I could see what they were doing but not hear them. She got her credit cards and the pawn ticket, and then came to that damn pill. A cop picked it up and walked to the booth, showed it to me and asked if I knew what it was. I told him that where I lived everyone knew what those things were, and that he knew it. I told him I found it in the bathroom at the drive-in. He asked if I was going to take it. I told him I hadn't decided. He asked if I'd taken any already and I said no. Then he asked if I'd been smoking "reefers." That really is the word he used! He thought he was hip. I said no and he shined a light in my eyes. He asked what

I'd been taking and I told him I drank some beer. And then he sent me home with my mother.

After a week Vicki left again, and she never again lived at home. She lived with girlfriends, shoplifted food and enjoyed her freedom. She was a wild kid, except that she had a conservative attitude toward sex.

I used to lecture my friends every day about screwing everyone they went out with. I was still a virgin, and I told them they were ruining their lives. They'd laugh and shine me on, but I was dead serious. One day Dan took a bunch of us to the zoo. I drank some sloe gin and it was my first drunk. Later we went to the little park at the back of the sanitarium; it was always empty at night. We brought blankets and all went off in different directions. I was with Dan. That was it. When I got out of the car Dan just said, "See you later." The insensitive bastard. I had just ruined my life. He'd never even told me he liked me. I found out later it was done on a bet. My friends gave me a hard time and told everyone we knew.

Everyone did feel sorry for me that it was Dan, instead of someone nicer who would at least care. I was crushed. The nuns had told me what happened to that kind of girl. I moved in with my aunt and uncle and I wouldn't leave the house, just took care of their kids. That lasted until my seventeenth birthday, when I went to a dance and ran into José, a friend of Dan's. He was ten years older, but nice, and we started going out every weekend. We liked each other a lot, but I loved Dan. This went on for a couple of months, and then one day Dan came over, casual, like he'd just been there yesterday. He wanted me to break my date with José and go out with him that night, which I wouldn't do. It wouldn't be right. Dan left, mad. That night we were at the drive-in and Dan pulled in and parked right in front of us. Dan came over the next day, and then every day, but on the weekends I still went out with José, with no sex. I was talking to my parents again, and we'd see each other. My parents were being nice without trying to make me come home, but my mom still made me mad. Like, I would steal clothes and she'd wear them and tell me they looked better on her.

Then Dan asked me to go to mass with him on Christmas Day. Christmas Eve I went to a dance with José and took some bennies and reds. José had to carry me into the house. So when Dan came to pick me up I was still loaded. I'd never taken reds before. My girl-friends helped me get dressed, and we all went to mass. After, we drove around all day and in the evening he took me to his mother's house for dinner. They seemed to have a lot of money, different from me. She was very nice, but I was afraid of her.

On New Year's Eve I went with José to a dance, on the next morning with Dan to the Rose Bowl parade, then drove around. Dan smoked weed constantly and was always getting tickets for driving too slow. He took me to meet his friend, a call girl who loved Dan and told me so. But he told her we, he and I, were going to get married, which was news to me.

José was upset that I stopped seeing him, and he never spoke to Dan again, either. I was in love and didn't care. We were ready to get married, but my mom said she wouldn't sign for me unless we had a big church wedding. So we did. Dan made me give up stealing from stores, because he made enough money selling dope. I never stole anything from a store again. He taught me all about sex, a good teacher.

Before the wedding, Vicki and Dan lived for weeks or months with a variety of friends and relatives, everyone making wedding prepa-rations. Dan's mother hired Vicki to assist her in her work as a hos-pital dietician. But then came another startling turn of events.

I was pregnant. I didn't want to have children, ever, and here I was pregnant already and not even married. To make matters worse, Dan was overjoyed. I had to quit working because I was sick. The day before, Dan and my mother got in a big fight, pulling me in dif-ferent directions and yelling at each other. But they worked it out. We got married in the summer, 1961. I was seventeen years old and four months pregnant. Dan was twenty. It was a beautiful wedding, High Mass, long white dress, chantilly lace, hoop, bustle and train. I was late. Dan was nervous. So was my dad. But it was nice. We had the reception at the home of a millionaire. Everyone got drunk and ate a lot into the night.

Dan got a job, first one in his life. My mother-in-law gave us furniture as a wedding present and we leased an apartment near her. I was really happy. Dan worked and I packed him a lunch. But then he got laid off and didn't look for another job. His mother paid him for helping her out. She wanted him to stay dependent on her. I kept house and cooked a lot and got really fat, gained forty-five pounds with the baby. Dan had a bleeding ulcer and hypoglycemia, so I had to be careful what I fed him. When I was about six months pregnant I got really sick and asked Dan to call my mom. For the first time in my life I asked for my mother, and the bitch wouldn't come. She said to call a doctor. When it was time for the birth I insisted on going to a Catholic hospital so the priest would be there to give me last rites, just in case.

Danny was born a month premature, and I did almost die and so did he. Dan was scared to death and started praying, promising God that if I lived he'd never use dope again. Danny was born placenta previa and that's what almost did him in. I passed out, and when I woke up Dan and my friend Dolores were standing over the bed, telling me how pretty the baby was. I really loved him.

For six months we were super-happy. Dan was still selling weed, but he wouldn't smoke anymore, which I didn't care about, but he also wouldn't let me take any diet pills to lose all that damn weight. Not even legal ones. So I joined a yoga class, starving and exercising with yoga. It took six months to lose it.

When we were first married I told Dan I wouldn't put up with all the infidelity his brothers' wives put up with. If he wanted to go out and run around, fine, but if he went out one night, I'd go out the next. Big words for someone who couldn't even drive! But I meant it, and he knew it. Because of that he would never go anywhere without me. Even when I just needed something from the store, he'd insist I go with him. He was a lot of fun. I really loved him; he was a great father. But he was also crazy. Spoiled. Our backgrounds were entirely too different. He was mama's little boy. I came from a big family.

Dan would go crazy whenever he didn't get his way. He would become very violent and hit me. He never really hurt me, but I didn't like it and wasn't about to take it. Dan was a Virgo; they are all perfectionists, I think, and I was not, but did things the way he wanted them done to make him happy. I really tried and was a good wife. After about a year, Dan's mother bought us a three-bedroom house, two baths, dining and family rooms. I had my sister Sissy come live with us to take care of little Danny while I worked for our aunt. Sissy was sixteen and in high school. This worked out well for her because my mom had left my dad and was living with some guy up north. My dad lost his office and all his property.

Sissy and I got along pretty well by then. I liked her. Then Lloyd, a friend of Dan's, came to live with us, separated from his wife. Most of the neighbors were retired, a mile from any store and I still didn't drive. I was lonely, though Dan and I went out a lot at night, to clubs and to see friends. But Dan would stay up late every night. I had a baby and couldn't do that. Also, it didn't feel like my home. It was like I was taking care of it for my mother-in-law. All the bills, even the utilities, went directly to her. She even bought our food. It was like playing house. Dan spent his time waxing his cars, cleaning the grills with a toothbrush. He wanted me to sit by him while he did it.

When my mother came over, we argued. Dan's friend Lloyd thought she was trying to seduce him, and she was. Dan couldn't stand her. She left the guy up north and moved back in with my dad and the kids like she'd been to the store. A few months later, she left again and took the kids with her. My dad just took it, and I'd get disgusted with him for that.

Dan got hooked on TV and got mad because I read too much. Lloyd would help with housework and laundry, like a brother to me. He stayed out of my arguments with Dan. Sissy didn't. I'd end up having to protect her from him.

Dan got too violent and crazy. It was better when he smoked weed. Finally I decided to leave. I loved him but couldn't take it. I rented a little room. When Dan got home he broke down the locked bathroom door to get Sissy to tell him where I was, but she told him to go to hell, and he gave her a black eye. For days I didn't leave the little room where I was staying with Danny. But then my uncle died and I had to go to the wake, and Dan showed up. He still had that power over me. I agreed to come home. Sissy and Lloyd moved out. Three months later, when I was winning at Monopoly, Dan socked me in the ribs, then went to bed to watch TV. He'd go nut-city and then a few minutes later he'd be over it.

We were becoming just like my parents. I knew I couldn't live like that, have a bunch of kids and raise them in that atmosphere. I planned, methodically. When all the plans were made I walked out with Danny, left a letter for Dan and moved in with a woman who had three children, to share the rent. She was a couple of years older than I. I was nineteen and starting a new life. We had my sister Dolly come to live with us, to babysit while we both worked. Dolly was thirteen then. I learned to drive and got hired as a barmaid. Soon I was the manager. I moved into an apartment in Los Angeles with my old friend and now sister-in-law Dolores. She and Dan's brother Gene were now married but he was in jail for drugs. I hung out in the bar with her, but everyone treated me like a kid because I didn't drink when I went there.

During this time I was seeing Dan, but he didn't know where I lived. I'd just meet him somewhere so he could take Danny for weekends. After about six months he found out where I was working and came into the bar and wrecked the place. He told me I had no business working in places like that, and if I didn't quit he'd tell them how old I was. So I quit and went to work in a restaurant. I had left Dan with the house and all the furniture his mother gave us. I hadn't wanted anything but out.

After a couple of months I left the restaurant and got a job in the bar where I hung out with Dolores. I liked it there because I knew all the people. Then one day, the police busted the place for gambling. I was underage and I had a bag of pills on me, so I was relieved they didn't arrest me. I decided not to work there anymore, but I still went in there every night. Dan found out where I lived, so I moved, but he tracked me down and one morning I woke up to the sound of the door coming in and there was Dan. He said if I didn't come back to him I was going to die. I called the police. He wouldn't leave. They came and took him to jail. Six hours later, there he was again, with a knife. Dolores called the police again, and again he waited and they took him. I called his mom and told her to leave him in jail this time. She did, and the judge gave him a year in prison for violating his probation. He'd sold some weed to minors and his mother had bought him out of it so he'd only got probation. This time he did the time.

While Dan was in prison, Vicki moved back into the house his mother had bought for them, and she resumed partying, becoming intimate with Ronnie, a friend of Dolores who had pursued her. Then she moved out; too many bad memories there. Her mother-in-law stopped making the house payments, but it took a year to foreclose, so for the duration Vicki ensconced her mother, her mother's latest new boyfriend and her siblings in the house.

Vicki's life as she described it was a roller-coaster of misadventures. She lived for fun, legal or otherwise, and never gave the impression of having underlying pain about anything. She was impulsive and open to any scheme that came her way, which is how she got involved in forging cheques. Her brother-in-law stole a cheque, and she signed and cashed it. At this point in her story I asked her to show me her skill as a forger. On first try, she duplicated my signature so precisely that I couldn't myself have told the difference.

It was so easy. I started opening bank accounts all over the place, getting IDs and cashing checks. Every Friday I'd open an account and cash all the checks by Sunday before the bank could discover the problem. I ran out of banks in the valley and went over to the other side of Los Angeles. I'd had an argument with Ronnie and wasn't seeing him, but he found out about the checks and talked me into stopping. There was already a warrant out for my arrest. The police in Inglewood saw my brother-in-law Gene and told him to tell me that I'd better quit "hanging paper." And they got me, arrested me at the hospital where I'd gone to see Dolores after she wrecked the car we used, which was Dan's but registered in his mother's name. Through all that they found me.

At the station they pulled out a folder with a blow-up photo of me and sixty signed statements from people who had identified me from the picture. My first night in a jail: single cell with stone slab for a bed; no mattress or pillow, only an army blanket. They gave us gruel in the morning, greasy, watery soup for lunch and a stew of sorts for dinner. I was arrested on Friday the thirteenth, age twenty.

The police asked me who was in on it with me, and I said no one. It was true. They offered a plea. If I'd plead guilty they'd ask the D.A. to drop the other fifty-nine counts of forgery, the three of fraud, and the three of perjury. I said okay. I pled at the arraignment and bailed out for four weeks until sentencing. The probation officer said he would recommend straight probation since I'd never been in trouble before and had a child to take care of, though Danny was staying at my mom's.

The day came and I told Ronnie and my mother, who wanted to go to court with me, not to bother. I was just going to go down there and get sentenced and then go to work. I parked in a one-hour parking zone and went to court. The judge said I was obviously not sorry for what I had done or I would tell them who helped me. He sentenced me to ninety days in county jail, four years' probation, and restitution. I was in shock.

They booked me under one of the aliases. I tried calling home, but no one was there. For three days no one knew where I was because they called the jail asking for me in my own name, and of course the people said I wasn't there. Finally I got another phone call. I asked my mother to keep Danny, get my car out of impound and move my furniture into the garage of my house where she lived, and she said she would. Ronnie visited every week until another guy friend, not a boyfriend, was coming too and Ronnie got mad. My grandpa died while I was in jail. I wrote to my husband, Dan, because my mother-in-law said he was worried about me.

When I got out of jail the people at the restaurant I worked for gave me my job back, even though I'd only worked there for three weeks before I went to jail. After a month or so, Ronnie and I made up. I got an apartment. Danny went to nursery school, and I worked, and Ronnie came over in the evenings. Danny resented him. He was as possessive as his father. But Ronnie and I decided to live together and got a bigger apartment. Then Dan got out of prison and would take Danny on the weekends. Ronnie pressured me to get a divorce, but I didn't want to. I didn't want to live with Dan again, but I didn't want to marry anyone else, either.

Dan found a girlfriend and moved in with her family. He hadn't picked up Danny for over a month, but then he called and said he was coming the next day. Well, he didn't show up, and I was really hot. I'd stayed home all day waiting, and Danny was upset. Two nights later Dolores called, when I was half asleep. "Vicki," she said, "Dan's dead. He was run over by a train."

I was dazed, and I don't know what happened then. The next thing I remember is the mortuary, the night before the funeral. I didn't cry. I just let people tell me what to do and I did it. I didn't go near the family. All our friends were there. I didn't speak to anyone. Lloyd, who had lived with Dan and me in the house on the hill, told me later he felt like hitting me because I just stood there and didn't show any emotion. I just didn't believe it. I couldn't. We never saw the body because they said it was beyond recognition.

When I finally accepted it I assumed he'd been in his car when he was killed. But he wasn't. The car wasn't around. He was lying on the railroad tracks when the train ran over him. I went to the police and asked what happened, and they wouldn't give me a straight answer. They tried to hint at suicide, but I wasn't going for that. Dan was entirely too vain to kill himself in such an ugly way, or at all. He wasn't suicidal. I told the police I wanted to go to court, and finally they showed me the report. Dan had been lying between the rails with his arms folded across his chest. All he had on was a pair of Bermuda shorts, no shoes, underwear, shirt or anything. Dan had never gone out like that in his life. He didn't even go barefoot around the house. He was fanatical about his appearance. I ironed his underwear with a crease, not my idea. And Dan wasn't a walker; what would he be doing walking around at night? The parents of his girlfriend, who was pregnant, lived six blocks from where he was killed. They thought he was the father of their grandchild, and he was living with them, but they didn't attend the funeral or send flowers or express sympathy of any kind. Gene later told us that Dan was having an affair with both the girl and the mother. We never found out what really happened.

Right after Dan's death I found out I was pregnant. Ronnie wanted to get married in a hurry now, and I didn't have the excuse of being married to Dan. Ronnie was overjoyed about the baby and I was depressed. I put off the wedding until I was five months pregnant, and then postponed it until after the birth because I didn't want to get married in maternity clothes. I knew I didn't want to spend the rest of my life with Ronnie, a nice person, but... We moved to a larger apartment and I waited for the baby to come. I couldn't work as a waitress, so I took a sewing class and a real estate class at night school. When I was eight months pregnant I picked a fight with Ronnie and left him. I rented an apartment with my sister Sissy and Dolly came, too, so she could be with Danny when I went to the hospital. I got on welfare for the first time.

Larry was born when I was twenty-two. He came right after we got to the hospital, a lot easier than the first time, and he was cute from the minute he was born. I called Ronnie and he came. Ronnie didn't believe in hitting women, so I wasn't afraid of him the way I had been with Dan. He was more than kind, and I went back with him. We rented a larger apartment and Sissy and Dolly came too. Dolly was still in high school. I got another waitress job close to home, and Sissy went to college and worked part-time. Ronnie worked in construction. There was always someone home with the kids. Danny loved Larry, he was just great with him, and they're still very close.

When Dolores and her husband, Gene, Vicki's brother-in-law, moved back in with her and it became overly crowded, Vicki asked Ronnie to move out. She'd accepted him into her life for the children, but she quickly tired of him. When he refused to go, she started going out with another man who bored her; she made the point with Ronnie. She found an apartment for Ronnie, rented it in his name, and he moved. Everyone liked Ronnie, and they were angry with Vicki for hurting him. She was undaunted, continuing to share her home with her sisters and with her in-laws—who, she soon discovered, were both addicted to heroin.

Sissy took an acid trip, and after she did it I wanted to do it too. I really loved it. I called Ronnie, and we decided to spend time together at his house. We took acid and went to the Farmers' Market and had a really good time. But when we got home Sissy told us the police had arrested Gene for possession of heroin. Dolores was nine months pregnant, and she was getting sick from withdrawal. It was awful. For four days we took care of her while she kicked and screamed and cried, and then she started having labor pains. She spent three more days in the hospital kicking and in labor until the baby was finally born. The hospital had to treat her for withdrawal.

There are repetitive themes in the lives of imprisoned women, including minimal formal education, unstable relationships and residency, children by different fathers, frustrated male partners who sometimes use violence, and substance abuse. Vicki's story incorporates all these elements, and like others she was matter-of-fact about it. Almost everyone in her life was in some way "in the life."

Gene came out of jail for a month until sentencing. He burglarized drugstores a lot and would bring all the dope home in the middle of the night, and I'd help him sort it. He also taught Dolly's boyfriend how to do it. They got a PDR, a physician's desk reference, that told us what everything was. I started sampling all the pills they'd bring home. I still didn't shoot dope, but all those pills were fun. We discovered we liked Percodan, a synthetic opiate. When Gene left for prison, Dolly's boyfriend kept on burglarizing drugstores, and I'd sell it. There was a lot of drug traffic coming and going, and I'm just glad none of my sisters, who were with us a lot, ever got picked up and taken to prison.

Sissy decided not to live with us anymore, and I went to work as a cocktail waitress in a nightclub where my friends went. I made a lot of money. Dolly also was working, so I brought my next sister, Bibby, to live with us. She's a very sweet, good-natured person, and it seemed that everything happening went over her head. I stopped selling dope and let two male friends move in and rent a room from me, and they sold the dope. They were both downer freaks. I'd get mad at them and give them bennies to keep them from stumbling around. I'd drive them everywhere they had to go to sell their drugs. Having two men as roommates was hard to explain to my friends, but they were financially helpful. I was boss, and we all knew it, and so we got along.

The pills weren't working for me anymore. I'd take thirty or forty a day just to feel normal, and I decided to quit. I slept for a few days, and when I woke up the house was a mess. I got mad at Dolly and told her to move. I had a tantrum and broke dishes. Dolly went home to Mom. Bibby stayed. I decided to keep taking pills because I couldn't go to work without them. Soon after, I got a bad case of the flu. My friend Lloyd came over and told me he had something that would make me well. I'd always been down on needles, but I told him to get me some, and he did. [I injected speed, and] the first thing I felt was the flash. My knees buckled, and then I felt really good, really good. I loved it. That was the beginning of the end. I loved that feeling. And it didn't leave me feeling hungover like pills did.

I got fired for dealing, though I wasn't, actually. But I got so many calls and people looking for my roommates that it looked like

I was. I moved again, with Bibby and the kids and a girl who didn't have any place to live. Dolly's boyfriend and his friends were still bringing me the dope they stole. I started testing all the synthetic narcotics, and I liked them all but codeine. Swan, my new gangster friend, told me I shouldn't take dope. Swan and his friend Dodge gave me a long lecture and scared me. I said I wouldn't do it anymore.

But she did. She broke the law to gain the energy she got from the drugs. She also broke the law in part because of that hyper energy. It was a self-perpetuating cycle.

Lloyd came over one day and asked me if I wanted to go out with him to burglarize washing machines. Gene used to do that, and Lloyd and I had gone with him a few times. We each took it for granted that the other knew how to do it. We went into the bathroom and shot some speed, then went off to commit our big crime. We discovered we didn't know how to do it. It took us half an hour to get the lid off. It took Gene about thirty seconds. We thought about fingerprints, so when we were running to the car we threw the lid in an alley and went back to wipe them all off. But when we pulled into the alley we were surrounded by police cars. They booked us for burglary, possession of dangerous drugs and paraphernalia. I called home and told Bibby to tell Swan I was in jail and to come get me. He was super-mad, but he got me out that day and I got a lawyer. When we told him what happened he said Lloyd should have been arrested for mismanagement of a circus, not burglary.

Swan said I had to hang it up, but I didn't want to. I was learning how to do burglary right. We were all shooting speed, and I was still selling jars of pills from the drugstore. When the traffic got too heavy I had to move again, to a beautiful house, four bedrooms and storage buildings, three of us and the children. I was selling dope and burglarizing, working around the clock, rarely sleeping. I fixed up one of the walk-in closets with carpeting, a table and

cushions on the floor. That was the only place in the house anyone could fix [inject drugs], so the kids wouldn't see it. I thought I
was being slick.

When my mom made Bibby come home, I hired a gay friend to
move in and take care of the kids. He loved the children and they
loved him. He was fantastic. He kept the house beautifully. I had
several other girls cashing checks for me. I'd furnish everything
and we'd split the profits. Sometimes I'd go with them, and one
day we were arrested. The checks were stolen, so they booked us
for burglary and forgery. I had stolen property in the house, and my
mother was there, so she got arrested too. It wasn't a pretty scene,
but they let her go right away.

On bail, the police watched everything I did, and I kept doing
what I did. I got arrested almost every time I turned around, on
bogus charges so they could take me in. Before long I'd built up
nine felony arrests in four months. None held, but on the tenth the
judge gave me a habitual-criminal hold. My probation was revoked,
and I requested the rehabilitation center because I knew I'd do less
time than in prison.

At the center we were treated like children in a boarding school.
We grouped for an hour a day, worked for three hours, and I spent
the rest of the time sleeping or reading. I had a good counselor, a
psychologist, sort of a father image. He had a small group called
"the ex group," and that was a frequent topic of our conversation.
He helped me see myself more realistically and gave me a desire
for a future, where I do something besides playing cops and rob-
bers. He said I needed to find new excitement that wasn't dangerous. And he told me I castrated men with my independence. He
steered me to the IBM program at the institution. I learned data
processing and helped the doctors with their research, which I
thoroughly enjoyed.

When I left the center I was not yet twenty-five. I moved in with
my father, Sissy and Dolly, and it was really great to be home. The
phone rang all day, old friends, everyone wanting to see me, and it
was fun to be the center of attention. The next day we had a party

with lots of people from the apartment complex. They knew where I'd been, but they were very nice to me.

While I was at the center, Ronnie visited and wrote to me, convinced that we'd start all over when I got out. I didn't discourage him, because I thought he could help me stay out of trouble. But it wasn't what I wanted. I just wanted to be free, completely free. So I didn't tell him when I was coming home. Of course when he found out I was home, his feelings were hurt.

The next week I borrowed my sister's car and got a job in a Jewish restaurant. I also went to see an old friend and shot some speed. When I later told my new boss that I was on parole for narcotics and forgery, he just said, "Will that affect your work?" I told him no, and from then on we were friends, although I didn't stay there very long.

One evening I got home from work to find Sissy in a rampage. It seems we'd been evicted that day, and she said it was all my fault. They'd lived there for a year before I came home, getting along with everyone, and now this. I hooked up with my old friend Lloyd, who was living in the canyon and needed his house painted, so I moved in with him and did the work. Ronnie had Larry, and Danny stayed with Dolly, who'd taken care of him while I was locked up, and they'd come out on the weekends.

Three weeks later Lloyd was cooking speed with some woman while I was puttering around the house, and they had to go out to get some more chemicals. Lloyd hadn't wanted me to be in the house when they were cooking speed, because if anything happened I'd be in more trouble than ever. He'd suggested I go to a motel while he was cooking, but I don't like to be by myself, and besides, I wanted to watch. Lloyd and the woman left and I stayed to make dinner and watch things. He told me not to let anyone in.

It all happened about 9:00 P.M. I was watching a television program and waiting for them to come back. We lived miles from anyone, so the front door was open but the screen door was locked. I saw an old man walking up the driveway and I thought he must be lost, so I went to the door to give him directions. He pulled out a badge and told me he was a narcotics officer and that he had a report of narcotics activity going on in the house. He was all by himself, or so I thought. He said he had to come in, so I just stepped back and closed the door in his face. I looked around me, wondering what to do—the whole kitchen was a lab and there was dope in every room. It took about five seconds and the door came in. Two men. The other had been hiding. He was much younger, and he was a really big guy.

They went into the kitchen and came unglued, like two kids in a candy store. They didn't know where to start. They called for more police, and every time our phone rang they answered it, trying to get more information. I hoped Lloyd would call so he'd know not to come home, but I soon heard his car in the driveway. They had me in a chair, handcuffed in front with a gun to my head, and they told me not to move. I didn't move, but I yelled. They opened the front door and Lloyd was standing there, looking for his key. They pulled him in, threw him on the floor, handcuffed him and had him sit on the couch. They also got another guy who was riding by on a bike and stopped in to say hello.

The officers stayed for a couple of hours. I got to thinking about the nice dinner I'd cooked, so I asked one guy if we could eat while they finished up. He said no. I thought, "What can they do, arrest me?" So I just got up and served dinner, Swiss steak. It was delicious, even with handcuffs. When they finally took us to jail they loaded everything into their cars, but they missed a frying pan full of speed on the kitchen table, a plate full of dope in the cupboard and funny money stashed in the closet.

When we got to the police station one of the narcs there recognized me and called my parole agent, so I had a hold right away. When we went to court the narcs messed up their testimony, and we were convicted only of possession, not manufacturing. My parole agent, the probation department and my attorney all recommended that I be recommitted to the rehabilitation center.

The judge had a reputation for being the Santa Claus judge. He sentenced about twenty men that day and didn't send any of them to prison. He referred Lloyd to the rehab center, and then it was my turn. The judge called me up to the bench, and my attorney talked a few minutes and told the judge he concurred with the recommendations to send me back to the center. No go. The judge said I had had my chance at rehabilitation, that I was a habitual criminal, a menace to society, a manufacturer and dealer in narcotics, and he wished he could give me more time, but all he could give me was the term prescribed by law and sentence me to prison, for an indeterminate sentence. He told me he hoped I'd do the maximum [fifteen years]. I was dazed, in shock, couldn't believe he was serious.

When I arrived at CIW, with armed escorts, I was twenty-five years old. The cell was depressing: six by nine feet, a narrow bed, open toilet, small sink, small desk. Concrete. At the center we had four to a room, so it was lived in when you arrived and the others would welcome the new roomie and make her feel comfortable. Here I felt very alone. When it was time for count I heard loud noises like machine guns popping off. It was the doors popping open for count, everyone back to their cells to sit on the bed and face the window in the door, so the guard could walk by and tick off every number. If one was missing there was a lockdown until she turned up. I've learned to live with that sound, and I don't hear it anymore.

I hated it here at CIW that first time. I was on the main "campus," like they call it. That's a laugh, but in some places it does look like one. The grass and trees and brick buildings look pleasant to the outsider. I was assigned to work in the kitchen, which I hated, and then I got a night clerk job, and I went to school during the day to finish high school. I also joined a group with the psychologist. I hated being locked up with 600 women and having to do so many years. I decided I would do anything if it would make me change my way of life, so I wouldn't have to come back—ever.

In 1971, Jessica Mitford published Cruel & Usual Punishment, *a muckraking book about prisons in the U.S.A. She exposed many negative practices, including using prisoners as guinea pigs in drug and surgical experiments. Vicki was a victim of just such treatment, though she volunteered for it.*

I heard about an experiment the chief medical officer wanted to do with hypnosis and drug addicts. It involved taking a drug called Anectine, which stopped the breathing and paralyzed you for ninety seconds, during which time he would give a suggestion to respond to in hypnosis. I volunteered. He told me it would be a terrible experience but that afterward he would be able to hypnotize me and teach me self-hypnosis to control my drug use.

It was the most horrible experience I've ever had in my life. I was lying on a table in the surgery room completely paralyzed. The only part that would move was my mind, and it was racing up and down my body trying to find a place to breathe. Terrifying. When it was over, air was the greatest high in the world. They helped me down, put me in a chair and put me under hypnosis. Later he taught me how to do it myself by concentrating on my hands. I could do it. I could shut everything out and nothing could bother me.

I finished my high-school general equivalency diploma. Then the medical officer asked if I would like to be his assistant and arranged for me to work for him. I handled permits, initial screenings, and helped with the procedures. I had to check blood pressure and pulse every minute. I also attended the weekly reinforcement sessions and handled reading assignments.

It was an interesting study, but unfortunately it didn't cure drug addiction. I worked with him for my whole first time at prison. It's the best work I've ever had. He was a great person and taught me all about the medical secretary field, hospital coding, surgical transcriptions. I watched surgery and worked with him on several other drug studies.

I went on parole in 1971, just after the big earthquake. It was such a gas just to be out, after three years. I never wanted to use dope again. I knew I didn't need it, and I was really happy without it. Dolly and I, with two friends, rented a big house. At first, they worked and I stayed home and kept house and did errands. I seldom went out, but it was good to know I could. Danny came for weekends, and he was coming home for good when school got out for the summer. He had his own room and liked the house a lot. It seemed best at first for Larry to stay with Ronnie.

About the time I started looking for a job, I came down with infectious hepatitis. I'd been exposed at the prison the month before. I was miserable, really sick. I refused to go to the hospital. It would have been like going to jail. I just stayed in bed. A friend came over and gave me some packaged ounces of stuff [heroin] to sell. I sold it to a couple of people, never even opened the package. I still wasn't using. I just needed money to live.

There was so much traffic in and out of our house that, when I was well enough, I got permission from my parole agent to live in an apartment with Pearl, a friend who was also on parole. I was still selling dope, but only to the same two people. I had a few ounces left but wasn't in a hurry to get rid of them. I still wasn't using. One night Lloyd came over so I sold him some, and then he asked me if I wanted some. So Pearl and I had some with him. That was the beginning of the end. We lay in bed and shot dope for about a week. And Lloyd just stayed on with us.

I started school the next day, but it was too late. I was already shooting dope, fixing every day, going to school, doing homework. We decided to go to Vegas for the weekend, and I got some speed so I wouldn't have to sleep. I hadn't shot any speed since I'd been home from prison, but it was my first love. So Lloyd got me some. I started shooting speed all the time after that. I really liked it, and I shot stuff, too. I kept holding my arm out.

I spent so much time at the dealer's that Danny finally got mad. He told me I wasn't spending enough time with him and he didn't like it. He told me he knew I was using dope and he wanted me to quit. He said he'd found a burnt spoon and he knew what that was for. He said he liked all the people who came around but he didn't like them using dope. I promised Danny I'd cut down on the running around, and I did. I started spending more time with him and taking him places. But then it came time for Danny to go to summer camp. A bunch of us were all together after Danny had gone.

Someone wanted some dope, so I offered to drive to get some. I was there for maybe ten minutes when the police arrived. There were many other people, and they took us all to jail. The dealer and I were the only ones convicted.

So here I am, back in state prison.

As a postscript, Vicki reflects on her experience of the criminal justice system.

In my experience, I have found the police and courts to be harsher on women. So many fewer women are involved in illegal activities. So when a woman is arrested she's given the attitude that she should be home. If she'd stayed where she belonged she wouldn't be in trouble. It's assumed that she's an unfit mother. Men are often released on their own recognizance so they can support the wife and children. A woman is seldom given this consideration even when she's the head of the household.

There's a lot of difference between men's and women's prisons. In the state there are about 600 women in just the one prison, and over 20,000 men in twelve prisons. We get more individual attention, which can be good or bad. The men have better vocational and educational facilities. They have a more complex classification system, with age, crime, number of times in prison, behavior and security risk all being factors. The men are treated more as adults, but they are dealt with more harshly. Their minimum and medium security prisons are very comfortable. The maximum, like Folsom and San Quentin, are ugly places, but I've known men who prefer them to the less secure places, which are more psychological.

In this system we're just being warehoused. For what? To protect society? Simply to punish? An alternative would be to assign a counselor-type person, not a psychologist but someone with an understanding, who would have a caseload of about ten people, see them frequently, talk to them, help them find a goal. Not like a parole officer, but someone who would take you places, introduce you to different types of people, walk you through the steps of making a new life. This would happen immediately after arrest or conviction. People could live communally in big houses while working with their counselors.

The guards have to follow so many funky, petty rules that anyone who is good quits because she can't stand it. If a guard tries to be more than a custodian for the warehoused women, if she shows any respect, she's called on the carpet and accused of "homosexual" behavior. I first came in contact with homosexuality when I was fifteen in juvenile hall. I gradually realized it was no big deal. I became best friends with a woman, a black woman, and then it developed into a real relationship and lasted a year, and it was very good. We remained good friends, even after we got out. I prefer to be with men, but I don't feel that heterosexuality is right for everyone, and I believe everyone should be free to choose what suits them without ostracism.

The parole board members are political appointees who are not qualified to judge us, but they decide how long we stay. And the parole officers have such big caseloads that even if one of them cares about what happens to you, she doesn't have time for you. When I was out the last time I just wanted to be free. In six years I'd been on the streets for a total of nine months, and I wanted to make up for lost time.

I have the feeling that nothing worse can happen to me. I knew what I was doing, and I knew it was wrong and that I had to pay the penalty. My own feelings are that it's wrong to take from individuals but not from big business. I have no sympathy for them. One department store I stole from, when they testified in court they declared the value of their loss to be four times what I took from them.

My relationship with my son, Danny, is based on honesty. He's ten. I respect his opinions as much as any adult's. I don't have to worry about him using narcotics. He knows more about life than most kids. He writes all the time and visits, and we talk on the phone at least once a week. Larry lives with his father, who's remarried and has raised him since he was a year old.

I don't let myself do hard time. I'm involved with a lot of people and read a whole lot. I've been in prison through my twenties. I see women get suicidal but I don't feel that hopeless, although it bothered me when they dropped me from the medical assistant program when they saw I was arrested for narcotics.

My eight sisters and brothers learned a lot from my mistakes— they saw what I got myself into, and we talked about it. I skipped school, flunked and dropped out. All the others finished high school, except one, and she's a dancer who has been all over the world. The rest are going to college with no help from anyone. Our mother wasn't any help. It was a condition of my parole that I not see her. She was the kind of person who would rather be lied to than face the truth.

I always hated women when I was growing up, except my sisters, because I raised them. But I thought women were all treacherous and phony. I had men who were like girlfriends to me. Here I learned that there are other women like me; not all women are on a phony lady trip. I mean the kind of woman who, if a man walks into the room, her whole personality changes. I always wanted to just be one of the boys, but now I found out that I can be one of the girls.

If you play you pay, but I feel I've paid enough. When I leave I have to make a new life for myself in a new area, and it is frightening not to be able to go home. I've spent so many years doing nothing. I know I have to develop different habits. I want to get as much education as possible while I'm still here, so when I get out I'm inspired to go further.

Reflections: AN

Twice in her story Vicki used the words, "That was the beginning of the end." Although punishment seemed always to come as a surprise, she was finally ready to convict herself on the evidence. She does not blame the tragedy that ended her estranged husband's life under shocking circumstances, but in fact it was not until after this event that she began to use drugs heavily.

Vicki was popular. When she came out of prison she was no loner rambling down an empty street, but rather was the centre of a welcoming family with new neighbours wanting to meet her. Her employers seemed glad to give her back her job. She gave unstinting aid in emergencies. She showed stamina. When motivated by a longing for freedom and challenged by the prison doctor, Vicki proved herself an eager student. She was also a daring and proficient participant in medical research, ironically undergoing an experiment aimed at curing addiction through drugs. The experiment failed to cure addiction—it was on the order of inventing a safe cigarette, food without calories and cars that can crash safely at high speeds—but her work with the prison doctor provided what Vicki had not found outside the prison: satisfying work, responsibility, opportunity for leadership.

In another time or place, with her organizational talents, energy, commitment to people and blithe spirit, Vicki could have been a research scientist or run a large family farm. In the end perhaps it can be said of her, as it was of her friend, that she was guilty not so much of crime as of mismanagement of a circus. Los Angeles in the sixties provided an ample tent, with more than three rings.

Reflections: KF

Unlike many women in prison who have been beaten down by their lives and by the prison system, Vicki was optimistic about her future, and she maximized her time in her third prison sentence. She had never in her life been able to stick with anything until she began working with the medical officer. As soon as she discovered her intellect, her life changed. She enrolled in the courses we offered at the prison, through the University of California, and she did very well. She read voraciously.

Vicki was released after five years, and this time she was prepared. She no longer craved the drugs. She had learned to moderate her energy, to find balance and pace herself. She said that before she went to prison she was constantly in motion, moving from one place to another, not able to sit still. She would have met the criteria for extreme adult attention deficit disorder, which could be said of many people—men, women and youth—who go to prison. She'd escaped much of the drudge of prison life by being useful to the doctor, which had elevated her sense of self as a capable woman and helped her settle down.

For years, Vicki's talents were wasted—misdirected, misused and exploited. Much of her energy was sacrificed to the pursuit of drugs. Prison perpetrated the absence of clear choices in her life. When Vicki began to find the same excitement in study as she had in illegal risk-taking, and the same clarity she formerly sought from drugs, she figured out how to make life work for herself and Danny. As a condition of her parole, she moved several hundred miles away from Los Angeles. She got an office job, rented a comfortable apartment, enrolled in night school and stayed away from narcotics. Danny lived with his mom and they took good care of each other. When I went to visit he joined in the conversation, cracked silly jokes that made Vicki laugh and served us fresh lemonade—a perfect young host.

Vicki and I talked on the phone from time to time and exchanged friendly letters until one day my letter to her was returned, marked "Moved: No Forwarding Address."

7

MARIE

I'M NOT AFRAID

MARIE WAS IN HER forties, a short, wide, feisty woman who was friendly toward those who treated her respectfully but had no tolerance for people who abused their power. She believed that girls and women who fight back, verbally or otherwise, are less likely to be victimized than those who cower. But even if that sometimes works with parents, peers, boyfriends or random aggressors, it seldom works with institutional authorities, such as teachers and parole officials, as Marie's experiences attest.

In the California Institution for Women, Marie was outspoken, but some of the staff and even the warden had a grudging respect for her. Unlike others in this book, Marie was not oriented to "book learnin'." She just called it as she saw it. Crisis is a natural state within a prison, and many women suffer nervous agitation from the frequent bells, sirens and whistles that announce the latest emergency. But Marie would pull up her weight and say, "I'm not afraid." She loudly complained when there was a problem, but her complaints were usually on target and expressed what others felt.

Marie was conspicuous in a crowd not only for her "big mouth" but also for her physical bulk, at 285 pounds. As she explains, the parole board demanded that she lose 100 pounds before they would consider her for a release date. Most women gain significant weight when on a prison diet; it's unrealistic to ask someone to lose weight on a vitamin-deficient diet of heavy fat and carbohydrates, with little protein or fresh fruit or vegetables. To make parole contingent on losing more than one-third of her weight on this diet was an especially cruel punishment. The worst cruelties and mind games come precisely at the point that a woman has earned the legal right to release. For example, some women were not released until they testified to accepting Jesus Christ as their personal saviour, even though coerced faith is oxymoronic. Still others were held in prison beyond their sentence unless they agreed to give their children over to the state. Given the powers of parole boards, some women serve virtual life sentences for relatively minor crimes. The women who are good prisoners get out with the least fuss. Marie was not a good prisoner.

I met Marie in 1972, while teaching and doing research at CIW. She didn't complete the university courses Jean Gallick and I took in, but she did work with one of our tutors and got interested in her own life as a way to study society. Jean and I both took a liking to Marie and to her down-home attitudes about everything. She had had some horrendous experiences both prior to and as a consequence of imprisonment, but she had a salt-of-the-earth strength that never betrayed her.

Jean and I worked together in the classroom (Faith, 1993), and she also assisted by taping several women's life histories for my research project. Marie was one of the women whom Jean interviewed, and as I listened to the tapes I was struck by how in her day-to-day expressions Marie was outspoken about everything except the personal details of her own life. But with Jean's encouragement, she talked freely about what she'd ever done to get in trouble and said she was glad to share her life with the world.

Marie's Story

I was born in rural Oklahoma in 1924. My father was a farmer, had his own farm; he was a good father. He provided for us the things he could afford. He sent us to school, wanted us to get an education. He was a good husband to my mother. There was nine of us, five girls. He grew cotton, corn, all our food—potatoes, peas, everything. He raised hogs, cows, chickens, turkeys. Eighty acres of land, and we didn't want for too much. My mother was a Baptist and my father didn't go to church much, but he seemed to believe in it. We'd all go to Sunday school. We had a good life. We never sassed grown people. If we did wrong, our father would whip us with switches.

My mother worked on the farm, all the cooking and washing, while we did the farm work. My father hired people to help, to pick the cotton and stuff like that. My aunt and first cousins would come out and stay with us in the summer, to help out. The boys and girls worked together. The boys did the harder work, like sawing wood. But we'd go to the field with them. We enjoyed it! After I left for Kansas City they sold the farm and came out here to California. I don't know why they sold it. They had gas wells but didn't have the money to drill. Out here my father, mother, brothers, sisters all worked at the shipyard at San Pedro.

I started to school when I was eight or nine. We had white neighbors growin' up in Oklahoma, and we'd play and eat and sleep at their house and them with us—no bearin' on color. We had different schools. They had to go up the hill, and us down. But we'd walk along together to and from. I went to a school with just blacks— very good school. The school was big, went to twelfth grade. The teachers was black. Cousins of mine taught there. They had doctors in that family too. My family had a good education background. I liked school, and so did my sisters and brothers. School was the only separation. The whites used to come down and play in our gym because we had the best gym.

My brothers and sisters and I got along beautifully. We'd have scraps and arguments, but we'd work it out. We each had our own horse, and we'd go riding. I liked being a girl, and the way our father would explain things to my mother and to us kids. They loved each other and stayed together until they died here in California. He passed away just two years before our mother. They had a wonderful life together. She missed my father, was lonely and hurtin', wished he was still livin'. But she had her kids around her, and grandkids, right until she died.

I quit school in fifth grade. The teacher and I had a few words. A boy and I was talkin' in class and she was goin' to whip us. I told her I wouldn't let her, so she sent us to the principal and he gave us five or six licks on the hand. She had whipped my older sister, with a belt buckle, and made her bleed. My father was mad, he didn't want no teacher cutting his children. I never forgot that, and I said I'd never let a woman whip me, and when the time came I didn't. I went home and told my father and said I would never go back. I had to do extra housework when the others were off playing. I learned how to cook and clean house. I was very unhappy to not go to school, but I wasn't goin' to get beat on. I was just sixteen. The teacher flunked me. I threw my report card in the wastebasket and haven't been back since. Most of my brothers and sisters finished school, or nearly.

I knew if I stayed home my father would make me go back to school. So I ran away. I took nothing. Just walked off. Waiting for the bus some people came along and took me to Tulsa. I stayed with some friends of my mother. A lady police officer, in Tulsa, arrested me for being in a tavern and lying about my age. I said I was eighteen. I wouldn't tell her where my parents lived. I didn't write to them because I knew they'd come and get me. At the jail they gave me blood tests and took smears. I didn't know about men yet. The first time I was in jail for about five days and they kept sending me back because I wouldn't stay out of the tavern. I like to dance and listen to music. In our time we did the Big Apple and things like that. I didn't drink but I liked to dance. We were having a lot of fun.

My first job was with a white lady as her housekeeper. But she drank a lot and had quite a few men coming and going so I stopped going there. I got another job as a housekeeper and kept that job three or four years. I enjoyed domestic work and I liked her kids. In 1943 I left Tulsa and went to Kansas City with a friend. The whites and blacks didn't mix in KC Missouri, but they did in KC Kansas. They could even marry in Kansas, but not in Missouri. I always wondered what was the difference.

This is where I met my husband, in KC Missouri. When we was dating, anything I wanted to do, he was for it. We met in the park in the summertime, when it was hot. We'd go to the zoo and things like that. We'd go to shows. He was my age, young too. I didn't know he would fight.

We were married after about a year. He was a Marine. After we got married he took me to meet his family. Very nice parents. We never had any children. It was beautiful for a while. He didn't let me work. I was a housewife, doing the cleaning, cooking, washing. We'd go out to dances, friends would invite us to parties.

In the second year we started to get along bad. Fighting. He was the jealous type of man. He could talk to the ladies but I couldn't talk to any man but him. The ladies' husbands would talk to me and it was stupid if I didn't answer. They'd want to know what was wrong. He didn't know what was wrong with him, why he was like that, liked to fight. He came from a good family. His mother and father were real nice. But then his mother quit speaking to me. Not his father or brothers and sisters. They knew how he was. His mother knew too, but it was her son. He beat me so bad; he had a stick. I was black and blue all over.

He was very quiet about strong feelings. If he had things on his mind he would never sit down and talk about it. He'd go out and get drunk. Sometimes he would say he would die before he'd go back in the service. [He fought in World War II.] He wouldn't talk about the Marines, just say it was hard. He used to fight me quite a bit. Beat on me. They'd put him in jail, then he'd be out, fighting all the time. It was pretty bad.

When my husband was away with the Marines I left Kansas City, in 1947, and came to California where my parents was, and sisters and brothers, in San Pedro. My aunts and cousins lived in Watts and I went there and stayed quite a while. When my husband came back he was a construction worker. He just showed up, didn't write or let me know anything. I was down in Watts, outside with friends and my cousin, and I see my husband coming down the street. He tells me, "Let's go home." So we walk to my place and he jumps on me and beat me so bad both eyes were closed, I couldn't see.

The landlady called the police, so he was arrested his first night in California. When the police came they took us both to jail. The lady officer had me pull up my clothes to show the police, with my husband standing there. He dropped his head. He always said he was sorry. He asked me to not appear against him. But then he came out and the very first night he beat me again. They didn't take him to jail, just drove him around all night in the squad car. The next morning they brought him back. The landlady let him in, with the police. I still couldn't see. They just left him alone with me. He was sayin' how sorry he was and how he was gonna take care of me. The next day he got a job at the post office and he worked for a while. But he was very, very mean.

Three years later, 1950, he jumped on me in a restaurant [right out in public], and I stabbed him twice [with a steak knife]. He died from it. I was hurt by what I'd done but I knew I couldn't bring him back. So I goes on to do the time. They carried me to jail on February 4, 1950. I was twenty-six. A friend in jail and I was talkin'. She was tellin' me how her husband would fight and beat her. I told her people would never believe us. Unless you've experienced it you can't understand.

At the jail I got sick, and when the officer came around and told me to get up and scrub the cell bars, I told her I didn't feel like doing it. She sent me to the sergeant, who told me that when I got to court the judge would give me county time. I asked her, "How in the hell do you know? You're no judge. It's up to the judge." I always ran off at the mouth, 'cause I will speak, no matter where I am or who it is. I don't care. She locked me in the cell and I lay down and cried from pain until hours later when they finally let me see the nurse, and she gave me something.

It was four months before the judge heard my case. And sure enough, he found me guilty of manslaughter and gave me two years in the county jail, ten years' county probation and a suspended sentence at the state prison. He told me he would modify the time if I was a good girl at the county jail.

At the jail the lieutenant was always trying to make me do something, and I'm the type of person you can't make me do nothing.

You ask, you don't push me to do it. They were trying to get me on my knees to scrub the cracks in the floor with a toothbrush. And I wouldn't do it. So they locked me in seg. I didn't care, I was already locked, another door wouldn't hurt. Four other women were in segregation, but I was the only black girl. The others got to making noise, rattling the doors so nobody could sleep; they opened all the windows, so it was cold. I had nothing to lay on but the floor. The lieutenant took away all the blankets and mattresses. I told her, "I don't give a damn," and I just lay down on the cold, cold floor. But I told her, "If anything happens to me you're going to have to be sorry." She kept me back there five days. I wouldn't eat.

When I went to court I told the judge I'd rather be in the state penitentiary than in that jail on the thirteenth floor of the hall of justice. I worked all day in the sewing room, and I was a trustee when the ladies' groups came in. The food was lousy. For lunch they gave us soup with worms in it, we couldn't eat it. And worms would be walking out of the old lettuce. It was horrible. After seventeen miserable months on the thirteenth floor I get my lawyer and we go down in front of the judge and he modifies the rest of the time and lets me go.

Given his leniency, at a time when this was uncommon, it seems clear that the judge understood that Marie was a battered woman who killed her abusive husband in self-defence. Between 1952, when she was let out of jail, and 1968, when she was locked up again, Marie lived in California near her devoted family. She worked as a domestic and had a couple of serious relationships. She was again the victim of violence, but now she left instead of enduring it until she snapped, as had happened with her first husband. She led a conventional life. She was not an alcoholic, but she loved to go dancing and would drink moderately when at the club. On one of these nights, tired and with several drinks in her, she was picked up for drunk driving.

In 1968 they brought me to CIW on a drunk driving charge, calling it a "Z" case because of my past record. I'd finished up my manslaughter sentence a long time before that, and had done the whole ten years' probation. No problems. When I was driving under the influence no one was hurt, there was no accident. But when after six months at CIW I went before the parole board on this new charge, they threw me over to 1969. The next year, at that hearing, they made the stipulation that I had to lose one hundred pounds before they'd let me loose. I also had to admit that alcohol is a problem for me, which I couldn't do. If I had, I'd be telling a damn lie. The third stipulation was that I had to get along with my peers. But it wasn't my peers I didn't get along with. It was the damn staff, because I can't stand nobody pushing on me. You don't drive me to do nothin'. I get along lovely with my peers. It's them I don't get along with. [The parole board] asked me, why don't I get married. Well, I would never marry another man. It makes no difference if you're married or livin' with 'em. I'm tired of 'em puttin' their fist in my face. Police don't do a damn thing to them.

They thought they could change me from being stubborn, as they call it. But they can't, they can't change me. They teach these women to lie. I went to the assistant warden and he said, "I used to work in men's prisons and we kept a man for six years because he wouldn't tell us what we wanted to hear." I said, "Hold it, let me tell you, I don't have six years, but I'll do every day of it before I'll let you make me tell a lie on myself."

The doctors here wanted me to get out on account of my heart. I didn't know it was so bad, but the doctor went to the board and said there was no guarantee I would live very long. He thought they wouldn't want it on their conscience. My mother and father both died with heart trouble. But I was denied parole, and that was three years ago. Just lately the doctor told the board about a white woman who had bad health, and that lady's going home next week. Nobody's dyin' in here but the blacks. They'd rather see something happen to me than let me out of here. They don't give me my medicine on time, but they always have somebody watching me in case I get upset and have a coronary. They used to give me disciplinary reports for cussing them out, but they don't bother me now; they don't write me up no more.

They don't try to help the women here. When a woman goes to the board and tells the truth they don't believe her, and tell her, "We'll give you six or eight months to think about it and come back and tell us what we want to hear." So the women do this. They said, "Well, they wants to hear this lie, so I'm gonna tell it, 'cause I wants out." I think it's a damn shame. It's a waste of taxpayers' money. And where does that money go? They give us food that's turned green, even in the hospital.

The people who run things here think we're stupid. But they're the ones that's stupid, and I tell 'em, "You're stupid. You ain't got no sense. You talkin' about everybody needin' a psychiatrist, well, you need to see one yourself." There's some women in this penitentiary that the staff likes more than others. They bring 'em things, like their baby to see, or dope. Staff don't like the way I talk, they say I'm too plain-spoken. The warden even said that to me. One staff told me I would die in here, but I said not until I tell what I know, that maybe somebody out there would listen. What would happen if people with money ended up in this place? They'd change it.

I needed a pair of orthopedic shoes and it took three years. The doctor put in my order but nothing happened. One day I stopped the woman who orders stuff when she was giving some people a tour of the prison. In front of them, I told her, "I never got the shoes the doctor ordered for me," and the next month I had them, after waiting three years.

After that 1969 hearing, the board didn't see me again until this year, 1972. I couldn't lose the hundred pounds, but I tried. I went into the prison hospital and didn't eat anything, just drank some juice, but I got sick with a high fever and my blood pressure running high. And then we had a hepatitis epidemic and they had to discharge me and most others. So I didn't lose the weight, but I still got to see the board this year. I told them I think I've done more than enough time, over four years on a drunk driving charge.

I don't think they're holding me because of my weight. They told me right out that they thought the judge should have sentenced me to first-degree murder when I stabbed my husband over twenty years ago, instead of manslaughter. That's why they're holding me. I asked them, "You mean to tell me the judge doesn't know what he's doing?" And then they backed off. Then they said I would have to appear in front of a full board, instead of just the two members as usual. I said, "I don't give a damn what you do," and I walked out of the boardroom. I wouldn't talk to them about the manslaughter. I don't remember too much about it and don't care to be talkin' about it.

When I walked into the boardroom for the full panel, the chairman said, "I see you're asking us for a discharge," and I said, "Right." He says, "Why?" I said, "For the simple reason that I've been here four years on a drunk driving charge. That's why. That's enough reason. You never kept no other woman here that long on that charge. Nobody ever put a stipulation to lose weight on a white woman. You must got a thing goin' with the blacks." You see, in the late sixties the blacks wasn't moving out of this prison at all. And they put the same stipulation on another black woman, who had a heart attack and died here for trying to lose that damn weight. Trueheart Lewis. It made me mad. I'd told her, "Trueheart, you can't lose that weight, a hundred pounds in a year." And I was so mad I wrote a letter to the board that said: "You must have a thing goin' with the blacks. Ever since I been here I've noticed that the black woman is doin' the long time. I can name two white women over 300 pounds. They never got that stipulation."

So at my hearing the chairman says, "We have no intention of discharging you." And I said, "Well, we don't have nothing else to talk about then, do we," and I gets up to leave the room. Before I got to the door I turned around and said, "I want all of you, I mean every one of you, to kiss my big black ass," and I walked out. I was so damn mad.

I met them in June, and on the second of July they sent me my discharge date. I leave six months from now, and they said they didn't want to see me no more, and I shouldn't come back.

I been sittin' here for going on five years and I never saw even one woman get rehabilitated. They don't help you. The women I live with are always considerate. If one of us is sick the others watch over her and help her out. In the hospital if you're too sick to get up to wash they just slam your food at you and you have to eat with dirty teeth, dirty face.

These people on the board aren't fair either. White women who have black husbands have to give up their small black children, they make them get rid of them, just bounce them out. That board is too much. Who gave them that much power, to tell you you can't go back to your husband, or live with your mother, or be with your children? That you have to go to a town where you don't know nobody? They mess with your mind. Women go haywire. One woman went to see her kids on a day pass and stayed too long. When they brought her back they added ten months to her sentence.

When you get a date they give you $68, you buy your dress and suitcase, you don't have bus fare or a place to live, and that's your hard luck. You try to find a job and you don't and back you come. Instead of building all these fences here, they should try to help these women. They don't try to help. They fix it so they have to come back. They're doing a damn good job of that.

I got three and a half months left to go. My sisters and brothers are waiting. I got a helluva family and I love them. They worry about me. They come to visit but when they leave it hurts. I don't want them to send me things. The prison got me, it should take care of me. I don't know how things'll be out there, after five years. I don't know what to expect. It will be real strange, but I'm not afraid.

Reflections

Marie's conversations were a running commentary on abuses that occurred as a matter of course. The injustices and cruelties were blatant. She accepted as a given, as did most of the women, that people are punished with confinement if they break the law. Few women protested the fact of imprisonment. They protested the inequities, and the sadistic actions that were sometimes inflicted on them contrary to the rules of law and official institutional policy.

Many authors, including myself, have documented abuses against prisoners. Black women did serve more time than white women for the same crime, with the same record. The medical facility did provide inadequate services and engaged in sometimes dangerous practices, such as drug experimentation. Some women were victims of plastic surgery gone wrong, at the hands of UCLA medical students who practised on the prisoners. The diet was thoroughly unhealthy. Women giving birth were chained while in labour, with guards in the room. Women were sent to segregation if they took food out of the "feeding unit" to have as a snack in the evening. Women were sent to segregation for "inappropriate touching," which could include holding hands with another woman. The most serious complaint was that women were vulnerable to sexual assault by some male guards and were locked in segregation if they filed a complaint. All rules were enforced arbitrarily and inconsistently; what might be tolerated one day could lead to "the hole" the next day. Some women were punished for offences that other women engaged in with impunity.

Marie served five years on a six-month sentence for drunk driving at a time when that offence was very rarely prosecuted. She was at the mercy of a parole board composed of retired military men and white women who had been middle-class housewives until appointed by the governor to help determine who deserved to be released from prison. Marie spoke her mind, held her ground, and was never institutionalized into submissiveness because she never acquiesced to the fear that permeates a prison. She lost years of her life, much of it in solitary confinement, because she wasn't apologetic and she wouldn't tell the authorities what they wanted to hear. Marie wasn't willing to barter with her dignity.

Reference

Faith, Karlene (1993). *Unruly Women: The Politics of Confinement & Resistance*, Chapter 7. Vancouver: Press Gang.

8

MATTIE & ME

CROSSING THE COLOUR LINE

THIS CHAPTER'S FORMAT DIFFERS from the preceding ones because it is, in part, my personal story. After Mattie briefly tells her story, I continue with an account of the friendship we shared, some of the events that transpired over the years and the reasons Mattie made such an impression on me.

Parables confirm for us what we already know, and Mattie's life reconfirms that the war on drugs cannot work. We know from the experience of Prohibition (1919–1933) that people cannot be prevented from ingesting what they crave, even if they have to become outlaws to get it. Harassing and punishing individuals according to which drugs they use does not reduce or deter drug use. Prison is largely a drug and alcohol culture. In California, at the dawn of a new century, over 40 per cent of women in state prison are being punished for a drug-related offence. In addition, women who are doing time for other crimes, and who have never been arrested for using or trafficking illegal drugs, are often nevertheless habitual users when on the street, and in prison, too.

A second fundamental message of this story is that "equal opportunity" is a primal myth in societies claiming to be democratic. The overwhelming evidence is that racism, especially in a class-divided society, poses significant barriers to political minority groups. To be sure, a black middle class, formerly confined primarily to a few black-dominant cities like Atlanta, now extends across the U.S.A. Many African-American parents can now send their kids to private schools to avoid the dangers of public education. After ordering public school integration in 1954 (Brown v. Board of Education), in 1955 the U.S. Supreme Court returned to the states the power to decide on how or whether schools should be desegregated. The busing of children from one district to another highlighted the more fundamental problems of residential segregation according to colour and class.

In the early twenty-first century, one in three black men in the U.S. is on probation, in prison or on parole, and black men comprise a majority of the 150,000 men in California state prisons. In a new millennium, decades after a spate of civil rights legislation catalyzed by organized mass protest in the 1950s and 1960s, a majority of African Americans remain subject to discrimination in employment, housing, education, health and criminal justice. Meanwhile, the gap between the rich and the poor has increased in the U.S.A., particularly among blacks, and segregation based on both class and colour persists. This is the backdrop of Mattie's life, and one can add to that the violence women of every colour suffer at the hands of abusive men.

Nowhere are the effects of racism more conspicuous than in prisons, where the disproportionality is extreme. During the 1970s, when I got acquainted with Mattie, there were a total of 600 prisoners in the California Institution for Women, then the only state prison for women. Over 40 per cent of them were of African heritage, even though blacks were then just over 10 per cent of the total California population. Three decades later, over 11,000 women in California are incarcerated in a new chain of women's prisons. In all of California, 14 per cent of the population is black, but although their numbers have radically increased, black women now comprise a lesser proportion of imprisoned women, just over one-third, because there are so many more Chicanas and Mexicanas in prison. Whites are now a minority.

The over-representation of political and ethnic minorities in prisons suggests, on the face of it, that people from these groups break the law at a higher rate than whites do. This appears to be the case with street crime, where poverty is the correlate of racism. And it is street crime, and very rarely white-collar "suite" crime, for which people are imprisoned. It is also the case, however, that ghettos and barrios are under stricter prosecutorial surveillance than middle-income and affluent neighbourhoods, which in turn receive the greater share of protective policing. Lawbreakers most apt to be convicted are those who lack the means for a defence, whereas corporate criminals are generally dismissed with a fine. In both Canada and the U.S.A., those arrested for street crime are commonly subjected to police brutality and often to lengthy jail time before their case is heard by a judge. The more aggressive prosecution of blacks (in both countries) exacerbates their vulnerability, as suggested by the crime of "driving while black," meaning that blacks are much more likely than whites to be stopped and searched by the police. To be black is to be under suspicion in a world dominated by whites. This is the world into which Mattie was born.

Mattie's Story

I was born on April 7, 1931, in Texas, dubbed Mattie Lou to combine the first names of both grandmothers. I remember when I was just a few years old my mother would let me sit with her at night when she sewed. She often sewed late into the night, and she'd let me stay up and make dolls' clothes. On this one night she was teaching me how to knot the thread to keep it from pulling through when we heard a car pull up in front of the house.

My mother went to the door and saw a car filled with white men. Thinking they had come to ask her to do some domestic work, she began to talk with them. But they were not looking for someone to clean their houses. They were looking for a black woman to molest. They tore off her clothes right in front of me and my older brother. Our screams might have saved her, because they stopped short of sexually attacking her. They went to their car and drove away, and Mama covered herself and gathered us in her arms.

We had another bad experience when my father was forced by the wrath of angry whites to flee our hometown because of a fight about the poll tax. My mother gave my father a big picture hat and told him to wear it so his tormentors wouldn't recognize him and would think he was a woman. He went to California. This was 1938. My mother, brother, sisters and I followed the next year.

They say I was a bright child, inquisitive and meddlesome. I began school when I was four years old in a one-room schoolhouse. I had already learned the alphabet and how to read simple sentences. When I was a third grader I entered the Los Angeles city school system. They wanted to place me in the sixth grade because of my reading ability, but my mother objected. They compromised and put me in the fourth grade. We moved a lot, and I attended four different elementary schools between the fourth and sixth grades. Eventually we moved to a government housing project which was built the same year the U.S. entered World War II. It was my mother's constant dream to "get my children out of this project." She did finally manage to purchase a home, when I was eighteen.

I was what is now known as a battered child. My mother told me that my father "spanked" me when I was four months old, for tearing a page out of his Bible when I was sitting on his lap. The beatings grew more severe with age. My brother and I and all our younger brothers and sisters who came along weren't allowed to attend movies, or school dances, or any group activity. I sneaked out, risking severe punishment, which I got pretty often. By age sixteen, I had run away eight times and was sent to juvenile hall on three occasions for running away.

Once my father beat me so severely, for coming in at 2:15 in the morning, that I passed out. My body was a mass of welts and cuts and my face was unrecognizable. I went to the police and they put me in juvenile hall for "protective custody." Three months later they put me back with my family, and I ran away within the week. I was returned home six months later, pregnant now and more bitter. I gave birth at seventeen to a baby girl, and my mother took control of her. It was as if she wanted to give all the affection she didn't give us to my daughter. I resented this. After my daughter's birth my father made one last attempt at violence against my person and I stood up for myself, for the first time. I didn't strike him or threaten to. I just said, "Daddy, you have beat me for the last time." I moved out of my mother's house with my daughter to live in a kitchenette. I got on welfare. Despite everything, I still got good grades in school, but I missed too much to graduate with my class.

We lived in the government project from the time I was ten until I moved out at eighteen. That's when I began my search for love in the wrong places. I started living with a man twelve years my senior, an ex-convict. He beat me also. I accepted beatings from him because I thought I loved him. He was generous. He was arrested and returned to prison.

I was alone with my baby and without money when I met the manager of a night club and he gave me a job as a dancer. He introduced me to marijuana, and at age eighteen I was arrested for possession. In jail I learned about heroin and decided that it must be good if people were willing to suffer so much for the use of it. I didn't become addicted as soon as some people do. In fact, I thought the addicts weren't telling me the truth about addiction. It was over a year of using now and then before I was using to relieve the symptoms of the beginnings of withdrawal. I had to support my habit, and I became a prostitute and then a thief.

In 1955, age twenty-four, I committed myself for a "cure," a ninety-day stay in the state hospital. They discovered I had a spot on my lung and transferred me to the TB ward of another hospital. Also during this time I discovered I was pregnant with my second child, a son. They sent me to a sanitarium where I remained until I was returned to the hospital for his birth. I left the hospital without authorization, and the health department picked me up. I was charged and convicted of violating the health and safety code, for which I served three months in jail.

I learned to live without heroin, but I was actively engaged in delinquent behavior, boosting, finding that stealing was more lucrative and more to my taste than prostitution. I had gotten a job in a sewing factory, but the police came and picked me up at my job for suspicion of till tapping. I was cleared, but my boss fired me anyway. I returned to my family.

Then I began living with my pimp, a man I'd known since I was a kid. During this time I was boosting and became addicted to heroin again. I gave birth to my third child in 1958, while I was out on bail for grand theft [of three men's suits]. I was sentenced to state prison at age twenty-seven. I served seventeen months and was paroled in 1959, returning to the same man. He had promised to marry me, and I became pregnant with my fourth child. Then he started beating me again, so I left him. I was arrested for petty theft and served sixty days in county jail. My child was born in jail, and I didn't get to see her until she was thirty days old. I was returned to state prison for violating parole.

When I was released ten months later I began to see myself and my life for the disaster that it was. I began night school to earn my high-school diploma. I terminated my relationship with my daughter's father. I got a house with my four children. I was on weekly naline testing and clean from heroin addiction. My relationship with my family was better than it had ever been. I reached out to my father, discussed my deep feelings, and a real father-and-daughter relationship began to develop. I was twenty-nine years old. I would like to say that everything was all right with me, but I was on welfare and supplementing my income through prostitution.

I met my present and only husband during this time. He was an ex-convict, but he was a Muslim. He told me things that made me feel really loved for the first time in my life. Although he was a Muslim he was associated with men who were committing burglaries, and an associate of his brought some stolen goods to my house. We were all arrested. The charges were dropped against me, but I was given a parole violation and returned to state prison for six months for "association with people of bad reputation and character."

Cyrus and I were married in November 1962. I had been free of drugs for over two years, including the six months I was in prison for the violation. In 1963 I gave birth to my fifth child, third daughter, the only one of my children who could not be termed illegitimate. I was proud of that.

When the tensions and financial pressures became too much it was natural to want relief. Later that year I was convicted of possession of three $10 balloons of heroin and sentenced to state prison again. I served thirty-nine months, with my husband serving time for the same charge. I received my high-school diploma while incarcerated, and they transferred me to the civil addict program, where I had intensive group therapy. I got involved in an employment training program and received a stipend of $52 per week, which I prided myself on living on without committing any crimes. I entered the Watts Skill Center, where I completed a clerical course. Through the center's placement program I got a job as a secretary to the director of a summer jobs program for youth. I also participated in the 7th Step Foundation and Prison Preventers, organizations that assist ex-cons and addicts in maintaining a drug-free, crime-free life. I was one of thirty ex-addicts who organized and worked for the first federally funded drug-abuse program in California.

I was an assistant in a Jobs for Youth program that was charged with misappropriation of funds. I was definitely not guilty. But over the protest of all the people I had associated and worked with, I was returned to state prison, to serve ten months for parole violation. I allowed this to put me into a tailspin, and immediately upon my release I started using again and was returned to the prison in quick order.

When I met the parole board in 1970 they informed me that tests I had taken showed I was very intelligent. I wanted to make that intelligence relevant to me. When I was released I was encouraged to enter college, which I did, majoring in sociology. I hope you can imagine what going to college meant to me, being poor, black, thirty-nine years old and an ex-convict. I was the only one in my family of four sisters and brothers who made it to college! But it was a short-lived dream. When my husband was released from prison we moved to San Diego, where I returned to drug addiction and was arrested for petty theft. I was sent to state prison for the eighth time on another parole violation, this time an indeterminate sentence. And here I am, four years later.

KARLENE'S STORY

When I met Mattie in 1972 at the California Institution for Women, some months before we started our class, she had been a prisoner there for the better part of fifteen years. Unlike most prisoners, who have long "rap sheets," Mattie had just two convictions—stealing clothes and possessing heroin. She did time primarily for her six parole violations. Although drug-dependent, she considered herself a Muslim and strongly identified with the Black Power movement.

Women at CIW didn't engage in the kinds of racialized altercations depicted in movies, and there wasn't much overt expression of racial hostility. There was a palpable tension in the prison for many reasons, but racial insults more often came from both black and white guards than from prisoners. The Black Muslim movement that found converts in men's prisons during that period did not take root at CIW, apart from with Mattie and a few others, but blacks and whites segregated themselves at meals and during free time, and black women organized an African-American Sisterhood. It wasn't an atmosphere of fear; no one expected a race war in the prison. Rather, the Sisterhood was a politicizing and healing process for black women to claim their identity, study their history and form bonds of solidarity with one another toward a different future. It was up to the "white girls" to keep their distance, just as blacks in the U.S.A. were required to keep their distance from whites for centuries.

The United States is a racialized society that legislated and reinforced segregation through an 1896 U.S. Supreme Court decision in support of the "separate but equal doctrine" [Plessey v. Ferguson, 163 U.S. 537 (1896)]. The "separate" was honoured, but not the "equal." The Jim Crow laws that followed from Emancipation ensured that whites wouldn't have to share public facilities with Negroes. Strict separation was enforced until the mid-twentieth century. The 1954 U.S. Supreme Court decision in support of integrated schools started an incremental process that is today in no way completed. The age-old struggle for civil rights accelerated for several decades, a cause for which many African Americans were still losing their lives in the 1970s.

When in 1972 my colleague Jean Gallick and I offered courses at the prison on "Women in Society," almost half the fifty students were African-American, with a number of Chicanas and Native women. For the instructors as well as the students, it was the beginning of understanding how race categories, class and gender intersect in the formation of personal and cultural identity. There was not yet a large body of second-wave feminist literature, but we brought in the most widely read of the early work, to mixed response. For example, after reading Germaine Greer's *The Female Eunuch*, women of colour critiqued it as an analysis of "white women's problems." The white women dismissed it as "middle-class women's problems." They reacted likewise to Kate Millet's *Sexual Politics*. The book to which they all responded favourably was the multicultural anthology of writings on women's liberation, *Sisterhood Is Powerful*, edited by Robin Morgan. Most of all they responded to the poetry of Pat Parker and Judy Grahn, and to Arlene Eisen-Bergman's work with women in Vietnam. The women in our classes believed in resistance against victimization and identified with women who organized for their rights. But they had not been infected by the idealistic notion that women's bonding with one another, just because they are women, transcends the injustices of racism, colonialism and class discrimination. All women are not created with equal opportunity.

During four months of research at the prison prior to our first class, I got used to the women's voluntary or customary separation by colour in the cafeteria and on the grounds. But I had never envisioned a divided classroom. It startled me the first day to go in and find everyone huddled in separate groups, each avoiding eye contact with the others. As a young instructor, I idealized the classroom as a hallowed space, located within the prison but operating independent of it, a free zone, no guards allowed, where open exchanges of ideas, inquiry, information and points of view could thrive in a fully democratic, safe, dynamic process of shared learning. That sure wasn't going to happen if the women wouldn't even look at each other, so I boldly started out by saying I couldn't teach a divided class, and I asked them to mix it up a bit. Right away one of the black women moved to a chair near the white group. That woman was Mattie, which surprised me, because I'd never seen her placate authorities, or whites, or anyone. I knew if she hadn't agreed with me she wouldn't have done it. Other women, black, brown and white, followed Mattie's move, still no one talking, until everyone was resettled and someone broke the ice by saying, "Okay, so we're integrated; let's get on with it."

At the beginning, some women in the class needed encouragement to speak their minds. Not Mattie. If she had something to say she said it; she was willing to risk conflict, speaking only when she was sure she was right. When racial tensions surfaced through careless or naive remarks, Mattie was often the one to see through the problem and find the lessons to be learned from it.

Most of the women in the class hadn't completed high school, which made Mattie one of the better educated. But the other women listened to her not because of schooling but because she was right too often to be doubted. She was an oldtimer who knew the score. It was her radical political views that made them uneasy. Black women who were trying to stay on the good side of the guards would urge her to tone down her militancy, at least in the guards' presence. Younger white women were intimidated by her, and they were critical of her for talking like a revolutionary and then going back to the needle. Mattie regarded them with patience, though not without sadness. What was important to me was that Mattie was thinking, and provoking everyone else into stretching their minds. I came to think of her as a special ally. And I was very upset when we locked horns.

One night in class we viewed *The Woman's Film,* a feminist documentary on how working-class women—black, white, Native, Latina, lesbian, heterosexual, young, old, single, married—were fighting for their rights, thumbing their noses at chauvinism in their jobs and relationships. About sixty-five women crowded into the room to see the film, including women who weren't in the classes. The room was sparked to life during the scenes of a job strike where police used force to break up a picket line; women were jumping up from their chairs, cheering out loud for their sisters on the screen.

When the film ended, everyone began talking at once: "They didn't show nothin' I didn't always know—that's just how it is out there—they got it, we don't, you try for your share and they beat you down." "It's good to see there are so many of them out protesting— something is really happening with women, isn't it?" "I can't wait to get out there—to get into all that."

Then Mattie started to talk very solemnly, and everyone stopped to listen to her. She said that black women who identi- fied with women's liberation were copping out, that black women coming down on black men divided black people—that "women's lib" was dividing black people, and diverting energy and the press away from black liberation struggles. She had no sympathy for "silly white ladies complaining about oppression while they sit drinking coffee in their shiny stainless steel kitchens when after centuries of exploitation black people are still struggling for basic survival."

Some years later, Mattie's position was articulated by numer- ous African-American women who recognized the dominance of white, middle-class women in the feminist movement and the fail- ure of that early movement to be inclusive of lesbians and women of colour. Minority women were always "welcome," but their interests were never addressed. Alice Walker, author of *The Color Purple,* cat- alyzed a "womanist" movement that was specific to points of view and life experiences of black women in all their diversities. Author bell hooks subsequently wrote about "black feminism." These and other critics of the white women's liberation movement elaborated the same points that Mattie had made years before. Hers was a prescient voice with a small captive audience.

On the one hand, I thought I did grasp the importance of black women articulating their own interests as distinct from those of white women, and especially as distinct from middle-class white women whose gendered codes carried class and colour privilege. On the other hand, contradictorily and idealistically, I believed we could all unite under the banner of "Women," a social category that became increasingly hard to define as the differences were accounted for.

Mattie's comments against white feminism after the film had moved the other women, and I should have let the conversation go where it might. I should have left it alone. But my instincts were poised against any more divisiveness, especially between black and white women, and I said so. A good teacher would have encouraged Mattie's critique and called for discussion. It would have led us all more quickly to a deeper understanding of the complexities of inclusiveness. Knowledge commonly grows from differences in perspective. Mattie understood this. I didn't, at least not when she put me to the test. The room took on a stifling, anxious feeling, with white women grumbling about how blacks get all the favours in the prison because they make the most noise, and black women hollering that "that'll be the day, when we get favours over the whities."

I believed, as "liberals" often do (though I'd have eschewed the label), that women needed to strive for unity with one another. Still, I was mad at myself for bad timing, and I was mad at everybody who was getting out of control. I was furious that Mattie and I were now the focus of a black/white polarity, her arguments reinforcing for black women the idea that women's liberation wasn't for them. White women who had come to see the film but who weren't in the classes, and who, before the film, had pooh-poohed "women's lib," were suddenly militant defenders of it and looking to me for validation. I did then raise my voice and make matters even worse. What I yelled out to Mattie, to be heard over all the loud voices, was that it was pointless for us to play "more oppressed than thou" in that situation.

Women in the prison sometimes played a game they called "more oppressed than thou." It was an amusement, relying on irony to induce laughter instead of tears. They'd go around a circle and cheerfully recite the ways they'd been oppressed in their lives. The winner one day, for example, was a Chicana lesbian, orphaned in childhood, physically disabled, a battered wife, a rape victim, poor, unskilled and addicted to heroin. The other women cheered as she piled on the oppressions, one atop the other. Nine. It was a kind of sick humour that discouraged self-pity. Common to the vast majority of prisoners is a very distinct continuum from victimization to criminalization. As the women often said, in words coined by Arina, a feminist clown who came in to entertain, "Lighten up, we've all had a lousy childhood."

But of course this incident didn't have to do with playing "more oppressed than thou," and even if it had, white women, whatever their problems, are free from the systemic oppression of racism. In effect I'd told Mattie to stop playing the victim, but she wasn't doing that, and she never did that. What she did was what many smart people had been doing for a century: she named and analyzed the ways by which the oppressions that originated in slavery could be collectively countered through reclaiming one's identity. After my dismissive comment, Mattie started to storm out of the room, with others ready to follow her. Again, I didn't think, just yelled over the din as the women were getting more agitated, "Mattie, don't you dare leave me in this mess." To my surprise and huge relief, she came back.

We sat down together, embarrassed when it got quiet, with everyone listening, as we began to speak from our hearts. Mattie said she was sick of explaining racism to white people, sick and tired of what it had done to her life, and she didn't want the job of educating the people who did it to her. We were both exhausted and discouraged, wary of each other. Then the buzzer sounded for lock-up, and Mattie and I stood to leave, grabbing a hug. Instantly both of us cried out, and we jumped apart. Her cigarette had come between us, burning my neck and her arm. Our yelps broke everyone's tension. We put out the sparks, laughing now and tending each other's wounds before the women all rushed off to be counted in their cells.

The film had obviously aroused controversy, and we had two more showings in the prison. These were open, so some of the guards attended. Their reactions were as mixed as the prisoners'. A white male teacher who had a reputation as an "MCP" (male chauvinist pig) said of the film, "This is very impressive, yes indeed. I hope it really makes them think, gets them caring about something important, gets them out of drugs and all that. These women need to find out about Women's Liberation. Most of these women would do anything for a man, and I do mean anything. We need to get 'em off that." A prisoner who was standing by came up and asked the teacher if he did his own laundry, and he conceded that no, he didn't. She harrumphed and walked off.

Within the class itself, women started opening up to each other like never before. White women talked about how they'd been taught to distrust "the coloured," told by parents to not befriend them or go into their neighbourhoods. They'd grown up being taught that all black men want to rape white women, a fear myth perpetrated historically by rampant accusations against and lynchings of generally innocent men, such as the landmark case of the Scottsboro Boys in the 1930s. White men's fear of black men's sexuality permeated the culture, and the modern justice system institutionalized the myth of the black man as sexual predator. It was not surprising, then, that white women objectified black men. For their part, black women said they hated white women "who steal our men for sex thrills." They also talked about the racism of judges in their sentencing, the parole board members who kept them in prison longer than white women with the same record and the police who tailed them after release, trying to catch them in a parole violation.

Reciprocal candour led to some deeper levels of understanding and acceptance on both sides. It was a crash course in overcoming stereotypes and objectification. Everyone practised speaking and being silent, declaring and asking, sharing information and listening and eventually laughing together. Each woman studied her own life, wrote it down and talked about it, exposing sore spots along with strengths. We called autobiographical work the "warrior exercises." Most of the women wrote of how they missed their children and regretted messing up their children's lives, and of how their own lives had been steered by the men they lived with and by unplanned pregnancies, as well as by their inability to get an education or move up the legitimate economic ladder. They wrote of love, giving it and receiving it, or not.

An integration of spirit occurred as the women's vulnerabilities surfaced. To a woman, they worked hard at their reading, writing and oral assignments, with a new sense of themselves as university students. Some of them required extra tutorials to learn academic skills. All of them had difficulty getting through the heavy reading assignments. I'd envisioned that a prisoner, alone in her cell, would have a lot of time to read. However, the cell units were extremely noisy until the 10 o'clock count, and then the lights were out. Still, everyone was interested in the readings and did their best to get through them. Most of the women were unschooled, but they wrote well and spoke well. Mattie was noticeably exceptional. As the weeks passed she gained affection and respect from the white as well as the black women. She was older than most at age forty-one, she had seniority as a prisoner, and she was a natural leader.

One night in class Mattie told us all that she had a parole hearing the next day. After class I walked with her back to her cell unit, and she talked about getting out, how she would put her life back together, stay clean, go to school, be with her family and, she hoped, work with addicts. Before she went inside, I promised I'd come to the administration building the next day when she faced the board.

When I arrived the next morning Mattie had already seen the board. While the three-member panel was deciding in private whether or not Mattie could be set free, Mattie was waiting in the hallway with several friends. She showed them our scars from the cigarette burn, and we hugged and joked about our fight, making small talk to speed the clock and ease the suspense.

Mattie seemed calmer than anyone, confident. One of her friends said, "Maybe they'll give you a gold seal, free and clear" [a complete discharge without parole supervision]. We were all optimistic. Mattie had already served more time than demanded by law, and she hadn't had any violations within the prison. Mattie said one woman on the board had remarked that she was pleased Mattie was taking the university class. They had asked her just a few questions and seemed satisfied that she was "reforming her ways."

They called her name less than fifteen minutes after her hearing. Very slowly, beautifully poised, Mattie walked down the hallway back to the board room, looking tall and sharp in her tailored dress, casually adjusting on her arm the new purse that had been sent from home. Just before she opened the door, she called to me over her shoulder, "Hey, wait there for me." As if I could have done otherwise, my heart was beating so fast.

Mere seconds had passed when Mattie's voice suddenly tore through the building, piercing, terrible, tormented screams, trailing into a long, crying wail and then words: "You motherfuckers, you goddamned white racist motherfuckers!" That wasn't her usual vocabulary. Now we could see her, bursting from the room, then clinging to herself against the wall, all the while screaming "NO—NO—No—No-no-no-ooh," a continuous sound of grief choking in her throat. A black guard ran out of the room beside where I stood with Mattie's friends, all of us paralyzed with the realization of what had happened. The guard rushed to Mattie, perhaps to help, but Mattie shoved her aside, and to her credit the guard didn't react. Mattie stood up straight and began walking up the hallway toward us, as slowly and proudly as she had walked away from us just moments before. But now there were tears streaming down her cheeks. Her screams had dissolved into stifled sobs and moans, but still her body didn't falter until she reached us. As she collapsed into a friend's arms, her purse slid off her arm and fell open onto the floor. There was nothing in it. Just an empty fancy lady's purse, for dignity.

Mattie's counsellor arrived, an African-American man, and the guards told him that the board had "shot Mattie down," giving her her "top," which meant she still had up to twenty-seven months to serve. As her friends led Mattie away, her counsellor followed closely behind, his fists clenched at his sides, muttering, "If I had my way the whole damn board would be black." I thought to myself that it wouldn't make any difference, if the guards were any example. Mattie later made me see things differently, but, at the time, I didn't see any of the many black guards catering to the black prisoners. Some behaved as if ashamed, as if the black prisoners reflected badly on themselves. I saw them bending for approval from their "superiors," the administrators, who were mostly white and who determined promotions and raises. Still, I respected the counsellor's fury on Mattie's behalf. And it was conceivable that black parole board members would have been more likely than white members to issue a fair judgement in Mattie's case, and with black women generally. Certainly people could expect more fairness in court from a jury of their peers, but most women couldn't afford a jury trial and most juries did not include blacks, Latinas or other minorities.

Mattie was a militant who never generalized about people. Not all white people were alike and neither were all prison guards. In fact, she had formed trust with a number of the black guards. They were upset by her parole denial, and she said of them:

I don't know that I could have made it through some of this were it not for the compassion shown me by black officers. I allowed them to communicate with me. Black guards are victims of the same racism that I am, and 30 million more blacks. The only variation is in our individual reaction to it. Malcolm X put it aptly when he likened it to the field nigger and the house nigger. I'm a field nigger.

The parole denial was a painful setback for Mattie, and at first I feared she might give up. That same week, two white women with more serious criminal records than she had received the short time that Mattie had expected for herself. She said she had realized, as a black woman, that she might get thirty to sixty days more than the white women, but she hadn't expected her time to be so extreme. At the time of Mattie's parole denial, black women in California with a narcotics history were serving from two and a half months to one and a half years longer than white women with a narcotics history, whatever their crimes of conviction (Engle Temin, 1973: 256–7).

One day soon after her hearing, I was encouraging Mattie to keep up with her studies. She said, "What's the use of having dreams if I'm just going to die in here?" But within the week she was back in class with no sign of feeling sorry for herself, her dreams deferred. She admonished younger women in class to "clean up your acts so you don't get stuck in this mess like me." Up to this point in her life, Mattie said, the most respectable thing she had ever done, which gave her pride, was to marry the father of one of her five children.

The women in the course all worked hard to prove to the prison authorities, the university and themselves that they could accomplish serious academic work even under the circumstances. As each woman took risks in exposing her vulnerabilities to the whole class, so did trust deepen across the colour line, and women began to form a group identity and speak of the class as a "sisterhood." They carried their copies of *Sisterhood Is Powerful* to the cafeteria, where the bright red-and-white cover attracted attention and spread the debate about women's liberation. These discussions around the prison resulted in a wide interest in the university program, which, following from these classes, was expanded and continued for four more years with dozens of volunteer instructors (Faith, 1993).

Whether feminism diverted attention from black liberation ceased to be the burning question when we started looking at the troika of race, class and gender, the interactive and reinforcing triple threats of colour, income and sex hierarchies. It was understood that while patriarchal traditions affected all women's lives, the degrees of harm varied substantively.

White women whose lives were limited to contact with other white people were missing out on the diversity that is part of the richness of life, but to the extent that they colluded with segregation they were creating their own problem. Their loss, witting or otherwise, could not be compared to being brutalized, terrorized and treated as inferior by white people and by the laws of the land. White women who had lived in poverty, as is true of most women in prison, did understand what it is to be denigrated by society at large and by people with privilege in particular. They knew what it is to bear the pain, fear, guilt, humiliation and desperation of not having sufficient resources to meet basic family needs.

Everyone had a litany of the ways sexism had affected their lives, with variances according to community, religion and cultural traditions. Not wanting to sound like man-haters, almost everyone named one or more men in their lives with whom they had trust and love (father, brother, son, spouse, platonic pal), but they also all had examples of being disrespected and abused by men. (Two of them, a working-poor black woman and a middle-class white woman, had killed their abusers, and that's why they were in prison.) There was no debate about the need for gender, racial and ethnic equality in education and employment, and Mattie was especially vocal about the harms of exclusion. Her vitality enlivened discussions. She worked hard, had a quick mind and, with her swift recovery from her parole hearing, showed an indomitable spirit.

My ongoing research at the prison included access to data in the official prison files, with permission from the women—who weren't themselves allowed to see the files. When I read Mattie's records, I saw a new entry that explained her parole denial:

> She resents all authority. She has a negative influence [as an organizer of the African-American Sisterhood]. Until she realizes that she cannot blame her problems on being black or on authorities she will fail in her life experiments... The doctor feels she is acting out aggressions toward her father and that she needs extensive therapy to develop self-esteem.

I thought it a travesty that the events that shaped Mattie's life—child-beating, racism, poverty, adult male violence, drug dependency—could be reduced to a simplistic Freudian analysis. As I gathered from other women's files, the doctor found virtually all criminally convicted women to be suffering from penis envy. If a woman was a cheque forger, the pen she used was a phallic symbol, signifying her "unresolved aggressions toward her father." If she injected a drug, the needle likewise represented the penis she wished she had, so she wouldn't have to be like her mother. In the good doctor's view, the pen and the needle both represented male power. Mattie had suffered at the hands of her father, but she had resolved her conflicts with him and had forgiven him many years before.

My own experience of Mattie was that she was self-respecting. She had shame about having had to prostitute herself, but she was also pragmatic about it. She pointed out that she could work all day at McDonald's for $2 an hour, or she could turn a trick in half an hour for $50, and with her large family it didn't feel like a choice. She told of having gone to court and being sentenced by a judge who had paid for her services in the past; he didn't recognize her.

Because the psychiatrist's opinion generally influenced the parole board's decision, Mattie could be held in prison twenty-seven extra months on the grounds, in effect, that she had grown up resenting her father and lacked self-esteem. As for her resentment of authority, she was never, by reputation or in my observation, pointlessly rude or uncooperative with staff, black or white. She didn't accept abuse from authorities, or from anyone. She was in that respect less easily managed than other women. However, this was not an indicator that she needed psychological treatment, but rather that she was psychologically healthy. After all those years she still wasn't institutionalized. And she had self-esteem, which is not easy to hold onto when you're held captive behind coiled razor and barbed-wire fences, with bars on the windows, human guards and laser beams, electronic doors and endless nights of stifled grief in a 6′×9′ cell. Even if a woman did need therapy to develop self-esteem, prison would not be the place to get it.

In the year following our class I saw Mattie only on occasional weekends, when I went to CIW to help coordinate the expanded university program. We'd take time to visit and share family photos, speculating on how long it would be before her release. And suddenly she was set free, fifteen months after her parole hearing, a year before her top date. Her friends said she was more surprised than anyone. For two years I didn't see her or hear from her; then, in 1975, I received a good letter letting me know she was reunited with her family and doing well. She had graduated first in her class in a substance-abuse training program. We corresponded for a while, then silence again, and then I moved from Santa Cruz to Los Angeles.

On a Sunday afternoon soon after I arrived, I was giving a talk on women and criminal justice. I'd just finished and called for questions when, in the back row of the crowded public hall, a glamorous-looking woman raised her hand. When she stood and smiled I recognized that it was Mattie. Clearly her life had changed. I learned that she was now the executive administrator of a drug-abuse program. We made plans to visit, and a few days later I was in her office, which she showed me with earned pride. A carpeted room with a large wooden desk and nice furnishings, paintings on the wall, plenty of windows—it was a room befitting Mattie, filled with colour and light. Her name on the door, her stylish grey suit with a flowered silk shirt, the obvious respect toward her from coworkers who came and went: Mattie was a success story.

Some months later Mattie's program sponsored a public forum on drug abuse and the criminal justice system, and she invited me to speak about the problems of addiction in prison. That day I was also able to testify in front of her colleagues, clients and family—her beautiful mother, her children and grandchildren and her proud father. I talked about some of the ways Mattie had been a positive influence on me and on the women with whom she had been incarcerated. I'd seen her keep her spirit alive through error and grief. She had stirred my heart. When I witnessed her with the young people in her program, I saw that Mattie the student had become Mattie the teacher.

Mattie and I lost touch again in 1977 when I moved north to Sonoma County to teach women's studies and to work with San Francisco Bay Area groups doing advocacy for women in the federal prison at Pleasanton, near Oakland. Sometimes I accompanied musicians and poets who were invited to the prison to perform, and I was asked to emcee a concert on New Year's Day, 1979.

By the time we finished with searches and clearances and made our way to the prison gymnasium, a large crowd of women were already waiting for the show to start. The performers were awaiting my introduction: Pat Parker, Gwen Avery, and the Mary Watkins and Linda Tillery bands, with their manager Laraine Goodman. I'd just adjusted the microphone and said "hello" into it when, from the bleachers at the other end of the gym, a familiar voice called out my name. There was a hush. I knew right away it was Mattie, here, in yet another prison, and my heart rose and sank in that split second. Then she was right there with me, about a hundred pounds of her, wearing a wig that made her look more like twenty-eight than forty-eight and came askew as we hugged and jumped for joy, happy to see each other, tearful, so sorry it was there that we had met again. We quickly collected ourselves, and I introduced the performers, leaving the audience bemusedly assuming, semi-correctly, that Mattie and I were, as one woman put it, "homies from the state joint."

That afternoon, while the music played, we caught up on news and danced. I met her new friends, and we enjoyed the serendipity of yet another reunion. Mattie looked younger, different, and was apparently feeling good, which perplexed me. I wondered if she was relieved in some ways to be back in prison. I'd known others who had grown so used to being in prison, so institutionalized, that it was the one place where they could feel at home.

THE YEAR FOLLOWING OUR reunion at the Pleasanton prison, I showed Mattie the first draft of what eventually became this chapter. She

liked the title and agreed with my interpretations until she came
to the above paragraph. She was extremely displeased that I would
wonder "if she was relieved in some ways to be back in prison." In
her own words, from a letter dated June 4, 1980:

> I get the feeling that you, of all people, would never wonder that
> I, of all people, would be relieved to be back in prison. It seems
> to negate all you have learned with regard to African Americans'
> position in this country. Malcolm X said, with regard to Afri-
> cans and prison, "Yes, I've been to prison, but if you're black and
> in America you're in prison." This is an ever-present truth that I
> live with each second of my life. Prison is only a microcosm of the
> larger society.

I did regret my thought that Mattie could ever be resigned to life
behind bars. So what had brought her back after four years? This was
the longest period in twenty years that she had managed to stay out
of prison. She didn't want to be in prison, but she had been unable
to stay away from heroin when her world fell apart. When funding
was cut for the drug-abuse program she administered, she continued to work full-time without pay, holding a second job as a halfway
house counsellor for income. The emotional and physical strain was
greater than Mattie's resilience, and she returned to narcotics.

Mattie wrote the following letter to the judge who had sentenced
her. In it, she pleads for a reduction in time to be served:

> After growing to the point where I was a contributing, valued
> member of society, I again allowed myself to fall all the way to
> the bottom of the pit I suffered so much to climb out of. In all
> my learning I hadn't learned how to ask for the same support
> I'd been giving steadily for over four years. I didn't want to show
> weakness.
>
> Honesty, acceptance and surrender are key. I'm being honest
> with you, as well as myself. I accept the past, but it can't affect me
> adversely unless I allow it.

Since I've been here I've served on the Inmate Council as representative of my unit, elected by the other prisoners. My duties are to take issues, complaints, requests and so on to the administration, and I served the maximum time allowed. I teach knitting and crocheting. I was in the drug abuse unit prior to coming to my present living unit. I spend my time in productive activity, such as hobby crafts and assisting women who are studying for their General Education Diploma.

I really feel that this current incarceration is the direct result of my not allowing myself to reach out for help when I needed it badly. I didn't have the honesty to admit that I needed support.

I am thoroughly remorseful for my involvement in this crime. They decided to give me four more years before considering me for parole.

I've written this letter in order to solicit your understanding. I freely admit that there has been a lot of delinquent and deviant behavior in my life. Please believe that my behavior was not malicious or vicious. I've learned a lot from my life, I have it in perspective. With what I've learned through experience coupled with the didactic training I've had, I have a lot to offer society. I can assist persons like myself who find themselves dependent on drugs.

My family ties are very strong but my mother is ill, and she has responsibility for my 16-year-old son. This is a plea for modification of my sentence.

There was no reply from the judge, and the sentence wasn't modified. Mattie remained locked up, but still she didn't lose heart. Her letters were encouraging: "There's so much beauty to be found in all the things we take for granted. Take the good from all situations." "I was reading Henry David Thoreau's writing on John Brown. He tells how most people just fade out of this life. They don't really die because they never really lived." And after the concert reunion, she wrote: "Everyone thought you'd done time with me. I explained you hadn't, but you hurt right with me.

And you came back like a bolt out of the blue. I can't help feeling like it is a good omen."

Mattie's most impressive accomplishment in the federal prison was her production of a major theatre event, *The Black Experience Past and Present*, performed in June 1981 on Emancipation Day. She wrote and rewrote proposals to get permission to do the show, coordinated rehearsals, worked hard on the script, made the costumes, did the staging, recruited performers from the outside for the music and, finally, with her allies inside, convinced the prison authorities to provide a soul-food feast for the prisoners that day.

About 200 prisoners and dozens of outsiders went to the auditorium. The cast included a few friendly guards along with fifty prisoners. The dramatized review of African-American history included smoothly woven vignettes and readings using the words of black liberation heroes. As co-narrator, Mattie was seated on the side of the stage, elegantly guiding the show. An African king and queen sat on golden, spotlighted thrones in colourful splendour. Slave scenes evoked moans and rumblings from the audience. When "Harriet Tubman" spoke we heard Harriet Tubman. A white male guard read the revolutionary words of John Brown while his real-life black captives sat in amazement at the irony.

Dancers gave movement to the soulful feelings that rose in the room, crowded with women of every hue sitting in rapt awe. When "Ida B. Wells" spoke we cheered her courage. "Sarah and Angelina Grimke" orated, and we heard from "Martin Luther King, Jr." and "Malcolm X." "Dick Gregory," in a snappy white suit and hat, brought the house down, and "Muhammad Ali" really was the greatest. "Nikki Giovanni" stirred us with her poetry, and women wept when "George Jackson" read a letter home. While "Angela Davis" spoke of capitalism and chains, a guard in the rear was absentmindedly jingling the heavy ring of keys on his belt.

The audience remained spellbound. When the program had nearly ended, Mattie walked to the mike at centre stage. She had brought her passion and spirit to black history and educated a roomful of displaced women, many of them black, through the voices of black heroes. Now she was offering her own voice. She told the audience she was going to sing a song she used to sing when she was eighteen, before she first went to jail. It was Mattie who stood before us, singing a mournful "Gloomy Sunday" a cappella, but it was Billie Holiday's voice we heard. Mattie had a musical voice. She had listened to that record hundreds of times, and she had it down. Everyone was moved. The audience cheered, applauded and rose to their feet in her honour.

Soul food and dancing followed the show, and Mattie was the life of the party. We skipped outside to get a prison-authorized Polaroid picture of us on the lawn, to show off the unlikely coincidence of our wearing almost-identical white suits, mine a last-minute loan from my friend Cris, who had often performed for prisoners.

On the drive home I kept seeing the women's faces aglow during the show. I'd seen that look on the faces of striking farmworkers shouting "Huelga!" ("Strike!") and showing their children that nothing matters more than self-respect. I saw that light in the faces of anti-war activists determined to end the killing in Vietnam and Cambodia. I saw it in the faces of Filipinos in L.A.'s Echo Park, and in the faces of lesbian audiences at concerts of "women's music." You see it wherever people come together in a united cause, and that's what Mattie gave them. In the prisons where Mattie spent most of her adult life, she inspired other African-American women to celebrate the good of their lives and the glory of their heritage. In an era of black nationalism, she was adamant about the necessity of black-only organizations. She was also, however, an effective force for coalitions between black and white women.

FOR THE NEXT TWO years in the federal prison, Mattie worked eight hours a day in the prison furniture industry. In her spare time she kept up with reading, correspondence, pottery and needlework. She sold fashions and ceramics to visitors so as to contribute to her family's support of her teenaged son; her other children were now young adults. She also organized a professional-quality fashion show within the prison, with beautiful women modelling garments of Mattie's own design and handiwork. My Aunt Irene owned a boutique in Calgary, Alberta, and when she came to the Bay Area where I lived for a visit with her daughter Bonnie, my cousin, we all went together to the prison. Irene was impressed with Mattie and the quality of her work, and she took a crocheted dress back to Canada to sell in her store.

Mattie never assaulted anyone or stole anything exceeding the value of three men's suits. Yet she was in prison for the better part of three decades due to her drug habit. Prisons exacerbate drug dependency. Black women are selectively criminalized, and the solution to "the drug problem" lies in more equitable distribution of resources, including health care. Prisons liberally dispense pharmaceuticals to quiet the women, who sometimes get addicted to these pills. Illegal drugs circulate in prison, as well, and women who had never used street drugs on the outside sometimes become dependent on them while in prison. Guards, visitors and male prisoners who do yard work at the periphery of women's prison grounds are all potential runners, smuggling in drugs or making a drop over a fence.

As illustrated by Mattie's story, and by numerous others in this volume, the war on drugs is futile. Those who feel a need to elevate their spirits, or be calmed, or feel normal, will continue to seek out drugs—and dealers, commercial or underground, will continue to supply them. We naturally crave that which makes us feel better. Law-abiding citizens en masse become habituated to refined sugar, caffeine, salt, nicotine, alcohol, and prescribed stimulants and sedatives. Alcohol is the drug most frequently ingested in association with illegal actions, especially acts of violence. A drug, whether illegal or legal, including alcohol, can be an ally if consumed in moderation by a person with a healthy lifestyle. However, this doesn't describe the lives of those whose immoderate drug habits lead them to prison. People with resources are sent to rehab; the others are locked up and punished.

For Mattie, the compelling struggle would always be against the racism that her imprisonment represented. Following is a letter she wrote to me in the early 1980s, while still in the federal prison:

At times it is difficult for me to realize that no one who hasn't experienced it can comprehend the vastness of racism. It's shot into our veins like a vaccine, omnipresent in every facet of our existence. Africans' attempts at assimilation into the dominant culture are incidental. Wouldn't it make sense that after hundreds of years of torture, degradation, dehumanization, a person or a people would acquiesce or attempt to? Acquiescence is one form of defense. We are also retrieving and embracing Africanism. We are African, always was, always is and always will be.

The mothers and fathers of those four little girls murdered in that Birmingham church bombing must still be writhing in agony, and the guilty party received just ten years, freed on appeal bond. Dessie Woods is languishing under a sentence of 22 years for killing a white man who was trying to rape her. These are the gross insults we live with. The cruelest of all, for which there can hardly be reparation, is the calculated destruction of our culture and our names.

Have you ever thought about the fact that the Ku Klux Klan has been in existence for nearly 200 years? Their headquarters have never been shot up by the FBI, like they shoot up African-American political headquarters. Have you ever heard of a black policeman going into a white neighborhood shooting to death a 20-year-old white youth, then claiming that he resembled a robbery suspect?

Instead of assimilating, some of us employ the more usual defense mechanisms: denial, flight or fight. We can't deny what's happening. We can't run—where to? That leaves Fight. "Power concedes nothing without a demand. Find out what people will submit to and you know the amount of injustice and wrong which will be imposed upon them. The limits of tyrants are prescribed by the endurance of those whom they suppress." Frederick Douglass said this in 1849. Quite appropriate today, don't you think?

While in her mid-fifties, Mattie was again released, and she returned to her family, with whom she had sustained close relationships over the years. She abstained from drugs and got her life on track again, although she suffered poor health. I moved home to Canada, and as the years passed we lost touch. My wish for Mattie is for drugs to be regulated rather than criminalized, so as to avoid racketeering, to eliminate the exploitation of women and the violence related to illegal drug deals, and to protect women like Mattie from criminalization and imprisonment. As for racism, is it too much to wish for widespread justice to be revealed through determined community efforts, and a radically altered political economy, within our grandchildren's lifetime?

References

Burkhart, Kathryn Watterson (1973). *Women in Prison.* New York: Doubleday, 256–7.

Engle Temin, Carolyn. "Discriminatory Sentencing of Women Offenders: The Argument for ERA in a Nutshell." In *The American Criminal Law Journal,* Spring 1973. Cited in Burkhart.

Faith, Karlene (1993). *Unruly Women: The Politics of Confinement & Resistance,* Chapter 7. Vancouver: Press Gang.

Poets Diane Ramsey (right)
and Norma Stafford (below)
at a recording session in
San Francisco, circa 1979.

Vicki, student and prisoner at the California Institution for Women, 1972.

Betty Krawczyk at a blockade against corporate clear-cutting of forests in the Walbran Valley, British Columbia, 2003.

Ann Hansen with Angel, Ontario, 2004.

Kathy, student and prisoner at CIW, 1972.

Angelique, artist and prisoner at CIW, 1972.

Lorraine Stick, Champagne Aishihik Nation, youth guide. With daughters Belinda (far left) and Ciara (second from right) and niece Jessie (far right). Yukon, 2002.

Centre: Patricia Monture, Mohawk lawyer, activist, professor, author. With her children (counterclockwise) *Brandon, Michael, Jack and Kate, and friend Rosie. Saskatchewan, 2003.*

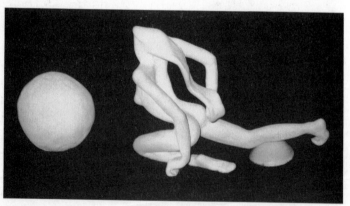

"Woman's Heart," sculpture by Gayle Horii. "Different from Atlas, who holds and controls the world, flaunting his power, the woman attempts to move the world with her heart. Different from Sisyphus, condemned to push the huge boulder in an unrelenting quest to reach the top, only to find himself at the bottom once more, women push forward though often still on their knees. Her arms signify the juxtaposition of the powerlessness that many women feel with the innate refusal of most women to use physical force as a method to control or to gain power."—Gayle Horii

*Karlene and Mattie at federal women's prison
in Pleasanton, California, 1981.*

9

BETTY

PROTECTOR OF THE FOREST

Betty Krawczyk is a committed environmentalist, an author, the mother of eight children, a grandmother, a great-grandmother, a tap dancer, four times married and a legend in her own time. Born in 1928, she was an anti-racist white girl who grew up poor in southern Louisiana swampland, with German and Cajun-French ancestry. To support herself, she worked as a waitress for many years, starting as a teenager when she walked picket lines on behalf of busboys and dishwashers. She has been a productive professional writer since the 1950–'60s, when in a decade she published more than 200 stories in popular "true confessions" magazines. She is not a prudish woman, nor lazy. When she had babies she got up at 4:00 A.M. to write before the day started. Betty says of those years:

> I loved writing confession stories. They dealt with the nitty-gritty of the working-class woman's life and I understood that life very well. The stories weren't always about romance. About half of what I wrote dealt with the social problems of poverty and racism, and the difficulties of being a wife and mother in the modern world. But after enlisting in the anti-war army I found I couldn't write these stories anymore. One can't really write what

one no longer believes and I no longer believed in the American dream (Krawczyk, 1996: 139).

Now in her seventies, Betty has the posture, gait, appearance and energy of a much younger woman. A feisty activist for much of her life, she is brainy, well read and an engaging speaker in public lectures and university classes, as well as at activist rallies. Politically, she was influenced early on by Unitarians, for whom spiritual action means responding to the needs of humanity and working for social justice. She was inspired by black activist Stokely Carmichael, and she demonstrated in favour of school integration; for doing that she was physically threatened by so-called Christians. She expanded her political education when she was in her mid-thirties by reading Marx and Engels and other socialist authors. The books she has authored are serious, thought-provoking and informative, and also funny and entertaining (Krawczyk, 1996, 2002). As she herself says, "Louisiana people are just louder, funnier, more talkative, and full of laughter than other folks" (Krawczyk, 1996: 16).

A woman who acts on her convictions, Betty has a long history of defending human rights. In about 1970, during the Vietnam war, her eldest son was recruited into the air force, with two of his brothers nearing draft age. Betty wasn't prepared to lose three sons to a war she opposed, so the family left the U.S.A. and moved to Ontario and then British Columbia, where for a time Betty homesteaded in the wilderness. By the 1980s she was a feminist who recognized that protecting the environment, promoting racial equality, supporting safety for women and children, and marching, writing letters and refusing to pay war taxes in protest against the U.S. invasion of Vietnam and Cambodia were all resistances against a patriarchal, white-supremacist, capitalist-driven disregard for the earth and most of its inhabitants, especially those who lack the reins in the global economy. Those holding economic dominance often dictate the decisions of governments, which function to protect the rich from the poor. At a time when Betty had seven young children, including a nursing infant, she was harassed by tax authorities who were angry that she was withholding war taxes from her (very small) income. Betty writes of how she realized, from reading Engels, that

> people had made the society we live in and, if enough people who didn't like the income disparity got together, they could unmake the present society and make another one more to their liking. This seemed to me a superior way of looking at the world than the religious view, particularly the Christian one. In the Christian world we are admonished not to fret about the poor because they will always be with us. Anyway, God will especially reward poor people after death if they have been meek enough in life (Krawczyk, 1996: 98–9).

For the past decade or so, Betty has been literally laying her body on the line, stretched out with other environmentalists on rural roads, creating human barriers to block logging trucks. She is an activist who is willing to be jailed to arouse public opposition to international corporations clear-cutting the forests of British Columbia. While denuding the forests, these corporations have reaped huge profits by selling lumber to Japan, the United States and Europe, among other places, for newsprint and toilet paper, among other products. Betty has an informed understanding of the profound ecological damage that occurs when animals and birds are rooted from their natural habitats and threatened with extinction, topsoil is washed away or contaminated, erosion is rampant, water systems are polluted, and First Nations peoples are cut off from their hunting, gathering and fishing traditions, negating their rights to their own lands and cultures.

Betty's first arrest was in 1993, when she was in the vanguard of protestors at Clayoquot Sound on the west coast of Vancouver Island, one of the last viable rainforests in the world and owned by the government. She was enjoying her quiet wilderness life in the Sound, and she was not at first receptive to the idea of protesting and disrupting the calm of her life. Also, she has a strong working-class conscience and did not want to imperil the loggers' job security. But with an understanding of the big picture, she did join the protestors against clear-cut logging. Her decision was triggered by a televised image of "maybe a dozen people with their arms locked together standing in a line across the Kennedy River bridge" to obstruct the trucks in the Sound (Krawczyk, 1996: 126). She contemplated going to prison, knowing it to be a possibility, and worried about her claustrophobia. "Will I be able to tolerate being locked up in a cramped space behind bars... without going mad? I shall soon find out. I will be on the blockade in the morning" (Krawczyk, 1996: 127).

In her book about the blockade, Betty analyzes the effects of capitalism, the unequal distribution of wealth and social power. She writes with the passion that fuelled her identification with the protestors:

> [M]agnificent old trees, hundreds, even thousands of years old, sacrificed for [profit]. I feel the same refusal to comply that had slowly built up in my heart toward the government of the United States over the wanton brutality of the Vietnam War. [H]ot anger washed over me again... because I have witnessed the landslides... I have lived with the body of the raped and beaten victim... the mountain range so ripped away that she bleeds all winter long in the form of collapsed logging roads, crevices carved down to the bone by the rivers of gushing rain... the landslides visible testament that the mountains are dissolving and melting into the sea (Krawczyk, 1996: 127).

The protestors, an international alliance of individuals and group representatives, gathered from Germany, England, Ireland and elsewhere, and from across North America, all of them recognizing the global effects of local forestry practices. They stayed around the clock day after day, sharing food and blankets and becoming a tribe, singing together to the accompaniment of guitars, fiddles and banjos. Betty was arrested for obstructing the logging trucks, and she had plenty of company; by summer's end, over 900 of the demonstrators, most of them young people, had been arrested. She describes how she felt, as one of twelve people in a line across the bridge:

> An eagle circles overhead. The morning mist is beginning to lift... beautiful as it rises above the river and over the trees, but I can't concentrate on the scenery as the alligator inside my stomach has gone berserk and I think I might be sick. But then people start singing and it is revival time again. I don't know the words to these songs, but they are compelling and repetitive, like gospel songs, and soon I am belting out with the rest, enjoying the solidarity, the unity of purpose with these people of all different ages and backgrounds whom I hardly know (Krawczyk, 1996: 129).

The group succeeded in turning the trucks back and also in attracting the Royal Canadian Mounted Police, who took them to the Ucluelet jail. Then ten of them, including Betty and three other women, were taken to the Nanaimo Correctional Centre, a men's prison. Through the night, every hour, a guard shone a flashlight on their faces. Betty couldn't sleep. The next day, when they were taken to court to enter their plea, she pleaded not guilty, explaining, "I was standing on crown land at the time of my arrest, which, other than what the First Nations People claim, belongs to all the people of British Columbia. If this is my land how can I be made a criminal for trying to protect its destruction?" (Krawczyk, 1996: 148).

Betty wasn't allowed to take her tap shoes to prison, so she relieved the stress by dribbling a basketball and shooting baskets. For court hearings the women were transported to Victoria, the provincial capital, in a small plane, bound in leg shackles and handcuffs. There they were confined in the city jail, which was a "nightmare, a dank dungeon of sunless stale air, cheap torn plastic mattresses... open toilets but no sinks... nowhere to go for a breath of fresh air" (Krawczyk 1996:170). The greasy food was entirely without nutritional value, and Betty threatened a hunger strike if they didn't start serving spinach. Even worse, men in the cells below them were frequently punished with pepper spray, which travelled the vents into the women's cells above. The women were confined in these conditions for several weeks, until one of Betty's co-defendants, Dr. Ron Aspenall, a physician, went to the court with the threat of appealing to Amnesty International on behalf of the women.

The group was transferred to the Burnaby Correctional Centre for Women. While still settling in, Betty received notice that her daughter Susan was suffering from a brain aneurism, and she attempted to gain release from prison by signing an agreement that she would not again impede the loggers, an offer the government had made in the court hearing. She had not been willing, up to that point, to make that promise, but now she was desperate to be with Susan. Although she was technically entitled, due to bureaucratic complications she could not gain release. This was when she recognized what it means to lose all choice: "I am a prisoner. Now I know what prison is. If you know you can get out anytime by signing a piece of paper you may be incarcerated but you are not imprisoned. But now I am definitely in prison. I cannot get out. My daughter may be dying and I can't go to her" (Krawczyk, 1996: 174).

Susan survived surgery and the crisis passed. Betty's large family are uniquely loving and loyal toward their mother. Susan told her mother that she hadn't wanted to be "responsible for causing you to give up your protest ... if you can help save some rainforest for the kids to come visit, then that's the very best thing you can do. So you just hang in, okay?" (Krawczyk, 1996: 176). Betty says that her children are always relieved when they hear that she's been taken to jail, because they know how unsafe it is for demonstrators in the woods, given the exigencies of nature and the animosity of loggers and the law.

While in the jail awaiting sentencing, Betty and the others were serenaded by a group of supporters outside their cells, their candles lighting the night as they sang. Popular opinion was strongly in favour of their release, although they were pariahs in logging communities.

After the first week of trial, Betty let go of the court-assigned lawyer and represented herself. The advantages were that she could object to anything that anyone said in the courtroom, and that she could cross-examine witnesses. In her statement to the court, she declared to Judge Bouck:

> Sir, there might be some satisfaction for me right now if I could equate MacMillan-Bloedel with the devil, but I can't. MacMillan-Bloedel, and other multi-nationals... have no parallel in human history. They are something new on the face of the earth and their power is awesome... The devil knows of good and evil. The devil has qualities one can speak to, wrestle with, cut deals with. MacMillan-Bloedel as a corporate structure has no human qualities of good or evil because it is a giant, mindless, soulless machine programmed to do one thing and one thing only—maximize profits from the forests. And because it is an entity with no human qualities the MacMillan-Bloedel machine can mercilessly butcher the forests with an immediacy and thoroughness that makes Attila the Hun look like a pea picker (Krawczyk, 1996: 196–7).

The judge was not impressed. Later he ejected Betty from the courtroom for yelling at him, but he brought her back the next day because it wouldn't look good to the public "to have a granny languish down in the dungeon cells while her own trial is going on" (Krawczyk, 1996: 197). After six weeks of trial, forty-four prisoners, including the four women, were convicted of criminal contempt, on the grounds that their protests threatened the sanctity of the law and civilized social order. The highest sentence was sixty days in jail and a $3,000 fine. Betty was sentenced to forty-five days and a $2,000 fine. They all had the choice of appealing or getting the time over with, and about half of them, including Betty, chose the latter. All in all, for the Clayoquot Sound actions, Betty served close to five months in a series of jails and prisons.

It started all over again in May 2000, when Betty was arrested in the Elaho Valley, 200 kilometres northwest of Vancouver, where she and a friend sang and danced in the middle of the road, blocking about thirty logging trucks. She was also arrested for another blockade. Before trial Betty complained about the uses of the justice system to destroy the environment. She complained about the sheriffs taking her shoelaces, handcuffing her, putting leg irons on her, forcing her to crawl into the police truck. And she complained about the Interfor corporation stealing the people's forests and stealing taxpayers' money by forcing a long, expensive trial. Many protestors had shown up to demonstrate against Interfor, but Betty was the only one to hold out on the blockade. She was soon rearrested and charged again with criminal contempt of court.

For the singing and dancing offence, Betty was sentenced to six weeks at the Burnaby Correctional Centre for Women, pleased it wasn't more though she still had another trial to face. This was her fourth time at BCCW, and fortunately, by now, Betty had lost her panic about locked iron doors and tight spaces. She was accustomed to the light in her cell that was never turned off, day or night. She was gaining an understanding of the divisive social functions of prisons, and she pondered the issue of drug possession, which was the reason many women were incarcerated. "I consider them political prisoners, too. If all the women at BCCW who had been arrested for drug or drug-related offences were released, I would be the only one left in my unit and one of the few left in the entire prison" (Krawczyk, 2002: 4).

A side crusade for Betty while she was at BCCW was protesting the evangelical effort by community volunteers to impose their religious views on the prisoners. In a meeting with them, she told them, "You are violating my religious freedom when you come into my space and start preaching to me without my consent... If I had my way, for every Bible and religious publication placed in this prison there would be small handbooks on the Charter [of Rights and Freedoms] and easy-to-read articles on what the Charter means and might mean to women in prison" (Krawczyk, 2002: 111).

This new jail sentence was made difficult when Betty was assigned a cellmate, depriving her of the space and quiet she needed to spread out her legal papers in preparation for her next trial, when again she would represent herself. She walked alone on the track on Saturdays, collecting her thoughts behind a high steel fence topped with coiled barbed wire. Upon release from her six-week sentence, Betty reflected on her experience:

> Jail time, the structure of jail time, recedes almost instantly once one walks out the gates. Now I do not have to be anywhere at any particular time unless I care to. I do not have to stand outside my cell to be counted, rise at a certain time, go to bed at a certain time, eat at a certain time, do certain chores at a certain time or go outside and exercise at a certain time. I do not have to wait my turn to make phone calls, to shower, to launder my clothes or to get my mail (Krawczyk, 2002: 117).

As much as she appreciated being back in the "free world," Betty was soon back in court, on the second of the Elaho Valley block-ade charges. The circumstances of the Elaho demonstrations were more dangerous than most. On one occasion, a mob of dozens of men, primarily loggers, trashed and burned the protestors' camp and physically assaulted three of the "tree huggers." Only five of the attackers were ever charged and convicted, and they were given suspended sentences, so none of them served even a day in jail. Betty made an impassioned statement to the judge that included a critique of the law's excessive concern with property rights and the government's short-sighted coddling of profit-grabbing private corporations. With reference to the loggers and their allies, that is, those who defended the rights of forest workers, she stated:

> In spite of my own union background and my working-class identification, my only response is this: care for the environ-ment must supersede temporary jobs. If the only jobs this society, this economic system, this country, this province can

provide are jobs that destroy the life-support systems of the earth, the entire economic system should be dismantled and we should start over again from scratch and try to create a saner system (Krawczyk, 2002: 135).

At the end of August 2000, prior to sentencing, Betty organized a "tent-in" on the lawn of the B.C. legislative building, refusing to leave until the premier of the province was willing to speak with her. She wanted a chance to plead for "citizens' claims of steward-ship" and a moratorium on clear-cutting. People gathered to listen to speeches and to laugh and sing along with the Raging Grannies, a group of older women in prim, old-fashioned long dresses and big gaudy hats, who sing amusing ditties against corporations, male chauvinists, the military, greedy politicians and corrupt unions. To the unionists who objected to the protestors' acts of civil disobedi-ence, Betty retorted:

[Their remarks] show that the workers have no understanding or even passing knowledge of the history of their own unions... It was the Wobblies who gained for all of us the right to orga-nize, and this basic right was won on the backs, on the flesh and blood, of men and women who knew firsthand the necessity of using civil disobedience. And a number of them paid for their determination with their lives... [They] not only wanted better working conditions and more pay, they wanted a better world for everybody.

The IWA [Industrial, Wood and Allied Workers] didn't resist the grapple yarders or the feller bunchers or other machines that sucked up union jobs. The IWA didn't protest the automation of the mills, which cost many more jobs. The IWA couldn't bow low enough in the dirt before all of the international logging com-panies, in their claim that we had to do these things to remain competitive.

...What the IWA accepted without question was the notion that the loss of jobs was primarily the fault of environmentalists, even when evidence to the contrary was right before their eyes. [The corporations] simply cut and run in this province, leaving behind not only communities that are devastated by the loss of forestry jobs but whole mountains and valleys that are repulsive to tourists because they are stripped of life ... [T]he very people who should be in the forefront of this battle—the workers—align themselves with their bosses [as if] their values and goals and fortunes are the same (Krawczyk, 2002: 161–3).

After nightfall, a guard asked Betty to remove the tent and move on, because it's illegal to camp on the legislature lawn. Betty took the position of Supreme Court of Canada Chief Justice Beverley McLachlin that Canadian law belongs to the people. As far as Betty was concerned, this was her legislature and her lawn. She reiterated that she would move after the premier met with her. The police were summoned and four officers came to remove her, each taking one limb, since she was not prepared to walk away on her own. They arrested her and carried her, upside down, to the police wagon parked behind the Parliament building, while she shouted slogans to the supporters who followed along.

The following morning, Betty had to appear in court for having camped on the legislature lawn, but at the jail they took away everything she needed for that appearance, including legal papers and her bra. The judge offered to release her until trial if she would promise to not occupy the legislature grounds again; she refused, making reference to the McLachlin position, as she did with every authority she encountered. After another night in the barbaric Victoria jail, she was shackled at her waist and ankles, handcuffed and taken to the Burnaby Correctional Centre for Women to await trial.

Betty, along with a group of her comrades, was also anticipating a mid-September decision by Justice Parrett, who tried them in the Elaho case. When they arrived for the hearing they were greeted by a roomful of supporters and the media. The judge addressed each defendant in turn, assigning varied degrees of guilt and levels of punishment. He saved Betty for the end, and, in part, had this to say to and about her:

What can I say about Betty Krawczyk? She at least has the courage of her convictions. She has never wavered from her open intention to force on others the task of arresting her and putting her in jail. Her goal in ensuring this end is to use her appearance, her age and her willingness to speak out as a vehicle to obtain media and public expression. She openly advocates public defiance of the law and the orders, and asserts the goals in which she believes. I have no doubt of her sincerity in those beliefs, as I have no doubt as to the result I am forced to impose. The evidence against Betty Krawczyk is overwhelming... The result of those actions gives me no pleasure, for Ms. Krawczyk is both personable and likable, but... I see no likelihood that she will swerve from the course she has chartered [sic] for herself. I find Betty Krawczyk guilty of criminal contempt of court (Krawczyk, 2002: 189).

Before sentencing, Betty gave yet another impassioned statement to the court, in which she pleaded for ecological sanity:

The Native people of old called the trees in the forests of old the Standing Ones. And we, sir, as well as the Natives, all of us, evolved together down through the ages with these forests, these trees; our very breathing is synchronized, we breathe in what they breathe out; they need our breath to grow and mature, become ancient, thousands of years ancient, fall down, become nursery logs and start the life cycle over again. When we make deserts of these forests we make deserts of our own hearts and spirits and degrade the entire human race...

I am a prisoner of my own conscience, sir, and only of my own conscience, and that makes me a free woman, a free person. And as a free person I refuse to enter into any sort of collusion with this court in terms of potential conditions or undertakings or electronic monitoring as part of sentencing...

[I will never assist] in my own punishment in ways that would force me to internalize prison, to internalize confinement, to internalize guilt, to internalize the power of Interfor and the Attorney General's office to punish me for trying to protect public property, property that every citizen has a right, and not just a right, but also a duty, to protect and enjoy and respect and love. Sir, you must lock me up, or let me go (Krawczyk, 2002: 208–9).

When Betty finished speaking and began walking back to the prisoner's box, the spectators gave her a standing ovation. It was not likely, however, that the judge would be moved to be merciful, and Betty figured he might give her as much as six months, even though others had been sentenced to just two or three months. It was a shock to everyone, then, when Justice Parrett sentenced Betty and one other defendant to a full year in lock-up, with no remission for time already served. She writes of feeling calm, with "an elder's fully awakened sense of responsibility" (Krawczyk, 2002: 212). As the sheriffs led her out, she yelled back at the crowd of supporters, "It isn't over yet!" And they called back, "We love you!"

As someone highly attuned to injustice, Betty was quick to observe the destructiveness of the prison system.

Most of the murderers here killed in passion or after prolonged abuse. Incarceration as we know it is, in my opinion, a crime against nature and the human spirit. The addicts belong in extended health care facilities with proper diet and exercise and hope for the future; the murderers belong in positions in the community where they can exercise the soul-cleansing practice of restitution. In spite of the fact that I witness little daily acts of care and compassion among the [prisoners] and staff, incarceration brings out the worst in everybody. To guard another human being in order to see that her freedom is curtailed is a disgraceful thing. It is akin to slavery. It elevates one over the other in obscene ways that degrade the mental and spiritual condition of both, and it should not be practised except in the most extreme circumstances, such as with serial murderers... Perhaps there should be strict limits placed on how long anyone can serve in the capacity of guarding another human being (Krawczyk, 2002: 187).

In early 2001, after four months in prison, Betty won an appeal and, without any conditions, was released from BCCW. She and I became friends, and I asked if she would be willing to contribute an essay to this book, focused on her experience of being in jail. As a friend and an inveterate writer, she readily agreed. One of Betty's strengths is her reliability, so I was surprised when her deadline came and went and her manuscript didn't appear. Nor did she return my call. Then I saw her name in the news, in reports of a new protest against clear-cutting. She was arrested and taken to court amid extensive media coverage. Soon thereafter I saw background images of Betty on television, in handcuffs and being escorted by a uniformed guard, a young woman. They were both smiling and apparently engaged in friendly conversation, while the newscaster explained that they were en route to BCCW.

I then received a call from Betty, from the prison; she explained that if I'd contact her literary agent, the agent would send me a draft of Betty's new manuscript, which included stories from Betty's previous times in jail. She offered me the liberty of excerpting from this material, and I have done so very gladly. In the following pages, Betty gives an account of what it is to live in a prison.

Betty's Story

The iron door to my cell has clanged shut for the last time. At least for me. At least for this trip. My trial is finally over, with all the attending media coverage of my logging blockades, and I am now on my way out of the maximum security part of the women's prison.

Burnaby Correctional Centre for Women is located in the boonies of Burnaby, British Columbia. Or what used to be the boonies. Now the entire section lying along this side of the banks of the Fraser River where the women's prison is located has been turned into an expansive industrial park.

My guard and I are heading over to the Open Living Unit, where I have just been transferred. I am pushing a large prison laundry basket in front of me. The laundry basket is borrowed from the laundry room of Section C for the occasion. It holds all of the worldly goods I was allowed to have in my cell in maximum security.

There are strict rules concerning what a prisoner may have in her cell. It's the same in Open Living. I've been housed there twice before. I know from experience that the cells in Open Living really do look more like rooms, even though they are not discernibly bigger, and that the guards there wear civilian clothing and are called "staff." The women who are called staff instead of guards usually make an effort to be, if not exactly friendly, at least approachable. Unlike the uniformed guard who is accompanying me at the moment with a rather stern demeanour.

She's young. And silent. No chit chat from her. She probably doesn't know what to make of me. A lot of the guards don't. Because most of them are aware of my crime, which was standing in the middle of a logging road and refusing to move, in order to try to help save some of the public old-growth forests of British Columbia for everybody's grandchildren, including my own, which inspires me, from time to time, to disobey a court order, which in turn lands me in jail. This time my quarrel was, and is, with International Forest Products, popularly, or unpopularly, known as Interfor, over the ancient forests in the Elaho Valley, just north of Vancouver.

So some of the guards appear diffident in my presence, or even embarrassed. It's because of my white hair and dignified stance. Most of the guards, like their superiors, seem to wish that environmental activists, especially seventy-two-year-old great-grandmothers like me, would stay out of BCCW. We protestors bring in unnecessary complications for prison officials and staff, and unwanted publicity...

Prisoners pushing laundry baskets piled high with clothes, papers, pictures, books and even plants are a common sight in the building, as women are frequently transferred from one unit to another. Other women, release papers at the ready, can be seen hauling all of the stuff they have accumulated in prison out to the exit door. One can usually tell from the women's expressions which prisoners are on their way out altogether and which are just being transferred...

[A]ny Canadian woman, regardless of age or class, would be safer from physical assault inside these prison walls than on the outside simply because there are no men here. Well, only a few. A man was in charge of the kitchen, the prison chaplain is a man and [so is] the assistant director of the prison. None of these men, as far as I know, have ever posed a physical threat or harassment to the women here. And in all the months I've spent in this prison, both in maximum security and in the Open Living Unit, I've witnessed only one fight between the women. It didn't get to a serious stage because the other women stopped the ruckus before the guards realized what was happening. Which makes me wonder.

What are all those vicious B-grade women's prison films about? Where are the bull dykes that rape and mutilate other prisoners; where are the vicious, murderous she-devils? Certainly not in the Burnaby Correctional Centre for Women... While the women here don't often physically attack each other, they frequently turn their anger and grief in on themselves. They slash frequently. Too many are suicide risks.

We pass another prisoner pushing a laundry basket... She's older, a haunted look in her eyes and prominent track marks on her skinny arms... [B]oth of us could be practising to be bag ladies... Like Pearl Bailey once said, I've been rich and I've been poor and rich is better. My own "rich" is strictly metaphorical, while my "poor" is literal, but in the immediate future the "rich" of the Open Living Unit beats the hell out of the "poor" of maximum security... [The guard] stares straight ahead, mindful of her duty. Or maybe she's having trouble with her man. Or woman. Or maybe her kid's sick...

Down the steps with the laundry basket, which is no mean feat, and then we're free of the shackles and steel doors of the maximum security building. Oh, joy! Oh, bright September sun, so bright I feel giddy, so warm I'm tempted to break out in song. But I restrain myself. I've learned that all prisoners are supposed to look and act as if in a chronic state of misery, which most are anyway. Unexplained expressions of joy are looked upon with the keenest suspicion...

I will have a room of my own that I won't have to share and a desk where I can organize my books and papers, and with a little luck recoup my word processor. On September 15, 2000, I was sentenced to a year's incarceration without remission by Justice Parrett of the Supreme Court of British Columbia. Writing retains my sanity and keeps me centred. And although I have already served over four months of an earlier sentence for blockading in the Elaho, I will need all of the sanity and centredness I can muster in order to endure another entire year. If I can just luck out now on the location of my new cell, I'll be okay.

But I don't. My new room is sandwiched between two devotees of Rock 101. The built-in wall radios in all parts of the prison will only receive Rock 101. My god! What were they thinking, the people who designed this prison? Don't they know that music has an enormous effect on the psyche? And that the women behind these walls already walk a thin line, jangled as they are by drugs, physical abuse and mental disturbances?... But I must get organized, which consists of trying to muffle the raucous sound from the radio panel with my towels, and then a pair of sweatpants. It doesn't work. I'll have to speak to the woman to the right who has her radio turned on high. Which I hate to do. I knock on her door. After a moment the door opens. She is young, as most in here are. She brushes lank bleached-blond hair off her forehead and rubs her eyes. She was napping, I think. Sometimes the medications, like methadone, seem to make the women dozy.

"I'm sorry," I apologize. "But I was wondering if you could turn your radio down. Do you mind?"

She stares at me. "Who are you?"

"I've just moved in next door."

I give her time to digest this information, as I know I look more like staff or a volunteer than a prisoner. Or some Girl Scout's grandmother. Actually, I am a Girl Scout's grandmother.

"Oh. What do you want?"

"Your radio. I was wondering if you could turn it down. It's a bit loud for me."

She rubs her eyes again and then blinks at me. "Oh. Well, I like it loud," she counters.

I stand my ground. "It's too loud," I repeat.

There's a long silence. She wipes at the wispy bangs on her forehead again. She is thinking. I am obviously not a regular-type prisoner. Who knows what kind of pull I might have around the joint? And then she shrugs. "Okay. I was going out to the track anyway."…

No dinner bell will ring to announce dinner. We must keep aware of the time. In the Open Living Unit prisoners are supposed to be on their way out of the prison system, so we are each given a key to our room, our cell. We are advised to keep our rooms locked when we are not in them. However, when we are in them, we must not lock them. The staff must be able to enter our rooms at all times. Without knocking. Privacy is not afforded the prisoners. Ever. Just as I am locking my door to go down for count and dinner, I hear my name called over the loudspeaker. They want me in the office. My stomach gives a little lurch… As the mother of eight children, eight grandchildren and one great-grandchild, my first thought when summoned is always one of disaster… [In the staff office] the officer is deeply tanned and has short blond hair. I will call her Blondie. I take the proffered chair and wait. Blondie is standing over me, pondering a piece of paper in her hand.

"Betty, you are of retirement age," she says finally in an accusing tone, looking down at me.

"Yes, ma'am, I am," I answer, wondering where this was going. "I'm seventy-two."

"This means you don't have to work if you don't want to," Blondie says.

I stare at her. Not work? But I'm in prison.

"Of course, if you want to work, you can. You'll get paid the same rate as the others if you choose to work."

Paid the same rate? Six dollars a day, that's a day, not an hour, for scrubbing toilets, or doing outside maintenance in all kinds of weather, or sewing endless prison uniforms for men in the tailor shop, or the acute boredom of pretending to be interested in ceramics, and at the very top of the pay scale maybe a few extra dollars that only the kitchen help receive, for working a split shift, a shift that takes up most of the day. This is a choice?

"But of course if you don't work you have to have some kind of a project plan and you have to keep busy at the same hours as everybody else."...

What an unexpected windfall! They're going to retire me! In the lineup in the dining room I get more curious looks. And then a woman comes in who I remember from 1993. She's a lifer. It's an odd thing, but this woman and a few of the others like her, who have done passion killings, are often the most balanced, stable women in the prison.

The main cook is Asian. She is not a prisoner, but all her helpers are. "I have no vegetarian food for you tonight. Tomorrow I will," she explains. I thank her for the beans and corn she dishes onto my plate, not really missing the square of tofu I am sure she has in mind when she thinks vegetarian food. And there is a bowl of salad greens on a back counter and a separate plate of raw carrots and celery. For drinks there is a choice of hot tea, cold powdered milk or a red drink that looks and tastes like Kool-Aid. And a big cookie. All in all, it is a filling and rather decent dinner [unlike the food in the maximum security building]...

Each table seats four women. My three dinner companions greet me with silent stares as I sit down with my plate. I ignore their stares and begin eating. There's something about prison that stimulates appetite... "You been here before, aint'cha?" the woman on my right asks suddenly, breaking the silence.

"Yeah, I have, in '93 and for a month last fall. Were you here then?" I inquire, gazing at her. She is tall, broad-shouldered, thirty-ish with round blue eyes.

"Naw. I've been in and out, but not in '93 or last year. I heard Bookworm say you'd been in before."

I nodded. Bookworm was the lifer, the woman I'd recognized in the lineup...

"How long you in for?" she asks.

Prison etiquette deems it impolite to come right out and ask what one's crime was, but it's okay to inquire of one's sentence.

"A year," I answer. "Without parole."

Her eyes pop. "Holy shit! You must be one big, bad mama."

I laugh. So does Blue Eyes.

[The women at Betty's table speculate on her crime.] I decide I might as well come clean now as later.

"I'm an environmental protestor," I blurt out.

"What the fuck is that?" Freckles demands.

"She stood in front of some logging trucks," Blue Eyes says with a knowledgeable air.

Freckles' eyes narrow.

"What logging trucks? And what the fuck for?"

I take a deep breath. "Well, in this case it was Interfor logging trucks and I was trying to bring public and government attention to the fact that our public forests are being destroyed by international logging companies..."

"You're a tree hugger," Freckles breaks in. Her voice is contemptuous.

"Some call me that," I admit. "And sometimes I actually do go hug a tree. Just for fun."

"Bullshit. People like you kill jobs in the forest industry. I'm from Port Alberni. My dad used to be a logger. That was before you tree huggers messed everything up."

"Well, I wouldn't say we're the ones messing things up in the forest and causing people to lose jobs. Do you know what a grapple yarder is, or a fellow buncher?"

"Shit, yeah. I told you my old man's a logger."

"Well, you ask him how many men these machines replace in the woods. And the mills... ask him how automating the mills has cost jobs. It's been machines that have displaced men, not people like me. People like me object to the clear-cutting. It's the clear-cutting that ruins the forests and the salmon streams and causes all the landslides. You've seen them yourself, all around Port Alberni. The forests have been so cut and damaged around that area it's plumb pitiful, and those are public forests, that means they belong to me and my kids and grandkids as well as to you and your family. Those forests belong to all British Columbians. Don't you want your kids to be able to go into an old-growth forest somewhere, and look at a massive cedar tree, or Douglas fir, or hemlock, and feel the power and the beauty of ancient trees, and smell the streams and ferns and moss, and hear all the animals scurrying around who live in the forest... "

"I don't have any kids," Freckles interrupts...

There are programs in the evenings that some women want to attend, other programs that some of the women have to attend. There is television, gym, and, as long as there is light outside, a walk around the yard. I head for the yard. Soon the days will darken too early for evening walks, and it is this outside activity that helps steady my nerves in this place.

The smokers are congregated just outside the front door of the unit, a dozen or so, but there are three other women walking the circular path outside, a couple in the lead and a single woman walking a few yards behind. I step into the path behind the single walker. I don't mind walking around in circles. In fact, it's rather soothing... I could almost imagine myself in the country, as long as I am walking toward the river. But when the path curves I'm facing the grey, looming structure of maximum security. Never mind, the yard is grassy and there is a Native healing circle enclosed in one end of the yard, with a bench and four little pebble pathways facing each direction, bordered with native plants...

The couple ahead are talking animatedly to each other, and at one end of the walk I see them touch hands and heads quickly, break apart, all within a heartbeat. There are firm rules over here about that sort of thing. In maximum it's common to see women walking arm in arm, or curled in the grass in affectionate attitudes with one another. This is a change from 1993. This time, when I was first admitted, I was given, along with the familiar soaps, comb, toothbrush and toothpaste, a small plastic bottle of bleach and a condom with instructions on how to make a dental dam [to curb the spread of HIV infection]. I was impressed by this progression. At least, I thought, the people in charge of this place are aware that there are needles in here and that from time to time some of the women may engage in sexual activity. However, in the Open Living Unit, a prisoner is severely censored and even sent back to maximum security for indulging in either sex or drugs. At age seventy-two I'm not considered a high risk for either, with no record of such.

After walking half an hour I head back to my room. I nod at the women standing around smoking and gossiping at the doorway, but I don't stop to chat. I'm too new. Give them a chance to get used to seeing me. Women in prison, because they have so little, are jealous of their turf. Besides, some of the women have a tendency to look upon me as a possible spy, or rat. At least at first. Anyway, I have letters to answer. I receive a lot of mail. From sympathizers and well-wishers. It's plumb heartwarming. Most of the cards and letters come from British Columbia, although a few come from other provinces and the U.S.A....

I have written all of two letters when I hear my neighbour to the right return to her room. Rock 101 fills my space, my ears, my brain. As if waiting for that very signal, the woman on my left turns her radio on too. High. High, high, high.

Bloody hell! Concentration is now impossible. Oh well, time for my exercises anyway. I kick off my shoes and start gyrating to this obscure heavy metal rock band that makes no pretense to musicality or even rhythm, just piercing, tightly wired grating sounds that seem more a shrieking cry for help than anything to do with music. And maybe that's what it is... But I go through my dance exercises anyway.

The women all gather in the dining room where the count takes place. We sit or stand, waiting for a staff officer to come count us and write the particulars down in the log book. This staff officer is very young. She looks like a high school girl. How odd to be counted and guarded by such a young-looking person. Why, I have grandchildren older than she is, I'm sure. I will call her The Kid. The Kid looks perplexed. She asks if anyone has seen a certain prisoner. No one has. The Kid calls the woman's name over the intercom. Everyone waits.

Then a bit of horseplay erupts at one of the tables. One of the younger women tried to tip over another's chair and there is a bit of a tussle and lots of raucous laughter. Just in time for Blondie to catch as she walks in the room.

"That's enough!" she barks. The offending table settles, sullen but quiet. Blondie and The Kid put their heads together. Blondie tells Bookworm to go see if the absentee is in her room. In a few minutes Bookworm is back with the hapless absentee in tow; the new arrival looks dishevelled and not quite awake. She is ordered to the office immediately while the rest of us are dismissed. As I'm leaving the dining room Freckles falls into step beside me. She tells me in a sort of guarded, respectful way that she talked to her father and he's heard of me. The tone she is using tells me that I will have no real trouble from her in the future.

I MADE A FORMAL grievance against [the religious fundamentalists who came to prison seeking conversions]. They ostensibly came to play ball with us, on the track field outside. After the first inning, while we were enjoying their pop and cookies, they started handing out religious pamphlets and preaching. The upshot of my grievance was that, in the future, they must hold all their religious services in the chapel and announce their presence as being a religious presence, just as other church groups did. Now here they were again, invading my space [on October 8, Thanksgiving Day]. And they haven't come empty-handed. Oh, no. They are bearing turkey with all the trimmings… "What are you all doing?" I ask the short,

stocky man. He pauses, his arms full of goodies. He is the spokes-
man for the group. He recognizes me, and frowns. And then tries
to hide his frown with a forced smile.

"We are going to cook your Thanksgiving dinner," he says
brightly.

"My Thanksgiving dinner?" I ask.

"Yes. Everyone's."

Damn. Now I have to assert myself.

"Not mine, you're not," I say angrily. "I didn't ask you to cook my
Thanksgiving dinner. And I won't eat it."

He stares at me blankly. A couple of people in his entourage have
heard the exchange. So have some of the other prisoners. I whirl on
my heel and beat it to the office, where I voice my displeasure.

"I want my regular prison meal for dinner," I demand. The
women on duty in the staff office seem bewildered by my complaint.

"But Betty, the church people are just being nice..."

"They aren't being nice," I insist. "They are being self-serving.
They want souls to save and laurels heaped upon their heads for
their good works... Is this just a way for the prison to save money?"

The guards look at each other. I can tell they can't fathom why I
am so upset.

"Look at it this way," I say. "While I am incarcerated here this
is my home. I have to abide by all the prison rules, and I'm willing
to do that. What I am not willing to do is put up with something
that isn't in the rules, tolerate people coming into my home who are
not prison staff and who I would not invite into my home on the
outside. Especially to eat with me. I'm boycotting the Thanksgiving
dinner."...

The guards stare at me. "You still have to come for count," they
say almost in unison.

And so I do.

[A month later] I may be old news inside the joint, but, on
the outside, news of my plight has spread. My mail has indeed
increased. I must really work to stay abreast of it, which runs me

into complications with the staff. Stamps are contraband. That means if you are caught with stamps you will be punished. Why? Because stamps have been known to harbour drug dust particles, deliberately placed, so that the licker of the stamps will get a high, or at least a buzz. And visitors are not allowed to bring in pre-stamped envelopes. Which means a prisoner must buy all of her pre-stamped envelopes from the canteen... [T]he canteen is not ordinarily stocked with large amounts of pre-stamped envelopes. I must place a special order.

The Elizabeth Fry Society is very helpful to me from time to time. I can go bitch to Julia, and she will treat my frustration concerning the mail-out procedures with the importance it deserves. Which means she will listen and verbally pat me on the head before she turns her attention to women who are struggling for their very lives. But it definitely comforts me to know that there are women working inside this prison who are not beholden to the prison for their jobs or their paycheques...

A staff member will be up shortly making the rounds of the rooms. She will poke her head into my room to see if I'm at my desk [which qualifies as work]... Because my hair is so white and I receive so much mail I have come, from time to time, to be considered as something of an authority on certain issues...

[Blue Eyes is] eyeing the pod of fresh hot red pepper on my plate. The red pepper is contraband, which is anything not issued by or approved by prison staff. So I never divulge how I came into possession of the pepper. But I must have it. I'm from southern Louisiana. I was raised on hot peppers. These few contraband peppers are what make my unpeppered meals tolerable. That is the magic of a hot red pepper. It can make a piece of cardboard taste middling good. And I don't think Blue Eyes even really likes the bloody pepper, but just because it is something forbidden and on my plate, she also thinks she must have it. Or a piece of it...

I cut off a small piece and stealthily shove it across the table in a napkin. If one of the guards sees I will have to explain where it came from... "Rats" are viewed with contempt by everyone. On several occasions in maximum security certain guards would invite me to "tell" on an infringer of the rules, and I would ask them in effect whether my white hair indicated some kind of feeble-mindedness to them, as even the stupidest of prisoners knows that "ratting" invites retaliation... I could spend the rest of my life in the joint. Which is why I am most anxious to protect my source of fresh hot peppers, which are manna to the Cajun soul...

[In the yard] I find myself scrutinizing every blade of grass, every little clover, every mushroom. There are quite a few mushrooms, at least half a dozen different kinds, encircling the young coniferous trees on the outer edges of the yard, and some strewn around the gravelled path. I wonder why there are so many mushrooms. Was the yard constructed over some kind of landfill?

Poplar trees lining the Fraser River are losing their leaves. The air has decidedly chilled. There is a railroad track that runs by the river and a drawbridge that rises to let boats go through. I can see the rail and boat activity more clearly now that the trees are becoming bare...

[M]ore to keep the peace in the environmental community than anything, I have agreed to have a lawyer for appeal. So I don't have to mess with researching case law anymore... or trying to come up with a new legal twist that might throw a monkey wrench into the works. Now all I have to deal with is my book [*Lock Me Up or Let Me Go*, published in 2002] and the mail. And I read.

I am totally satisfied with my new room... I am no longer tormented by Rock 101. [M]y neighbour's radio is on her opposite wall... Free of grinding, raucous heavy metal and silly, sexist, inane remarks by the radio commentators who command the Rock 101 station, I can actually think.

And I have a view. Really. It's a view. My desk is by the window, and I can look out over the wide expanse of lawn and see the trees guarding the riverbanks most any time of day... [and] glorious multi-coloured sunsets in the evenings. Except when it's raining...

It's a bitch trying to call long distance from this joint. A prisoner can only call collect, or else go through a request process that is tedious and humiliating… And of course we can't receive calls. As the lineup for the collect phone is often discouraging, I turn to my favourite form of communication, the letter. I go down the list [of the eight children], writing in longhand to Joe in California, Susan in Pennsylvania, Andy in Toronto, Mike in the wilds of Manitoba, Margaret and Rose Mary in Ucluelet, and then when I get to Barbara Ellen's name I just kiss the spot in my address book where I have scribbled her new address, the one that simply says On Journey. Barbara Ellen died five and a half years ago. From breast cancer. I am tired out by the time I get to Marian… so I decide to go down and see if the local phone is still busy. It isn't. I dial our number. Marian and I share an apartment in Vancouver when I'm not in prison. Marian answers.

"My face is falling," I say in salutation.

"No, it isn't. That's just your imagination," she answers. She knows that I am referring to the fact that the authorities won't allow me to have my Vitamin A gel… Like many other personal articles, my face cream is not allowed…

"Are you eating?" I ask. "I mean, eating well?"

"Actually, yes. And you?"

"It's okay. But I want gumbo. A filet gumbo. With cornbread."

She laughs.

ALTHOUGH THE GUARDS DON'T have to knock, some do out of courtesy, but it's only a brief half second before they poke their heads in.

"Were you reminded of your press interview tomorrow at one?" the guard asks, handing me a slip of paper. She is one of the regular staff members, young, plump, pretty, with deep dimples when she smiles. Dimples tops the list of staff favourites by the prisoners.

"Yes, thank you," I answer, taking the slip. In order to give a press interview I must be taken over to the maximum security building, where there are controls for that sort of thing, and I have to be accompanied by a guard. So far the prison has been very accommodating to me about this, even though it means extra work for them.

And there has been a flurry of requests for interviews by newspapers, magazines, radio and even television. I'm glad.

I am trying to embarrass Interfor and the government and the B.C. judicial system as much as I can. I want to embarrass the hell out of them. They need to be embarrassed; they should all be ashamed of themselves. And Greenpeace is gearing up to coordinate my protest with their overseas campaign. So yes, I am very happy to give interviews.

Reflections

Betty is happy to give interviews, and the press is happy to accommodate her. There is no question that the publicity attached to Betty's protests has educated a good share of the general public on local forestry practices and on the need for preserving a balanced environment. Between 1993 and 2004, Betty was arrested and incarcerated eight different times for contempt of court, for blocking logging roads, putting up a tent and holding a rally in front of Parliament, and holding sit-ins in government offices. She has been invited to speak in Europe and is a leading voice among environmentalists.

In October 2003, Betty was sentenced to six additional months in prison without parole, having been already confined in the prison on remand for almost five months. On the outside, Betty's supporters organized a "Free Betty Ball" with bands and speakers, including one of Betty's daughters. On the inside, Betty got along with everyone, including the staff, even though she described their treatment of the women as "barbaric." Women looked up to her, and she was active in the life of the prison. For example, when the Native Sisterhood organized a powwow, Betty participated energetically, and visitors who saw her dance that day couldn't believe she was seventy-six. She also used her energy to be of use to the women around her as an advocate. She complained in a letter to the solicitor general (11-11-03) about the problems of overcrowdedness, with two women in a $5' \times 8'$ cell. She stressed the neglect of women suffering serious ailments such as HIV, hepatitis C, sexually transmitted diseases, skin and respiratory problems and "a plethora of mental and emotional disturbances that underlie many of the addiction problems."

In February 2004 a note I'd sent to Betty was returned to me, stamped, "Not Here. Return to Sender." I learned from another woman in her unit that Betty's son in California was gravely ill with cancer, and a compassionate judge had given Betty an early release so she could go to her son's bedside. Shortly thereafter I received a letter she'd written in her son's hospital room. While he slept, she contemplated the ways that destroying old forests contributes to polluted air, water and soil, and to the runaway cancer epidemic. Her personal pain was cut with her political anger.

Betty is a remarkable human being. She stays high-spirited while incarcerated because her crime and punishment signify the strength of her convictions, rather than something of which she is ashamed. She finds peace and freedom within herself, no matter where she is. Betty Krawczyk is a respected elder who has more than earned her place in a global pantheon of strong, brave women.

References

Krawczyk, Betty (1996). *Clayoquot: The Sound of My Heart*. Victoria: Orca.

Krawczyk, Betty (2002). *Lock Me Up or Let Me Go: The Protests, Arrest and Trial of an Environmental Activist*. Vancouver: Press Gang/Raincoast.

10

ANN

BUILDING A REVOLUTION

HISTORICALLY, SOCIAL REVOLUTIONS follow a pattern. Political dissidents mobilize resistance to the status quo; they are kept under surveillance, and, if not assassinated, they are criminalized, imprisoned and often tortured as enemies of the state. When they have enough grassroots support, they emerge from prison as the popular leadership and are installed as the new government. This is a frequent cycle, exemplified in recent decades by Vaclav Havel in Czechoslovakia and Nelson Mandela in South Africa: from protestor to guerrilla warrior to criminal to revolutionary hero to head of state—until the next radical turn of events. Most contemporary states have evolved from such political rebellions, and most of the front-line players are men. However, women, too, have been very active as revolutionary forces over the course of centuries.

Emma Goldman, Elizabeth Gurley Flynn, Margaret Sanger, Dorothy Day, Barbara Deming, Joan Baez, Angela Davis, Bernardine Dohrn, Kathy Boudin, Susan Saxe, Assata Shakur, Emily Harris—these are a few of the many women who have been political prisoners in the United States during the past century. Among them, they have worked for the legalization of birth control; an end to poverty; equitable distribution of resources; cessation of war; an end to patriarchy, racism and imperialism; and the advent of universal freedom, equality, peace, social justice and respect for the environment. Canadian women have likewise worked hard and taken risks for social justice, but few have been imprisoned for political actions. Most notably among them, Ann Hansen caused a stir in Canada in the 1980s, with the consequence of long imprisonment.

In contrast to conventional revolutionary cycles that uproot tyranny, Ann's crimes were committed in the context of one of the world's most stable liberal democratic governments. She was not attacking her country. She and her comrades were not seeking to take over the government. Instead, they aimed to directly interfere with the work of multinational corporations profiting from the war industry, pornographic degradation of women and damage to the environment.

As Ann relates, her political work required moving underground and living a clandestine existence with false identities, weapons for self-defence, and daily risks. She has been both branded as a terrorist and applauded as a life-affirming revolutionary woman. Unlike terrorists, she and the others had a clear intention not to cause harm to any person. Properties, not people, were the target of their attacks, properties that signified violence against women, environmental destruction and the threats of nuclear war. They wanted to stop the Canadian government from employing Litton Systems to manufacture and test cruise missile guidance systems on contract with the U.S. Department of Defense, and to that end they sabotaged the plant. A series of mistakes resulted in injuries to ten people, an accident for which Ann and the others were ill prepared.

Although I did not yet know her name, Ann made a big impression on me on November 22, 1982, when two Red Hot Video stores in Vancouver, British Columbia, were firebombed after closing for the night. The media devoted considerable attention to the events, and I was surprised at the expressions of public support for the Wimmin's Fire Brigade, which took credit for the actions. These stores notoriously specialized in videos showing brutal and obscene violence against women and children. My own first thought was "good riddance," and this was a common attitude from conservative women as well as from feminists.

The firebombing was one of numerous precipitating events resulting in new legislation to limit and regulate commercial pornography in Canada. Public hearings produced dynamic debates between radical feminists, who sought legislative limits and social controls, and socialist feminists, who, together with libertarians, were concerned with freedom of expression protections. The Wimmin's Fire Brigade, composed of Ann and other women, had not waited for the debate: they took direct action. Their position was that "lawful attempts to shut down Red Hot Video have failed because the justice system was created, and is controlled, by rich men to protect their profits and property... As a result, we are left no viable alternative but to change the situation ourselves through illegal means. This is an act of self-defense against hate propaganda!" (Hansen, 2001: 487)

Following their arrest in 1982 for the Litton bombing, the three men and two women involved in that action became known as the Squamish Five, because they were arrested on the Vancouver-to-Squamish highway. While they were still being held in the province awaiting trial, I accompanied a criminology class to the jail, where the students and the prisoners interacted and shared refreshments. Ann was quiet but congenial, and she seemed bemused at the curious sight of wide-eyed university students coming into the jail with cake, lemonade and rock 'n' roll tapes.

The five were tried for the Litton bombing; all were found guilty and sentenced to prison for terms of varying length. A common response to the bombing was "I agree with their reasons but not their methods." Ann and the others took the opportunity of the trial to do political education via the media coverage. These young defendants were intelligent, articulate, passionate in their beliefs and courageous in the face of prison. The impression grew that it was Ann Hansen who was the key strategist for the group. She was singled out by the press as the leader and deemed by the court to be more culpable than the others. She was sentenced to life, but she was released in 1990, after seven years of an advanced education in how the criminal justice system operates.

In 2001, twenty years after the crimes, Ann was recruited by a friend from prison days, Gayle Horii, to represent Strength In Sisterhood (SIS), a national support and advocacy network of former prisoners. In a guest lecture to my criminology class in 2002, an audience of future lawyers and policy-makers found Ann "inspiring" as she recounted what she'd learned through her prison experience and social justice work. The following night she gave a talk to a packed house following a public showing of a film about the Squamish Five, speaking reflectively about the times, then and now. She is unassumingly eloquent, a genuine force for change.

In 2001, Ann published a thorough, engaging and well-received autobiographical account of the making of a revolutionary woman, titled *Direct Action: Memoirs of an Urban Guerrilla* (Hansen, 2001). Her tour to promote her book took her all over Canada, and, just as she had in the courtroom two decades before, she used the opportunity to generate political debate. As a young woman, she had challenged the Canadian government's collusion with the U.S. war industry, corporate environmental degradation and abusive pornography. In her account below of the events that led her to prison, Ann raises basic questions about how best to alter an unjust world. She lets us see important moments in the life journey of a woman who is attuned to the spirit of nature and is committed to social justice, as shown by actions much louder than words.

Ann's Story

What is left of my childhood are a few strong memories, coloured by sights, sounds and smells that have left an indelible mark on my mind. I think these memories provide the emotional and spiritual foundation upon which my political analysis in later life was built. I have come to believe that human reason is a slave to instincts and emotions, regardless of how sophisticated the former may seem.

I remember one evening galloping like a wild horse through my dad's evergreen fields as the sun was setting. I was fuelled and consumed by the smell of the moist spring earth, the feel of the cool evening air in my lungs and on my face, and the sounds of the red-wing blackbirds collecting grass for their nests in the fields. The life forces were pulsing through me in a powerful way. I could have exploded with joy. Finally I stopped galloping and paused to face the sun as it was setting. It doesn't sound like a momentous event in my life, but it is impossible to put into words the powerful feeling that memory has retained all these years.

It's funny, but I have no profound memories from inside our house or of urban settings. Maybe that's because we didn't venture into downtown Toronto very often, and spent our vacations at Georgian Bay on Lake Huron. My mother and father are post–Second World War immigrants descended from a long line of Danish peasants. On both sides of my family, there is an old family farm that had been passed down through the families for generations until shortly after the Second World War. My parents were steeped in pastoral farm memories, and instilled in my four younger siblings and me a deep love of nature.

My memories of real-world events in my childhood, such as school, family outings and my home life, are not as vivid as those of my imaginary world. I was not a voracious reader, but the books I did read provided rich backgrounds for my adventures. Even though I had never met an Eskimo or an Indian or owned a horse, I felt more identified to them through the books of Farley Mowat and Jack London and Anna Sewell's *Black Beauty* than I did to any people in my real world. My memories are dominated by solitary adventures of long dog-sled journeys through arctic storms, evenings collecting wood for fires amongst various Indian tribes, and countless days galloping around on my black stallion through the woods and fields. Amazingly, all these imaginary adventures took place in the abandoned fields around my home in a small suburb north of Toronto. I say abandoned because we grew up surrounded by old farms that had been bought by speculators to sell off for industrial "parkland" as soon as Toronto made its next expansion north. In fact, this process of paving over my beautiful fields and woodlots was the most devastating memory of my childhood—a testament as well to the idyllic nature of my youth.

As a teenager I was always attracted to rebels, outlaws and revolutionaries. *Rebels.* A trip I took with my high-school friend to the University of Waterloo in 1966 was probably the most formative experience of those years. We stayed with her brother in the university residences filled with radical hippies smoking dope, preaching "free love" and talking about "bringing down the system." These exciting, rebellious people were my self-proclaimed role models. At one point there was a gathering in the student union building at which political speeches were made demanding... I don't remember what, but I do remember the passionate voices, the idealistic words, and a motorcycle being driven right through the front doors into the middle of the building. That night we tagged along with my friend's brother to another political meeting in some apartment above a store in downtown Waterloo. Once again the content of the speeches escapes me, but a small bonfire on top of a huge sheet of aluminum foil inside the apartment does not. The flames licking the air dangerously and the bearded faces reflected in the dark left a lasting impression on my adolescent mind. These long-haired men and women in sandals and beads were the closest living thing I had met to the Indian and Eskimo friends I'd hung with in my youth. But unlike my imaginary companions, these *real* people had explanations and solutions for all the industrial destruction I had so painfully witnessed of the once pastoral setting of my childhood home.

Outlaws. I was never one to blindly obey laws and, in fact, had a healthy fascination with those who didn't. I say fascination because it wasn't based on some sophisticated analysis of the criminal justice system; it was simply some instinctive admiration of those who robbed from the rich rather than resigning themselves to eating crumbs. I remember once taking a job with a friend of mine, repossessing a truck that had been stolen by a born-again Christian dope smuggler named Willy from our friend Roger, who also happened to be Willy's ex-partner. We were absolutely poverty-stricken and decided to take the job of repossessing the truck for the generous sum in the late sixties of $500.

We decided to hire another friend, Bob, to be the getaway driver, since my partner Eddie and I had no vehicle. Bob arrived in his Volkswagen carrying an impressive forty-five calibre handgun concealed in a brown paper bag in case we needed enforcement. The sight of the gun sent a shot of adrenalin coursing through my veins, since I had never seen a real gun of any kind before and hadn't known anyone else who owned one, either.

The job would involve driving to a large nudist camp Willy owned and luring him into his house so that my partner could repossess Roger's truck using his spare set of keys. The reason that Roger didn't just take back his truck was because Willy had a reputation as a dangerous man, as well as being a born-again Christian operator of a nudist camp. There was a rumour floating around that a dead body found on the property a few years previous was the work of Willy, but due to lack of evidence the cops couldn't lay charges. Willy also kept a loaded shotgun hanging above his fireplace.

We drove up to Willy's, and I knocked on his front door under the pretext of wanting to buy a membership to his nudist camp. As soon as he opened the door, I stepped boldly in and started talking. Within minutes I had him giving me a guided tour of his house, although he appeared somewhat suspicious of my odd behaviour. Suddenly Willy retreated from the bedroom, back to the front room where a large picture window faced the driveway. There was Eddie, centred in the middle of the window, driving very slowly down the driveway in the stolen pickup truck. Willy grabbed the shotgun from above the fireplace, ran outside and leaped into his bright red sports car. I followed close behind and leaped into the Volkswagen beside Bob, who had pulled his forty-five out of the bag. Down the road we raced, losing ground rapidly to the cloud of dust up ahead until it disappeared over a rise. By the time we headed over the rise, the pickup truck was parked by the side of the road with Willy standing close by, his shotgun pointed at Eddie's head. Bob cocked his forty-five. Suddenly Willy lowered his shotgun, got into his car and drove off in the direction of the nudist camp. As we turned around to watch him disappear over the rise, we were surprised to hear the truck spin its tires and continue at a break-neck speed down the road.

Much later, after successfully rendezvousing at Roger's place, we learned that Eddie had used Willy's keys, which he had left in the truck's ignition. After Willy had pulled the keys out of the ignition at the side of the road, Eddie had just used his spare set to start up the truck again and make his getaway. Sadly, we never did get the $500, so Bob went back to Roger's and hucked a brick through his window.

When I reflect back upon this story, it helps me understand why I identified at a young age with revolutionaries who engaged in militant actions, whether they be urban guerrillas or activists hucking bricks through Nike storefront windows. It's not that I subscribe to the simplistic notion that militant actions are the only legitimate ones. No, I have always been a firm believer that a revolution can only be successful if the people use every diverse tactic available, from legal forms of protest all the way across the spectrum to militant actions of sabotage. However, those who choose to be militants should not only have a revolutionary analysis, but should also be able to thrive on the danger and excitement that are the essence of an illegal lifestyle. When I look back on my early twenties, I can see that not only the political analysis but also the lifestyle of the urban guerrilla appealed to me.

Revolutionaries. I had come of age during the height of the Vietnam War protests and witnessed the defeat of U.S. imperialism by the Viet Cong using the tactics of guerrilla warfare. Despite years of battering by the French imperialists, the strength of guerrilla warfare, combined with the indomitable spirit of the Vietnamese people, was able to achieve victory against the overwhelming might of the American military machine. This lesson did not pass me by.

And even though I was just a child when Fidel Castro and his band of guerrillas rode victorious into Havana, the Cuban Revolution remained fresh on everyone's mind at every anti-war protest of the sixties. But I learned another important lesson during those years. I could not help but notice that the American imperialists did not respect the will of either the Vietnamese or the Cuban people. In fact, they did not respect even the will of their own people. It seemed obvious to me that they would stop at nothing to protect their interests and the ideology of capitalism all over the world. They would shoot down innocent Vietnamese peasants, carpet-bomb Cambodian rice fields and even shoot down white American student protestors in Ohio. So at a young age I came to believe that the ruling classes would never give up their wealth and power through peaceful protest and moral persuasion. These tactics were useful, but alone they appeared utopian and ineffective. The most peaceful response that I witnessed from the ruling class in times of crisis was for them to pack their money bags and flee.

These events set the stage for my intense interest during the late seventies in Germany's Red Army Faction (RAF) and Italy's Red Brigade guerrilla group. I voraciously read everything I could get my hands on about them. I discovered that they were Marxists, a political ideology I had studied in university and found to be the best analysis to describe the sources of the oppression all around me. The marriage of Marxist analysis with guerrilla tactics seemed a winning combination within the context of the times: the Algerian and Cuban revolutions and the Vietnam War, to name but a few.

So I set off in 1979 on a quest to meet and perhaps join the urban guerrilla movement in Europe. Through an odd set of circumstances, I eventually ended up living in a Parisian apartment with a group of RAF supporters. I spent the next three months completely immersed in support work, attending the trial in Germany of an RAF defence lawyer and participating in every demonstration and political event I could. For the first time in my life I felt part of an exciting, dynamic movement of political activists who were determining history, not merely being passive objects in the path of capitalist events.

I made a personal commitment to do whatever it took to stay in this vibrant country, until a young German fugitive from the RAF appeared at our apartment door. I was so enamoured with her every word and movement that she couldn't help but notice, and one day she took it upon herself to give me a word of advice, which I interpreted as a personal prophecy. She explained to me that it was important that young activists build the revolution in their own countries, because we would be most effective where we knew the language and culture and had a personal history. Pausing for effect, she gave me one last piece of advice: "People living in the 'belly of the beast' are in the best position to strike the most fatal blows to American imperialism." I took her words to heart and flew back to Canada with the sense of a noble mission to find other like-minded souls with whom to build an offensive militant force for a future revolutionary movement.

Considering that militant Canadian revolutionaries in 1980 were scarce, I was once again lucky to meet a like-minded soul that summer while spray-painting Prison Justice Day slogans in Toronto. This young man and I experienced an instant affinity. By the fall of that same year, I had relocated to his communal house in Vancouver, where we began to lay the foundations for a future guerrilla group in Canada. Our plans were much bigger than reality would allow. After a solid year of talking, organizing and carrying out small illegal actions, we realized that our plans would have to be scaled down or abandoned. In our minds, the latter was not an option.

Scaling down meant coming to terms with the fact that there were only three of us who would be willing to live a totally illegal lifestyle isolated from friends and family. We were willing to make this extreme sacrifice in the hopes that our actions and political communiqués would spark other militant actions, no matter how small. The way we saw it, the political movement could continue supporting guerrilla movements in Third World countries, wearing Che Guevara T-shirts, and watching radical films, but as long as they didn't engage in strong resistance tactics, the state could accommodate their culture of revolution indefinitely. We decided to call ourselves Direct Action.

On May 30, 1982, we drove off early in the morning to catch a ferry to Vancouver Island, where the Dunsmuir substation was nearing the final stages of completion. In the back of our pickup truck were 350 pounds of commercial dynamite, as well as blasting caps and detonating cord, stolen from an isolated dynamite magazine along the Squamish highway. Our mission was to cause as much damage to the transformers and oil-pumping station at the Dunsmuir substation as possible.

We had chosen this as a target because it was part of the nearly completed $1 billion Cheekeye-Dunsmuir transmission line, designed to increase the flow of electricity from the British Columbia mainland to Vancouver Island in order to facilitate the expansion of the pulp and paper industry. The main beneficiary of this hydro mega-project would be the MacMillan Bloedel pulp and paper conglomerate, but there were also victims, the main ones being the ravaged forests of the Island and the communities through which the clear-cut right-of-ways would pass. To make matters worse, the financing of the line was not coming from those who would benefit, the private pulp and paper industry, but rather would fall on taxpayers' shoulders through loans from public pension funds acquired at below market rates.

We also chose to sabotage this substation because there had been a protracted popular struggle to prevent the construction of the line or, at the very least, force the government to justify the need for the line through public hearings. The Cheekeye-Dunsmuir Alliance, spearheading this struggle, had employed every legal tactic imaginable, but to no avail. Finally they had resorted to civil disobedience, pulling up surveyors' stakes along the right-of-way and using their bodies to block bulldozers. But as soon as they were arrested, the surveyors and bulldozers continued razing their path of destruction across the Georgia Strait and along the Sunshine Coast. We believed that using sabotage to damage the substation's expensive transformers and oil-pumping station would demonstrate to people that direct action could be effective if the legal struggle failed. We also wanted to demonstrate that laws should be disobeyed if they are not used to defend justice but instead to protect the interests of the rich and powerful. Unlike the European guerrilla groups who had inspired us, we had decided to limit our actions to property destruction, because we wanted to hit the capitalists in the area that would hurt them the most, financially. In our analysis, a capitalist economy is not affected by the destruction of life whether it be human or not, as evidenced by its own anti-life corporate policies.

As the crimson sun began its final descent toward the horizon, we cut a hole in the mesh fencing surrounding the substation. The line had not been electrified, so we didn't have to worry about our action causing residential blackouts. As the final rays of light turned into darkness, I could see my partner's silhouette moving about connecting the detonating wire-like umbilical cord between the behemoth-like transformers. Finally, in the near darkness, I could barely see him pause as he turned on the disarmingly innocent-looking red switch of the electronic timing device, which would set off the blasting caps at the end of each "umbilical cord," igniting enough dynamite to cause a house five kilometres away to shake as though it had been hit by an earthquake.

In terms of sabotage, the Cheekeye-Dunsmuir action was a success. All four transformers and the oil-pumping station had been irreparably damaged, to the tune of $5 million, but even this success was tempered by the fact that the line eventually was completed, only two months behind schedule. Politically, the action was less successful. Few people outside of British Columbia understood why we had carried out the action, and, even in B.C., much of the Left was critical.

By the fall of 1982, Direct Action had expanded from a three-member guerrilla group to five, and we were planning on sabotaging the Litton Systems plant in Toronto, which manufactured the guidance system for the cruise missile. The reasons for targeting the Litton plant were much easier to understand. Most people were aware of the cataclysmic effects of nuclear war. Opinion polls of the day indicated that well over 50 per cent of Canadians were opposed to manufacturing or testing nuclear weapons for the American military. We hoped that this action would be more successful politically.

Similar to the Cheekeye-Dunsmuir transmission line, there had been a protracted popular struggle in Ontario to stop the manufacture of the guidance system, and there was a growing movement against testing the cruise in Alberta. The similarities did not end there. The government chose to ignore the opinions of the majority of the people, and not only signed agreements to test the cruise on Canadian soil but even gave Litton $48 million in grants and interest-free loans through the government's corporate welfare program, known by the ironic acronym DIP (Defence Industries Production Department).

When we flicked on the switch to the timing device of a 550-pound dynamite bomb packed inside a van parked against the Litton plant, we reasoned that the nuclear disarmament movement could continue organizing indefinitely while the military marched on: business as usual. [Prime Minister Pierre] Trudeau had made his case eloquently, if deceitfully, in various venues that Canada would sign on to test nuclear weaponry for the United States because it was part of our obligation as NATO allies. His arguments were deceitful because he was aware that the cruise was not a NATO weapon, but rather an American defence weapon. Meanwhile, Litton Systems Canada was busily preparing a bid for a new contract to build a more advanced version of the cruise missile guidance system.

This time our zeal to execute the bombing overwhelmed our sense of caution. After surveying the Litton plant at night, we had come to the realization that there was a small night shift working in the building we wanted to sabotage. Rather than target another site, we decided to set up a series of safeguards to ensure that the building would be cleared before the bomb went off. The most notable aspect of this action was that nothing happened as predicted. First, the security guards who worked in a glass-walled tower overlooking the Litton compound did not see us drive the van up onto the flood-lit lawn against the building. Second, our phone call to the building, warning of the bombing and the need to clear the plant, was ignored. And thirdly, the bomb exploded fifteen minutes earlier than expected, just as the bomb squad arrived and started talking together, using high-powered walkie-talkies that we later found out set off the electronic timing device prematurely.

The unthinkable happened. Ten people were injured, some seriously. We had spent so much time meticulously going over our security precautions to ensure that no one got hurt that we really did not consider the possibility anyone would. We struggled between thoughts of suicide and thoughts of exile. Even though we knew in the back of our minds that injuries were inevitable in any serious resistance struggle, we also knew that our careless choice of target and our decision to leave the responsibility for civilian safety in the hands of the authorities were grave mistakes. We delayed sending out our communiqué and added an apology and explanation as to the reasons for the injuries.

There was a tangible lack of open support for the Litton bombing. However, the fact that 15,000 people showed up in Ottawa for a Refuse the Cruise rally two weeks later, a record number for the times, suggests that the bombing did not frighten people away from openly agitating against the cruise missile, but rather drew the public's attention to the issue. This theory was bolstered by the record number of demonstrators who also showed up to participate in a demonstration and acts of civil disobedience at the Litton plant less than a month after the bombing, despite warnings of a massive police presence.

The biggest political booster for the Litton bombing came from a most unlikely source, Ronald Keating, the president of Litton Canada. In an interview published in the *Globe and Mail* newspaper, he complained that the Americans had not awarded Litton Canada a new contract to manufacture the advanced version of the guidance system because they did not like the bad publicity generated by the protestors and the bombing.

Although the Litton bombing was regrettable in that people were injured, it did not deter us from proceeding with our militant campaign. We reasoned that destruction and death, inherent not only in nuclear war but also in capitalist industrialism, far out-weighed any injuries caused by popular resistance movements. We did not view ourselves in isolation, but rather saw ourselves within the context of a larger global resistance movement, where militants should learn from their mistakes rather than use them as an excuse to remain passive in the face of planetary destruction.

When we got back to Vancouver after the Litton bombing, we were contacted by some women involved in a growing campaign to shut down a franchise of violent pornography video stores known as Red Hot Video (RHV). Once again, they had exhausted every legal channel conceivable—from letter-writing campaigns to public appeals urging B.C.'s Attorney General to use hate crime laws to shut down the stores. The women who approached us were disillusioned and wanted action. If the government was not going to use the law to shut down Red Hot Video, they argued, we had no choice but to shut the stores down ourselves. I and another woman from our guer-rilla group joined up with this group of normally law-abiding women to organize some kind of direct action to close down Red Hot Video. We decided upon firebombing three stores simultaneously in the early hours of the morning when no one would be inside, and then issuing a joint communiqué. The three separate groups of women would decide autonomously the logistics of each firebombing.

Not surprisingly, the Wimmin's Fire Brigade (WFB), as we called ourselves, was quite popular. Unlike the high-tech bombings of Direct Action, people could relate to the firebombings of the Red Hot Video stores. They were the kind of action that anyone could do without becoming a fugitive, stealing explosives, designing timing devices or carrying out robberies. After the smoke cleared, the Wimmin's Fire Brigade had burned down one RHV in a strip mall, plus a couple of adjacent stores, and partially burned down a second; a third store was left unscathed when some cops drove by just as the women were about to throw their Molotov cocktails.

Although the WFB had not intended to burn down the stores adjacent to the RHV in the strip mall, we felt that there would inevitably be some collateral damage in the struggle against violent pornography. It was utopian to believe that any resistance movement would have no casualties.

The political success of the WFB could be measured both in terms of its ability to close down RHV and in its popular appeal. After the firebombings, radio phone-in shows and letters to the editor in newspapers expressed the laudatory view that the WFB had been more successful in closing down RHV than the B.C. Attorney General had. Finally, on the day of our arrests [later, on the Squamish highway], the RCMP raided the Victoria RHV store and laid obscenity charges. The timing of this raid gave the impression that the cops felt compelled to act in order to redeem their reputation. Within a year of the firebombings, every RHV except one had closed down, moved out of B.C., changed its name, been crippled by legal fees or been burned down. Even at our trial [as the Squamish Five] in the spring of 1983, dozens of women demonstrated outside the courthouse wearing red fire hats and claiming to be members of the WFB.

By early January 1983, we were deeply engrossed in the final stages of planning for a Brink's truck robbery. Little did we know that our shortage of money would intersect with the hourglass of time running out on the Squamish highway, high above an ocean precipice. Unknown to us, we had been under physical surveillance since mid-November and our house had been wiretapped since just before Christmas. On January 20, 1983, as we sat at a roadblock waiting for a highway road crew to move their equipment, we witnessed the crew transform instantly into a heavily armed SWAT team. As we were thrown to the ground with handguns to our heads, more armed men in camouflage came pouring out from behind rocks and bushes. And so ended the militant stage of our campaign.

For the next year and a half, we were imprisoned in the sprawling provincial prison complex known as Oakalla. During that time, my political identity remained the driving force behind all my decisions and actions. I wore a necklace to court that had a tiny assault rifle inserted in the crosspiece in the women's symbol. We flaunted our disrespect for the criminal justice system by refusing to stand up every time the judge entered or exited the courtroom. When the judge declared that I was a threat to Canadian society, I added a dramatic exclamation mark to my life sentence by hurling a tomato at him.

I remember watching a feature film in Vancouver, about a year before our arrests, called *P4W*. P4W is an acronym for the Prison for Women in Kingston, Ontario. Even at that time, I assumed this would be the place I'd end up in if I wasn't already dead. I watched the film with fascination and concluded that P4W seemed an interesting place. The prisoners seemed as intelligent and dynamic as any women I had ever met.

When I walked onto B range in P4W for the first time, it was with a mixture of fear and excitement. All newcomers were placed on B range, a row of open-barred cells in an archaic setting reminiscent of the old Hollywood prison movies. B range was known as the fish tank, because the prisoners on A range could observe the newcomers through a thick plexiglass wall separating the common rooms. Prisoners develop the uncanny ability to see everything around them without moving their heads. Everyone has to learn to live by their wits alone, with no one ultimately but themselves to count on. And so it was of utmost importance to see everything without appearing to be watching.

Whenever I walked into the common rooms of B range, I would carefully observe, from the corner of my eye, beautiful women in fashionable clothes with fancy hairdos and impeccable makeup draped over other women, affectionately holding hands and occasionally kissing as they watched TV. It was like watching a gigantic silent movie on an IMAX screen, because the indoor/outdoor carpeting of the common rooms muffled all the sounds. Passing through the doors of the common rooms onto the old two-storey ranges was like breaking through a weird sound barrier, as suddenly you entered a world where women strutted their stuff rhythmically to the pounding beat of ghetto blasters punctuated by laughter and shouts echoing off the old cement walls. Some women sauntered down the ranges with an unmistakable sexual machismo. Others, who were more timid, seemed to scurry like mice trying desperately to make it from A to B without being seen or heard. The one thing everyone had in common was a lack of destination. "All dressed up with no place to go" had a whole new meaning.

It didn't take very long to realize that the P4W filmmakers had not had access to the bowels of the beast. Even though the film had documented the prisoners going about their mundane daily activities, it had only hinted at a darker side. In the film, a vivacious young woman speaks with her hands while the camera pans down the sides of her companion, focusing briefly on her thin white arms criss-crossed with welts from old scar tissue. Sometimes the young woman's eyes would fill with tears and she would turn her head away from the camera, unable to express with either her hands or her voice the depth of suffering going on inside and outside her head.

By the time I had spent two weeks in P4W, I realized that the laughter, the comradeship between the women, and the fancy clothes and decorated cells were desperate attempts to survive in a world where insanity is only a word and a wall away. It took me just as long to realize that we had no rights. The guards and administration were all-powerful. Getting the outside world's attention demanded near-death experiences, such as thirty-day hunger strikes or the accidental release in 1995 of real film footage of women prisoners in segregation having their clothes ripped or cut off with scissors by the male riot squad.

A world away... One particularly warm spring afternoon, I went out in the yard with a couple of Native women. I only mention their race because I think it is important here. We were acting crazy and laughing just a little too loud, like children who have been cooped up too long. When we came in, the guards ordered us to see the nurse. She said the guards in the yard had reported that we were behaving as though we were on drugs or drunk. We were ordered to provide urine samples. The Native women complied but I refused, because I knew my lawyer would be eager to challenge this new practice. Despite providing urine samples, the Native women were put in segregation for "being under the influence," even though their test results would take days to determine.

One woman became very, very angry, so angry that her pupils became dilated, which the nurse interpreted as confirmation of her diagnosis. Wrongly accused, the woman began to vent her anger, swearing at the guards who had put her in segregation. Each time she swore or disobeyed any "direct order," another charge sheet would be passed to her through the bars, driving her closer and closer to insanity. By the fall of that year, she was still in segregation. Twenty years later, she has only been out on a few passes, although remarkably she has managed to maintain her sanity. As I sit and write these words, there are four women I knew from that time period who are still in maximum security prisons. Three are Native.

It was also common practice for guards to pass on reports about prisoners they considered "management problems" to the prison psychiatrist, who inevitably sedated the women with psychiatric medications such as lithium or Elavil. Caseloads for the prison psychiatrist were so heavy that drug therapy was used to treat everything from anger to depression. It was always easy to spot the women on psychiatric drugs, because their eyes, the windows to the soul, were vacant, and they moved about as though in slow motion. These women were forced to take their medication, often sinking deeper into depression, trading off their feelings for being unknowingly more manageable to the guards.

A wall away... I will never forget Rocky, a gentle yet disturbed childlike woman trapped inside a huge, muscular body. Her awesome strength and repressed anger, in combination with her legendary personal history, instilled fear in the guards. The story surrounding Rocky's crime was that she fell in love with a guard on the street and moved in with her. One day she came home unexpectedly to find her lover in bed with another woman and killed her.

One day they took Rocky to segregation for some petty charge. A small ventilation grill in each of our cells opened up into a plumbing/electrical corridor separating the segregation unit from the range, thereby allowing sounds from segregation to travel freely into our cells. One night we woke up to the unmistakable sounds of Rocky screaming, "I am not an animal!" over and over again. This was followed by crashing noises, which we later learned were the sounds of Rocky tearing her steel cot out of the cement wall to which it was bolted and using it to smash up her cell. Then came the sounds of heavy boots jogging up stairs, jostling, water gushing, and finally a long series of wails, I imagine similar to those one would hear near a slaughterhouse. We knew what was going on. The goon squad had been called in to subdue her. They had used a high-powered water hose to knock her down, then had rushed in and handcuffed her to the cell bars where she would stay until they were convinced she had calmed down.

Months and months passed while Rocky remained in isolation. What had started out as a relatively minor charge had quickly escalated into a series of charges. This phenomenon was not uncommon. Once prisoners were in segregation, some guards would aggravate them by refusing to bring toilet paper or smokes. These seemingly small things would assume greater importance within the deprived world of isolation. Sometimes the women would have emotional or mental problems that made it very difficult for them to control their anger at the best of times and almost impossible in isolation. Many nights the sounds of howling and screaming coming through the vents from segregation would wake us up. We would lie in the dark silence listening to these sounds, which articulated all too clearly the feelings we shared in our souls.

After what seemed like an eternity, Rocky appeared on the range again one day. I stopped to talk to her at the barrier as we waited for lunch and didn't notice anything different about her until she started to talk. She strained and searched for simple words like "lunch" and "supper." At first I thought she might be on some kind of heavy sedative, but her eyes seemed clear and her movement normal. Then I learned she had "volunteered" for routine shock treatments. How "voluntary" could this decision be, when presented as the only way out of what appeared to be indefinite imprisonment in isolation? She said she liked the way it blotted out a lot of bad memories. She felt it was a small price to pay for peace of mind. I felt that having her brain fried on a monthly basis was too costly a price even for peace of mind, but when what she really got was a vacant mind, the transaction was nothing less than criminal.

After seven years in the prison system, I was released to the halfway house in Kingston. In my own estimation, I had survived the prison system without too much damage. Sometimes damage is palpable. A woman can wear it on her skin and in her eyes so that there's no mistaking the toll that prison has taken. Others appear the same, but the damage is like a tree rot that isn't visible until the tree falls down suddenly one day in a storm. For me, it was daily experiences that changed me slowly, imperceptibly, like the slow drip of water over the years cutting a deep chasm in a granite rock face.

There were signs that I had changed. I watched TV every night to escape reality and especially liked the mindless comedies that demanded nothing of me but a laugh. I also took the time to dress more fashionably and even streaked my hair and put on makeup on Saturday nights. My new dress code reflected my new identity of ex-prisoner as opposed to my former identity of radical feminist.

I often liken the bonds that prisoners share to those experienced by war vets. These bonds are created by intense, traumatic experiences endured for many years that no one else can understand. In surviving these experiences, prisoners over the ages have evolved a complicated but separate subculture that only those who have lived it can understand. After I got out, I found relating to the radical and feminist communities difficult, because people seemed so academic and theoretical. So much of what they said came from their head and not from their lived experience.

However, there was collateral damage from living amongst my prison friends. I can't blame it on anyone, because I think the slow drip of prison time on my soul had gnawed a hole in it that was just waiting to be filled. It didn't take long to find the perfect antidote to that empty feeling. It happened one evening in the halfway house when a friend asked me if I wanted to try some morphine. I had always had a bit of a fascination with opiates. Even as a teenager, descriptions of heroin sounded more appealing to me than not. In prison I had injected heroin once and had an immediate attraction to the high. So it came as no surprise to me that the instant I injected the morphine, I felt a sense of calm euphoria that stayed with me for hours.

By nature I am a tense, driven personality who finds relaxation and peace of mind difficult to achieve. The opiate family instantly gave me that sense of calm energy that I found so elusive naturally. Probably the fact that I was striving to live a so-called normal life with a job, an apartment and the pursuit of material goals didn't help matters. Even as a young adolescent, I had always questioned the values of our capitalist society and been attracted to those who rebelled and lived alternatively. It was not in my nature to conform and embrace the values of consumerism. In retrospect I can see the signs of my inner sickness reflected in the decisions I made at the halfway house. I chose to spend the money I had saved to buy a huge, gas-guzzling z28 muscle car.

I got a regular job in a sweatshop that mass-produced kitchen cabinets. I often described my days in that shop as worse than those in prison. The owner would often degrade people by calling them "morons" and throw tools around in a fit of rage if workers made mistakes. We had choices: we could either put up with the abuse or look around for another job. For someone fresh out of prison on parole, getting another job was not easy.

By that time I had moved out of the halfway house into a small apartment. At first I used to get up in the middle of the night and just sit in that empty apartment, appreciating my freedom and the simple things like being able to go outdoors and look at the stars. But that freedom came at a price. I couldn't very easily quit my job or I would not be able to pay for the apartment.

My early experiments with morphine in the halfway house had now become a weekend habit, which I would look forward to with much anticipation. It was a wonderful way to cap a week of degradation and meaningless labour. After about a year of using morphine every weekend, I found myself anticipating Friday night with an urgent craving that was physical in nature. It wasn't just excitement anymore, it was a drive. My stomach would churn, my palms would sweat and my heart would beat crazily as I drove home from work. If there was no morphine around on Friday night, I would feel desperate and depressed. Many a night I found myself sitting with my friend outside a dealer's home waiting for hours for him to show up. I would be unable to do anything else until I had scored.

After about a year working in the cabinetry sweatshop, I decided to start up my own custom cabinetry business with a talented young man I had met at the shop. Pretty soon we were making good money—enough to buy a new car, a van, machinery and lots of heroin. Five years into our business, we were scoring on our way to work in the morning, fixing in the washroom at work, scoring again at lunch and then one last time in the evening on the way home. As any drug addict knows, we were rarely doing drugs anymore to get high but needed the heroin to function; hence the expression "using to straighten out."

In retrospect, I think my heroin use escalated from an experiment to a habit because I had lost my identity and was living a lie. No one in the business community knew that I had been politically active or done time. My family and parole officer interpreted all the trappings of my bourgeois lifestyle as signs of success. But for me it had no meaning. The heroin initially gave me the sense of euphoria and excitement that I used to get from pursuing political ideals and goals. But as time passed, it became a habit, and so much more. It had become a physical addiction. The world looked black and white to me. I would wake up every morning wishing I was dead, and I toyed with the idea of driving into the cement overpasses all the way to work. When we were sick and waiting for the dealer to call, I used to say that I would be disappointed if God called instead.

I eventually became so plagued with thoughts of suicide that I began to try everything to get over my addiction. I used to go home to my mother's, where I knew I couldn't score for the weekend, but after twenty-four hours I would always end up driving back to Kingston at five in the morning. Then I tried going to a couple of thirty-day treatment centres. The second one really helped, by giving me a kick-start at detoxifying and providing me with the mental tools to cope with my cravings, but soon I was using again.

The final solution for me was a combination of going on the methadone program and closing down our business. Methadone is a synthetic derivative of heroin that is distributed legally through methadone clinics in ever-diminishing doses, until the addict is finally off the stuff entirely. Some addicts never go off methadone, because their addiction is perhaps too severe to overcome. We closed down our business because we found it almost impossible to break the habit of coping with the pressures of running a small business through using heroin.

After we closed down our business, I began writing about my experiences as an urban guerrilla. Through writing, my political identity began to re-emerge, and I found myself beginning to crave activism again. We also had bought a small farm and a few horses. Slowly I felt myself becoming stronger. Each morning I went out to feed the horses, never tiring of the smell of the air, the sounds of the birds and the miracle that is nature. Living surrounded by the natural world was the food I needed to fuel my drive to work with others to change this society, from one that is based on the life-destroying values of greed and power to one that values nature and the equality of all life. I feel, even at this relatively young age of fifty, that my life has come full circle. I am back to living with nature and dedicating my life to preserving what is left on this miraculous planet.

Reflections

A majority of people in liberal democracies claim to want to live in a safe and healthy environment, with equality and justice for all. However, at the high echelons of an advanced capitalist system, it is economic interests that prevail, at whatever cost in human life and to the natural environment. Ann's story is a call not to arms but to the imagination. To paraphrase poet Audre Lorde, how do we dismantle the master's house without using the master's own tools? How do we directly oppose corporations and complicit governments that cause massive harm and death without using some defensive measure that may in turn cause harm?

Without defensiveness, Ann suggests that collateral damage is to be expected in revolutionary actions. Direct Action was distinctly not terrorist in its intentions. The group's members did not intend to incite fear in the public or to cause physical harm to anyone. They were literally attempting to "dismantle the master's house" by sabotaging his tools: woman-bashing porn shops, environmentally destructive technologies and instruments for the purpose of mass destruction.

I appreciate that Ann observes a person must have a certain temperament to be a guerrilla fighter, and that she recognizes there are other ways to be useful to social movements. Ideology separates terrorists from liberators in the public mind, according to whether or not one accepts the official version of who is causing harm. To my mind, Ann Hansen exemplifies the spirit of a true liberator. The level of her commitment invites the question of what the rest of us do to achieve justice for all and to protect the planet.

Reference

Hansen, Ann (2001). *Direct Action: Memoirs of an Urban Guerilla*. Toronto: Between the Lines.

11

CHRISTINE

ACTIVIST AGAINST U.S. IMPERIALISM

CHRISTINE LAMONT SPENT almost ten years in prison in Brazil for participating in a kidnapping intended to raise funds for the independence movement in El Salvador. I was keenly struck by her story when it first began appearing in the Canadian media in 1990, because I was reasonably well informed about the U.S. assaults on the lives of people in El Salvador and Nicaragua. My brother-in-law Carroll (AKA Carlos) Ishee, who grew up in a civil rights family in Mississippi and was an activist against the Vietnam War, died in the early 1980s in El Salvador. Like Christine and her partner, Dave Spencer, he was assisting the rebels in their resistance to U.S. intervention. He and his companeros were shot at and killed by U.S.-trained soldiers from a low-flying U.S. Huey helicopter. His wife, my sister LaVaun, helped coordinate resistance support from the United States with CISPES (Committee in Support of the People of El Salvador). After the accord, she and her daughter and members of Carroll's family went to El Salvador to reconfirm their commitment to that country's freedom. Subsequently, LaVaun returned on a medical mission with members of Carroll's family. Along with millions of other internationalists in North America and globally, we all marched to protest U.S. imperialism in the region. Reading about

Christine was inspiring to me not because she'd been implicated in a kidnapping but because it was clear that she was fully committed to justice, at whatever risk to herself.

Christine is a tall, dark-haired woman with fine features, a fair complexion and unassuming ways. Nothing in her background could have pointed to such a dramatic outcome for her life. She was born in April 1959 in Boston, the second of four children. Her parents are Canadians of English, Irish and Scottish heritage, her father a surgeon and her mother a piano teacher. When Christine was three years old, the family moved to Fort St. John in northern British Columbia and then to the B.C. Lower Mainland, near Vancouver. There, Christine enjoyed what she calls a "small-town middle-class life." She took music and ballet lessons, played sports and received parental encouragement for her activities. At a young age she developed a social conscience, and she and her friends organized a children's club to raise money for the poor. She was also, at an early age, committed to the protection of the environment.

In 1977, having completed high school, Christine spent a year in Edmonton with her older sister. The following year she returned to B.C. and studied arts for a year at the University of British Columbia; she left undecided as to professional goals and unhappy with the conservative nature of the university and her student cohort. Thus began a series of jobs over the course of five years, including one as an employee of a wholesaler of Asian imports. Christine travelled several times to Thailand, and in these travels she observed inequality on a global scale, "not as a function of place and culture, but as a function of politics and economics."

In 1984, at age twenty-five, Christine returned to university and majored in political science and Latin American studies. She became a serious student of the "mechanics and results of imperialism," and she came to feel obligated, given her theoretical knowledge, to become an activist and learn on the ground. In time she became a regular participant in the solidarity movement, helping to produce a weekly program on community radio. She was involved in a sister relationship between Canadian student unions and AGEUS, the main university student union in El Salvador. She co-organized a delegation of Canadian students who travelled to El Salvador for international meetings. Her political work came to dominate her time until, in 1988, she left the university before completion. She and her partner Dave continued their activist activities and also travelled to Nicaragua. They moved there the following year.

In Nicaragua, Christine and Dave worked with a collective producing internationally distributed radio programming in support of the Farabundo Marti Front for National Liberation (FMLN). When the FMLN requested that they participate in a kidnapping operation in Sao Paulo, Brazil, they agreed. Their task involved setting up a "safe house" in which the victim would be held during the ransom negotiations. The group included two Argentines, five Chileans (including one woman), one Brazilian and two Canadians (including Christine, the second woman). When the police arrived several days after the kidnapping, five of the ten people who were arrested were at the house with the victim, who was released unharmed.

In 1990, all ten defendants were convicted, and their prison sentences ranged from eight to twelve years. Later the prosecution appealed the sentences, and all were raised to twenty-eight years, more than double the average penalty for first-degree murder. Protests ensued, with the Canadian government seeking a solution and many private citizens writing to the Brazilian authorities requesting Dave and Christine's return to Canada. During this period I had occasion to meet Christine's parents, when the three of us arrived at the same time for a visit with Claire Culhane, the legendary Canadian prison abolitionist, in her hospital room following a heart attack. The Lamonts struck me as dignified, kind and intelligent people who were very grateful for the considerable support for their daughter's return to Canada.

In 1998, having served eight years, the group engaged in a hunger strike to protest being denied parole on the basis of nationality. Their objective was to be expelled from Brazil, according to judicial precedent. Instead they were transferred to another prison, with a promise of day parole. When this promise had not been met after six months, they resumed the hunger strike, and this was eventually successful. All were returned to their home countries and the Brazilian to his home state. Christine and Dave were transferred to Canada in November 1998, under the terms of the Transfer of Offenders Treaty, a Canadian creation. The treaty, like those Canada has in place with numerous other countries, allows prisoners to serve out the sentences they receive abroad in their home countries. In Canada, Christine and Dave were imprisoned in British Columbia. Three months later, one day following Dave's release from the men's prison on the word of the National Parole Board, Christine was released from the provincial women's prison on full parole on the word of the provincial board.

In this chapter Christine explains her involvement as a revolutionary ally of a beleaguered people seeking to reclaim their land, defend their lives and rebuild their country with socialist principles and respect for human rights. Her perspectives give context and substance to the events of 1989, which were reported in the media in often sensationalistic and superficial ways. She reveals herself not as an adventurist jumping onto a radical bandwagon but as a serious-minded woman committed to challenging serious social imbalances.

Christine Lamont's account follows just as she wrote it for this collection. She tells the story of what she experienced, explores the meaning of and reasons for her political convictions and reveals her uncommon willingness to act on these convictions. We learn who she is and what she lived through. Her experience invites strategic dialogue about how best to be politically effective in advancing human freedom, equality and justice in exceptionally reactionary times.

Christine's Story

My journey into and through the prison system for women began on Sunday, December 17, 1989, in the metropolis of Sao Paulo in Brazil's southeastern region. I was one of ten people under arrest, each of us for our part in the kidnapping of Abilio Diniz, a wealthy Brazilian supermarket magnate.

The surrender of the part of the group I belonged to was the end result of a thirty-six-hour standoff with police. This had begun on Saturday at about five in the morning, when a handful of police brought Humberto, the leader of the operation, to the house where Dave and I and three others lived. From the street, Humberto began shouting for his brother, Horacio, inside. Horacio recognized his voice in an instant and, grabbing several firearms as he sprang out of bed, was downstairs and at the door within seconds. Through an extraordinarily audacious manoeuvre, Horacio was able to help Humberto get away from the police and into the house, and to slam the door behind him. Although Humberto was still in handcuffs, the two immediately descended to the underground room that had been constructed to conceal Abilio Diniz and brought Diniz up to the second floor.

The rest of us were by then wide awake and had scrambled into clothes. We armed ourselves from the cache while we threw mattresses, furniture and boards up against the windows. Within a few hours, 400 police agents of every title and description had surrounded us. They were in the neighbouring houses, on all of the nearby rooftops and perched in the trees across the street. They cut the electric power to the house. Negotiations with the police began immediately and were carried out through the second-floor bathroom window facing onto the street.

All the while, Humberto recounted for us in bits and pieces what had led up to this. Since the day before, one or two at a time, he and four other members of the group had been taken prisoner and were being brutally tortured by the police. [International human rights monitors at that time considered the extreme and frequent tortures and brutal killings inflicted by police on prisoners in Brazil to be the worst of any criminal justice system in the world. *KF*] Humberto, the only one of the five to know our location, had withstood the beating and electric shock administered to him, but when, with a view toward extracting information from him, the police escalated their torture of Maria Emilia to include a near-drowning technique simultaneous with the electric shock, Humberto had decided he had no choice but to try to negotiate a solution from the house where the hostage was. During the first day, there was a brief exchange of fire, in which a bullet nicked the top of Humberto's head. There was another exchange during the pitch-black night, as the police tried to storm the house from the roof. At other times, we could hear police sawing on the metal grates over the windows downstairs, trying to gain entry through the main floor. Despite these provocations, the negotiations continued every few hours.

Dom Paulo Evaristo Arns, the highly respected cardinal of Sao Paulo and a renowned human rights advocate, assumed the role of principal mediator. On the second day, the police brought the four they had in custody to the street below to assure us they were not still being tortured. That being the day of the first presidential election in which the public would participate since the Brazilian military dictatorship fell, the police had dressed our companeros in campaign T-shirts of the leftist Workers' Party (PT) candidate, Luis Inacio "Lula" da Silva. This was but one of several ways in which the police used the massive media coverage of the negotiations to skew the election in favour of the right-wing candidate, Fernando Collor de Mello. Although we will never know exactly the extent to which this attempt to falsely link the kidnapping to the PT in the public's mind was actually successful, the fact is that Lula lost the 1989 election by a small margin. Naturally, this political disaster ensured we would receive no support from the PT for many years to come.

Thanks largely to the efforts of Dom Paulo, an agreement was reached in the late afternoon of the second day. In return for the release of Abilio Diniz and our surrender, the physical integrity of all of the prisoners was guaranteed, and we were promised a fair trial. All in all, it was the best we could hope for. As we well understood, we were lucky to be coming through the ordeal with our lives.

At the conclusion of the negotiations, we exited the house one at a time. We were frisked and put on a bus, where we were greeted by a close personal friend and employee of Abilio Diniz and joined by various consular officials and the cardinal, each of whom had been waiting out the negotiations. When all of us were secure on the bus, Abilio Diniz walked out of the house on his own, shaken and drained but physically unharmed.

Upon our arrival at the police station, the ten of us were brought together. Due to the compartmentalized nature of the work, some of us met others in the group that day for the first time. There were two Argentines, five Chileans, a Brazilian, and my partner and me, Canadians. Most had been imprisoned at other points in their lives for resisting the dictatorships in their own countries and were now in exile from Argentina and Chile. Ideologically, we were internationalists, activists and militants of the revolutionary Left. We had carried out the kidnapping in an effort to raise funds for the Farabundo Marti Front for National Liberation in El Salvador.

BACKGROUND

There was little to explain such an odd mix of nationalities and personal characteristics in our group, save the purpose for our association. By design, there was not a Salvadoran among us, and while the police had learned of the operation's connection to the Chilean Movement of the Revolutionary Left (MIR) during the torture, they had not discovered that MIR was acting in solidarity with the FMLN.

We unanimously opposed revealing the Salvadoran connection for fear of jeopardizing the delicate situation in El Salvador at that moment. The FMLN was engaged in what it hoped would be the final offensive, the objective of which was to depose the U.S.-backed regime and to set up an interim government with the goal of returning political power to the people of El Salvador. We would not have been where we were if we, too, had not believed in the possibility of the campaign's success and had a partisan interest in the outcome of the war.

The FMLN held the moral high ground in the civil war. The armed struggle itself had begun many years earlier, after the military government had shut down the civilian mass movement's attempts to effect change through exclusively peaceful means. By the late 1970s, soldiers had begun to open fire on demonstrations in the streets of the capital, San Salvador, where protests involving more than a million people were organized to demand basic economic rights and social justice. Confronted with this widespread, pacific pressure for change, the U.S.-backed dictatorship had unleashed a wave of repression virtually unprecedented in the western hemisphere.

However, popular support for the FMLN was not merely a reaction to the dictatorship's violence but, rather, the result of years of hard work and extraordinary commitment to inclusive and ethical political principles. It had, for its part, treated captive enemy soldiers with respect and as equals, acting according to international conventions governing the rules of war. In many ways, the FMLN's conduct was remarkable, since these policies were practised in the face of escalating state-sponsored violence including the deliberate bombing of the rural civilian population, continued assassinations of leaders and members of the urban-based civilian mass movement, and the torture and murder of captured FMLN combatants by government troops.

Even more importantly, the FMLN had set up locally run community governments in the zones of the country it controlled, which, by 1989, made up about one-third of the national territory. There, the FMLN had thoroughly demonstrated its integrity and responsiveness to the needs and will of the rural sector. It had also maintained very close links to the many organizations that comprised the mass movement and had incorporated the interests of workers, women, teachers, students, human rights groups and others into its political platform. The FMLN itself comprised five political organizations encompassing a range of leftist ideologies. Thus the political alternative the FMLN put forward represented the aspirations of those whose interests were embodied in a truly broad-based consensus.

The FMLN's proposed alternative to then current political-economic arrangements was not, on the face of it, particularly radical. They proposed a mixed economy that would allow El Salvador to continue in the international capitalist economy and small-business owners to continue with their pursuits. Only key sectors of the economy would be nationalized. However, control of its own basic resources would allow El Salvador to develop infrastructure and social policy prioritizing a fundamentally different set of interests. The public interest would be redefined, and the new government would promote the policies envisioned by the majority.

Of course, this was indeed very radical compared to the arrangements that existed at the time the war began. Essentially, fourteen families of the ruling elite controlled the country's fourteen provinces, owning much of the corresponding territory. Perfectly satisfied with the arrangements they had with international capital under the neo-colonial political system of the day, the ruling class as a whole vigorously opposed such change.

Even so, there was much more to this struggle than domestic interests. The so-called Cold War had not yet ended. The Cuban Revolution had withstood all the pressure the U.S. applied and, in 1979, the Sandinistas had taken power in neighbouring Nicaragua. With El Salvador on the verge, and Guatemala and Honduras on deck, then U.S. president Ronald Reagan declared El Salvador to be the "line in the sand"; the communist threat to what Reagan referred to as freedom and democracy was to be stopped in El Salvador at all costs. Those costs were considerable: short of sending in its own troops, the U.S. spared nothing to support the Salvadoran regime. Military aid included advisers who essentially ran the war. U.S. military personnel trained El Salvador's troops as well as the infamous death squads, and the U.S. provided military equipment weaponry and financing to the tune of US$2 million a day. No country on the planet save Israel received so much U.S. aid at that time. So it was that this tiny country, scarcely more than a dot on the globe, and with a total population of only 5 million people, became the eye of the storm not only for the U.S. government but, on the opposing side, for those with an interest in independently chosen and created alternatives to the neo-colonial system.

It was for all of these reasons that many who opposed the U.S. intervention in other nations' affairs on principle, and who were appalled by the brutality and human rights violations of the Salvadoran regime, moved beyond a strictly oppositional stance and became proactively supportive of the FMLN. The Salvadorans inspired millions of individuals around the world, and many organizations as well as governments, in their varying capacities, became involved in the struggle. Long before we were arrested, there was a genuine international movement in solidarity with the people of El Salvador that spanned Europe as well as South, Central and North America.

The group I was eventually involved with reflected this geographic diversity, while the general ideology of the solidarity movement explains why the Chilean MIR was willing to co-organize the operation with the FMLN. Our operation was not business as usual for the FMLN, and it was not representative of what anyone else working in the solidarity movement was called upon to do. It was an extreme measure conceived of in light of the requirements of the final offensive, and we were all aware that we had been asked to act under exceptional circumstances in a time of extraordinary need.

THE TRIAL AND APPEALS

Our trial was set to begin two weeks from the day we were arrested. This left us very little time to prepare but, to contest the timeline, we would have had to risk losing the judge randomly assigned to the case, who was reputed to be fair-minded and not corrupt. The conundrum we faced was whether or not to argue we were political. After election day, the police and the media had changed their tune, and they were now presenting us as a band of greedy and utterly evil thugs. The immediate reason for abandoning the "terrorist" line was that, in Brazil, political cases are tried by a different court than are other crimes. In the wake of dictatorship, the sentence range for political kidnapping had been set at three to eight years, whereas the sentence range for its "common crime" equivalent was, at the time, eight to twenty years. Naturally, we wanted to avoid not only the higher sentences but also the ignominy of having acted out of self-interest. As the dust cleared, our lawyers realized that the prosecution, lacking aggravating factors conforming to penal code definitions, would use our alleged greed and ruthlessness to push for maximum sentences across the board.

The truth was that we were political but couldn't say who we were for all the damage this would do to the FMLN or the MIR at that time. We were unanimous on this point, yet we had to provide some explanation of what we were doing. Under Brazil's inquisitorial system, we were compelled to testify but, by way of compensation, we were free to answer the judge's questions any way we chose. Perjury is not an offence for the accused (although it is for the prosecution), so we invented an unlikely but plausible scenario in which we claimed to be a new internationalist group intending to effect political and social change in the southern region of South America.

Our defence also involved two other main elements. We all pleaded not guilty except the three who, during the negotiations with police, had proved beyond any doubt that they knew about all aspects of the operation. This, too, may have seemed unlikely, but it was nevertheless plausible because of possible variations in the way information could be compartmentalized. Our lawyers also argued that we should not be tried at all, because the evidence on which the prosecution's case was based had been obtained illegally, through torture. The prosecution's story was that there had been no torture, despite the many media photos clearly showing otherwise and the fact that, in the two weeks since her arrest, Maria Emilia had developed pneumonia. Sifting through all of this, the judge acquitted us on the secondary charges but convicted all ten for the kidnapping itself. The sentences he gave us ranged from eight to twelve years, depending on the role he believed each of us to have played.

Bleak as things looked to us then, our situation would get much worse in the years ahead. The full account of further judicial proceedings and the story of our families' unrelenting efforts to gain our release are full of twists and turns far too complicated to relate here. But I can say that the political support work was based on what happened next on the judicial front, which was that the prosecution appealed. By then, the various interested parties had a better grip on the reins. Our case went to a notoriously punitive tribunal, which accepted the prosecution's arguments in their entirety. The three men on this tribunal voted unanimously to maintain the convictions and reverse the acquittals, and they handed down the maximum sentence to everyone for everything. All of our sentences shot up to twenty-eight years. Our lawyers, of course, did their best to assure us that these sentences couldn't stand, and they committed themselves to carrying the case forward through the courts. Legally speaking, these sentences were unprecedented in their severity and were in demonstrable violation of Brazil's penal code. Yet they were upheld in our next two appeals.

BEING IN PRISON

We were, of course, in prison for all of this. I was in the women's section of the notorious Carandiru. The eight men were in one penitentiary, the two women in another. For the first year, Maria Emilia and I were held in solitary confinement. Except for the several weeks Maria Emilia spent in a cell in the prison clinic, while her pneu-monia morphed into a permanent abscess in her lung, we were kept for the rest of the first five months in separate sections of the "hole." Each floor of cells had a small walled-off section at one end of the corridor. Behind a heavy locked and bolted door was a row of four barren cement cells, narrow and deep, with high ceilings. A small window covered by a mesh steel grate was on the back wall of each and, although it allowed in light during the day, the window was too high up to see out through. Most of the time, no one was in any of the other cells, so we sometimes spent days on end without hearing another voice.

Prisoners accompanied by a guard would bring our meals three times a day and deliver these through a slot in the door. As we later learned, the administration had threatened them with disciplinary action if they talked to us. Nevertheless, most of these prisoners did not obey, and their guards didn't care. Although we barely spoke the language [Portuguese, Brazil's official tongue], these women would offer words of support and encouragement, give us updates on each other and generally try to provide us with whatever it was we most urgently needed. They did not really know what to make of us at first. According to the rules, we were being treated unjustly, and that was their concern. On their own initiative, some of the women lobbied hard to get us into the general population and, in the meantime, did everything possible to help us any way they could.

At the five-month mark, Maria Emilia and I were moved to regular cells, one beside the other, although the rules regarding our isolation from the other women continued in effect. Nevertheless, we were relieved that we could sometimes speak to each other apart from our meetings in the administration building with the lawyers. Also, the cells were infinitely better than those in the hole. Conforming to United Nations standards for single-person occupancy, they were much more spacious. These cells also were pure cement, but the floors were covered with hardwood, the walls were painted, and we each had three shelves. The beds were the same, built-in cement slabs with a foamy on top, but the toilet and sink were set off by a half-wall, and we no longer felt we were living in a bathroom.

There were, of course, some problems. Many of the cells were damp. Over the years, I would lose track of how many of the books my family had sent me I ultimately lost to mould. The giant flying cockroaches were not only unpleasant but noisy enough to wake us up during the night. They were difficult to hunt down, because we did not control the light switches for the cells, and aside from the candle ends the Catholics would slip us following special mass celebrations, we had no other source of light after 10:00 P.M. Occasionally, especially during the rainy season, rats made their way up the pipes and emerged in the toilet bowls. As the toilets had no seats, much less lids, this presented an obvious hazard. The cardboard covers we improvised were ineffective at keeping the rats out. It was not until about 1995 that a change in the canteen policy permitted us to buy large bottles of pop once a month. En masse, we started filling these with water and placing them inside the toilet bowls, which alleviated the problem somewhat. A far worse problem with the toilets, especially once the double bunking began a few years after our arrival, was that often, for months on end, we had running water only about one hour a day.

Toward the end of our year in solitary, Maria Emilia and I were gradually allowed more contact with the other women in our cellblock. Our integration into the general population was difficult at first, because the language barriers were still quite substantial. Naturally, our Portuguese had improved very little while in isolation. However, for other reasons, the women were confused about who we were. Sensationalistic media reports, together with visits from our families and especially from the [Canadian and Chilean] consulates, had misled them into thinking we were wealthy, "important" people. Some had seen us, on our rare times out of the cells, walking together around and around the "patio," the small, fenced-in cement courtyard connected to the cellblock, well within sight and firing range of the tremendous stone wall patrolled by the military police, which separated us from the men's state penitentiary where our companeros were prisoners. Some of the women had conjured up some very mistaken ideas about what had brought us there and what we were planning next.

On top of the other factors, the police deliberately promoted misconceptions. For example, through the prison staff, they planted the completely false rumour that our "organization" was coming to pick us up in helicopters and everyone nearby would be mercilessly gunned down. This slander, of which we knew nothing at the time, exacerbated the problem somewhat, but many of the women saw through it. The "divide and conquer" campaign was, overall, pretty clumsy and, by and large, a failure. We found most of the women to be open and friendly. Some, without the least hesitation, tried to bring us up to speed on who was who, often introducing themselves in a way I found quite comical at first; that is, not only by their names but, in the prison system's shorthand, by the number of their penal code violations. Eventually, as we gained facility with the language and were allowed to participate in regular activities, the other women got to know and accept us. To nobody's surprise, we got along just fine.

One of the first things that had impressed me, but which I only came to fully appreciate over time, was the level of solidarity amongst the prisoners. Often, this was apparent in small things which, it became clear, were constant features of the routine. On any given day, women were lobbying the guards for some minor concession for somebody else or for special attention to the needs of someone who was, for one reason or another, prevented from effectively making her own case. This included, for example, trying to get a "suspension of privileges" lifted, getting someone who was on the list to see the doctor actually seen, getting a needed change in work placement or pressuring the administration to get someone's parole application paperwork moving. This may not seem particularly extraordinary support, and it is the kind of thing one might naturally expect to see among friends. But in fact, it extended far beyond individual friendships to include everyone there.

We, strangers, and foreigners at that, had been beneficiaries of this solidarity, but it also extended to those very few women who had done some terrible thing, who had harmed or killed a child, for instance, something nobody understood and of which, certainly, nobody approved. In North America, women in these circumstances can wind up cut off from the other prisoners' support, segregated supposedly for their own safety. In Brazil, because there was no administrative segregation, the other prisoners got to know these women and realized perfectly well that something had gone terribly awry somewhere along the line, that the women, individually and personally, were not at fault. The mainstream prisoners, who were mostly in for money crimes or, increasingly over the years, on drug charges, not only made allowances for the ways a would-be marginalized woman might sometimes inconvenience them but went out of their way to take special care of her. A woman's strange behaviour, often nocturnal, might provoke quiet, exasperated grumbling on occasion, but generally even this would take a light-hearted tone. The woman was one of us by virtue of being in the same boat, and she was always treated with respect and included in group activities; she would have whatever it was she needed if this was within the power of the other prisoners to provide. This lack of extreme isolation is one of the most significant differences between Brazilian and North American prisons for women. I believe it is the single most important reason that there are so many fewer suicides and incidents of self-injury in the Brazilian prisons than there are in Canada.

By the time Maria Emilia and I were fully integrated into the regular regime, we had already met quite a few of the other women. However, because our communications with them had always been restricted, to varying degrees, we started to get a better sense of who they were only once we were allowed to work. Our first job was for a private sector company that sold clothespins, and we sat in a room at tables with about twenty other women jamming metal springs into the space between the plastic prongs. We were paid by the sack, so the women worked fast, but this did not prevent a lot of leisurely conversation. Some of the talk gradually revealed personal backgrounds, and we found out, for example, that many women were from the Nordeste (Northeast), the poorest area of Brazil, where most of the African slaves had been brought in to work on the sugar plantations. In fact, the majority of the women in prison had at least some African heritage. Land ownership, in the Nordeste in particular but also elsewhere in Brazil, was still, in the 1990s, semi-feudal, and some of the women had come to Sao Paulo looking for work. Many others were from families whose earlier generations had migrated to the city for the same reason.

Other main topics of conversation were the television soap operas and the local news, the main source of which was right-wing law-and-order radio talk shows. These were constantly on in the room where we worked all day, and it took me ages to figure out why the women listened to them. Eventually, I realized that these shows were a twisted equivalent of community radio, in that they allowed the women to keep tabs on what was happening in their neighbourhoods.

This mix of personal stories and the general topic of crime often brought up for discussion women's attitudes toward the events that had landed them in prison. I admit to being surprised at how great a majority took complete and utter responsibility for their actions. Very few considered themselves also to be victims; they did not blame their actions on the often horrendous violence they had grown up in the midst of, or on the fact that they were often the sole providers for any number of dependants, be these their own children or other family members. Many had begun their "criminal careers" very young, in the sex trade, and, although the repression of sex workers in Brazil is carried out by means other than imprisonment, they took responsibility for leaving that work and resorting to other illegal means of making a living. What it seemed to come down to was a sense that their choices were based primarily in two areas: first, on having chosen to engage in one particular type of crime over another (or having searched until they found some legal way to scrape together some, if not enough, money); and second, on having selected, for example, one target over another as a source of revenue to steal from. Given their options and the foreseeable consequences of each, the women's decisions never seemed to me to be much of a choice.

Eventually, Maria Emilia and I got jobs in the state-owned clothing factory, making uniforms for prisoners, for the orphanage/detention centres for street kids, for the public utilities companies and, once only, for the police. The police uniforms were a failed experiment; the quality of our work, usually quite good, plummeted. But apart from this one exception, given the opportunity to make money legally, the women demonstrated truly phenomenal speed, skill and diligence. Each month, without fail, most of the women sent their earnings out to their families. The sum was not enough for a family to live on but, on average, it was the same as minimum wage in the rest of the country. This allowed the women inside to keep at least some semblance of their usual financial relationship with their children and families. What became absolutely clear was that if any of these women had been given half a chance to live productive, dignified lives on the outside, they would never, ever have been in prison.

The school was another place we got to know the women. It went for two hours a day and ranged from basic literacy up to grade eight, which conformed to the levels of education the majority of women had missed thus far in their lives. Some in the prison administration had argued that Maria Emilia and I were past that level and therefore shouldn't be allowed to attend, but we justified our enrolment on the basis of needing to study Portuguese. Of course, we genuinely did need to study, but the more compelling reason for attending was that the school was a sanctuary away from the generally repressive ambience of the rest of the prison. The school was staffed and controlled by regular teachers from the state's public education department, and very few saw their role as even remotely disciplinary. On the contrary, most saw it as an important aspect of their work that they provide a forum where we could freely discuss any hot-topic prison issues and they could teach whatever interested the majority of students.

As far as I was concerned, the other women's interest in learning English was rather misguided. Nevertheless, for a while we had an ESL (English as a Second Language) class going in our room. This proved much more interesting for me than I had anticipated. The beginning level of second-language courses (the teacher rounded up materials) always involves going through basic information about oneself, and it is, therefore, an incidental way of becoming aware of the group's biographical information. In the section on familial relationships and marital status, for example, it came out that every woman in the class except me was a widow. This revelation closed down any more English for the day, as it launched us into talking about how this could be. It turned out that six of the women's partners, out of a total of eleven, had been killed by the police. This was more than a lot to think about in terms of how the patriarchal system worked for those at the bottom of the pyramid.

I do not mean to imply that all the women in the prison were widows. Many were in relationships when they entered prison, but these were very difficult to maintain once inside. This was obvious enough on Sundays, visiting day at most of Sao Paulo's penitentiaries. The one time both of my sisters came to visit, they lined up in the morning to get in to see Dave and noticed that most of the adults, among the thousand or more waiting, were women. When they came to see me in the afternoon, they had expected to see mostly men and children, but here, too, by far the majority of adult visitors were women.

It is a common observation that the women in men's lives more often stick by them than happens in the reverse situation. While there are certainly broader reasons for this, the different policies for prison visits by gender in at least these two penitentiaries speak to the relative priority the issue is given by the administrative personnel. At the men's penitentiary on the other side of the wall, visitors could bring in food, stay all day and have their visits in the cells. At the women's penitentiary, visitors were not allowed to bring in anything; those first in line could stay a maximum of three hours, and everybody was herded all together into the gym. It was a horribly uncomfortable atmosphere, without enough chairs to go around. It was often impossible to carry on a conversation face to face; in order to hear over the din, one had to have one's mouth mere inches from the other person's ear. Another key difference was that the men were permitted to have conjugal visits every second week; the women prisoners, never. What became clear to me was that the women's prisons not only reproduced the patriarchal relations on the outside but reproduced them in an exaggerated form.

The only other regular contact we had with the world outside besides mail (no phone calls permitted) was on Saturdays, when volunteers were allowed in to conduct activities. I was surprised and distressed to find that feminist organizations took little interest in working with women in prison, who are undoubtedly among those who suffer the most prejudice under patriarchy. Fortunately, the branch of the Roman Catholic Church oriented by liberation theology is still very active in Brazil, and it is very clearly feminist in attitude and action. The women involved in this sector of the church not only worked with us directly but had many contacts with other progressive organizations and individuals, religious and secular, concerned with society's most marginalized groups. They saw our various needs and, over the years, organized people on the outside who set up groups inside. We had, for example, a singing group and another hodgepodge group of artists, artisans and other people who brought in supplies for various projects and who also simply became our friends. Both of these groups contributed immensely to the well-being of all of us who participated.

My personal favourite, however, was the theatre group. It was set up by two Argentine women, both of whom had fled the Dirty War years before, and they worked with us almost every Saturday for about five years running. As a group, we created our own plays, which at first were pretty much fantasy comedies. These were truly fun and, as such, provided an extraordinary reprieve from what was otherwise often gruelling boredom. While we always maintained the fun aspect of the work, in later productions, as we became more solid as a collective, we addressed themes that were truly important to us as women and as prisoners. For example, we did a play about our vision of a housing and work collective run by and for ex-prisoners, a resource we knew was vital to some of us if we were to make it on the street after release. The theatre group was a space for creative output and natural political development. Like the other groups, it also allowed us to connect with each other and to form close friendships, and it linked us in a very profound way to people, life and the world outside.

This was what we had for regular group activities, aside from having our meals and watching TV together in the evenings, both of which were often done in enforced silence. But it is to their credit, in my opinion, that Brazilians take a realistic view of the very limited potential of prisoners to "benefit" from their incarceration. The punitive element and a bit of lip service to rehabilitative ideals aside, the authorities are generally not under the illusion that they are doing much more than warehousing people. The de facto mandate of the prison system is to provide prisoners with an opportunity to get the basic education they haven't received on the outside, to teach a few work skills if possible and to keep the convicts off the street until their sentences are up. Therefore, the Brazilian system neither requires nor offers "anger management" workshops, "cognitive skills" training or any of the other programs—useful and entertaining or not, as the case may be—that come and go in North American prisons. This is not to say that the authorities don't go through the motions of trying to identify the "mental disorders" academics often theorize are the "cause" of crime, especially the cause of women's crime.

My own introduction to the prison "psy" professionals came early in my imprisonment, with an outside-office-hours summons to the prison clinic from its psychiatrist, "Dr. Pedro." Everyone had been locked down for the night when I was taken from my cell in solitary confinement and escorted to the clinic, a separate building inside the compound. It was dark walking over and, at that time, I was still deeply afraid that the prison administration would give the police who had tortured my companeros access to all of us inside the prison.

Once inside the main door to the clinic, I was directed to walk upstairs alone. Only one office was lit, the door to which was open. The man behind the desk was bundled up in a ski jacket on this hot summer night as, I would later learn, he always was. He spoke reasonable English, and he directed me to come in and sit down. Then he said nothing. I asked him if he was Dr. Pedro. He insisted he was not but refused to tell me who he was. I walked out.

Back downstairs, I tried as best I could to explain the situation to the nurse. She rolled her eyes at this apparently new prank in the doctor's infamous repertoire of tactics for assessing the mental stability of prisoners. She accompanied me back upstairs and formally introduced me to Dr. Pedro, whereupon he quizzed me on my knowledge of the botanical names of Canadian trees and mushrooms. This was the theme of all future interviews I would have, though never at my request, with this man. I later learned from the other women that he usually interrogated his "patients" about their sexual histories. Of particular interest to him were the positions in which the women had had intercourse and with what kind of partners, by familial connection, gender and species.

As far as I can tell, Dr. Pedro got away with this type of conduct because he always prescribed the tranquilizers the women asked for, which was fine by both the prisoners and the staff. Of course, a prisoner's dependence on medication would be noted on the psychiatric evaluation Dr. Pedro wrote for the judge, who would decide a woman's application for parole without ever having set eyes on her. While the prolonged use of medication would reduce her chance of success somewhat, more often than not the notation simply provided the judge with a convenient excuse to deny parole should this be his decision based on other factors. However, in general, Dr. Pedro wrote favourable reviews, and writing these reports and prescriptions was essentially his role at the prison. If, however, he summoned a woman to his office on a whim and she refused to see him, she would be disciplined, and her refusal would go on record and form part of any future parole application. Men in the prison next door, as I well knew from Dave and the others, were never subject to such coercion.

It is perhaps obvious that Dr. Pedro was a special case, perverse and lazy and very possibly a lunatic himself. Nevertheless, it is my opinion that the "psy" professionals in Canada are in their own way just as bad, and the results of their interventions even more sinister. They operate on the same sexist assumptions and look for the same false causes, the difference being that, in Canada, nobody is rolling their eyes. On the contrary, in order to get out of prison, women have to prove that they buy into the pathological labels they are assigned or, at minimum, effectively agree that they are liable to develop a pathology if left to their own devices. Women in Canada have to pay for their freedom with proof they are working on their "issues" by participating in programs and counselling that they are often required to continue, on threat of reimprisonment, even after their release. Although the "mental health issues" women are presumed to have, in my opinion, have nothing to do with what got them into prison in the first place, nobody acknowledges the elephant in the room. As far as I can see, just as in Brazil, the women in prison here [in Canada] did what they did because they were caught between a rock and a hard place. Pathologizing women is a convenient out; if it is just something about the individual women that is to blame, then there is no need to deal with the rocks or the hard places.

In many ways, I think a thumbnail sketch, as I have given here, can be misleading no matter how accurate the specifics. I can say that my day-to-day life in prison was, among other things, an opportunity to learn more than I probably could have learned anywhere else on earth about class, race and gender relations in a society like Brazil's. I not only had the honour of getting to know the women at the bottom of the pit our system creates, but I got a pretty fair taste of what it's like to live there. I sincerely doubt anyone could go into a women's prison with a class analysis and not come out with that analysis in many ways expanded and enriched.

The most important thing I learned is that, packed into these grim and unjust places, are truly magnificent women capable of tremendous solidarity and acts of kindness, who can be recognized by their strength and uncommon grace. I had never met women like these before. Yet, almost paradoxically, I learned that these women live by the same values most people do. They respect other people and want respect in return; they think it is right to look after those who are damaged or fragile; they want their needs and those of their families to be met, and they are willing and able, given the opportunity, to work hard for that; they want to live in a dignified manner and have some joy in their lives. Sometimes these things take a slightly different shape inside the walls than they do outside; sometimes not. But at the core, these women are not the "other" they are often thought to be.

Although I spent very little time in a Canadian prison, too little to really get to know its inner workings, it was nevertheless readily apparent that here, too, was a group of compassionate, intelligent, creative women. Not surprisingly, they were in for essentially the same reasons. Our system denies these women the means by which to live happy, productive, dignified lives and to have their own and their families' needs met. Many of the women who return to prison after being released do so for no better reason than that this condition remains unchanged. Perhaps it is even that much more true for them upon getting out than it was when they went in.

LOOKING BACK

In 2004, it has been more than five years since the ten of us began the hunger strike that got us transferred out of Sao Paulo and led to our release. It has been fifteen years since Dave and I made our decision to participate in the action that took us to prison in the first place. Writing this piece has taken me back there and made me reflect on the entire experience.

To this day, it is difficult to think about any of it as somehow detached from the political context in which it took place. Reflecting on the Salvadoran struggle in broad terms, I still feel that what I had hoped to contribute to was valid and just. The objective had been to replace a fundamentally unjust political arrangement with an alternative based on national consensus as to the form political, economic and social change should take. There was never any question as to which side we were on. Even so, our decision to accept the task of participating in a kidnapping in support of this aim was something of a matter apart, and neither simple nor straightforward.

Certainly, on the one hand, there was nothing appealing about the prospect of taking part in a kidnapping, the idea of which was as revolting to us as it would have been to anyone else. It went against the grain at a visceral level. At precisely the moment we were wholly committed to participating in the building of an authentic alternative to a system that was wrong and unjust, we were asked to take part in an action that was seemingly unjustifiable. On the other hand, I did not think I knew better than the FMLN leadership what it needed. It was clear that fighting a war against the U.S., let alone winning it, was a very expensive endeavour. In 1989, the war in El Salvador was entering what may well have been the decisive phase, and the proceeds of the kidnapping were anticipated to be about US$30 million. At that particular moment, that much money would have had the potential to make a real difference.

Yet there was more in the equation than the above factors. It was impossible to avoid thinking about all the other ways of making worthwhile contributions to the struggle. The student work and the radio projects Dave and I had been involved with in Canada and then in Nicaragua were, like all the solidarity work going on, valuable and necessary, and this had the advantage of being ethically pure. In that work, we did no harm to anyone, nor did we drag anyone else into it with us. We had not needed to observe strict security measures requiring that we lie to our families and friends about where we were and what we were doing, or to cut off all contact with them for an indeterminate period. We hadn't had to think about how our deaths would affect them, certainly a distinct possibility should the [kidnapping] operation go awry. It is perhaps ironic that we did not consider what our imprisonment would mean to them, since that was, in the end, what would consume much of their lives over the coming decade.

Those in the FMLN who asked us to take part in the operation knew full well the nature and implications of what they were asking, and they gave us ample opportunity to decline the request. The fact is, nobody wants to do this kind of work. We had the option of staying where we were, or of walking away altogether. Because we were Canadians, those choices were open to us; neither our survival nor our personal well-being depended on our participation in this struggle. However, it was precisely because of who we were that we were asked to do this work. Despite our lack of skills and experience, our race, class and nationality were a good fit for the task. We could take advantage of biases, part and parcel of the neo-colonial system we opposed, to get certain things done without raising much suspicion.

However, what it ultimately came down to, as far as I was concerned, was a review of the decision I had made long before, as had Dave, when we began to work in solidarity with the Salvadorans. At that time, we had freely chosen to take our First World privilege and put it at the disposal of those who were fighting for something which we, too, believed in and supported. For the vast majority in the solidarity movement, the identical commitment left people where they were, doing tasks that were sometimes difficult but ethically uncomplicated. Very rarely did such a commitment take one into a grey zone, but it did us, and in that zone we had a decision to make. The stakes were high and we took our chances. We made our decision knowing we would have to live with the consequences. We still do live with certain lingering repercussions, as thousands upon thousands live with their own particular versions of the war's aftermath.

When people ask me if I am sorry for what I did, they usually want a simple, categorical answer. I can tell them in all honesty that I am sorry for the anguish, heartache, work and expense I caused my family. I am sorry that our operation lessened the chance of a leftist electoral victory in Brazil in 1989. I believe that a better analysis of the situation on the ground could have averted this turn of events. Finally, I am sorry for the horrible psychological distress I caused Abilio Diniz and his family.

All of this is true, yet I knew in advance that the experience would be painful for all concerned, and I regretted that fact before I participated in the kidnapping. Moreover, it remains to be said that I do not regret having tried, as best I knew how at the time, to contribute to the making of a better alternative for millions of people. It is much easier to stick with the oversimplified answer than to explain that, rather than my remorse, a complex combination of changed political context and personal circumstances is society's guarantee that I will never constitute a threat to anyone again.

I think back to those days and those that followed quite often, and I interpret my own experience to be one among the great many that comprise the collective experience of an era now over. This is not to say that I don't see the many parallels to what is going on today, or that this past doesn't inform my perceptions of what may be coming down the pike if we, as a society, keep moving in the direction we are headed. I am encouraged to see that others have figured this out for themselves without taking the road I travelled, and are working at the grassroots level on new ideas for building a more just society.

Still, my own journey has given me experience and insights for which I am deeply grateful. These are things I value and do not wish to forget. Much of what I hope to accomplish now is inspired by knowledge hard-earned. I would not recommend the method to anyone, but I cannot imagine having learned all I did any other way.

Reflections

Two years following her release after three months in British Columbia's Burnaby Correctional Centre for Women, Christine re-entered university, and this is where we met. She completed a Bachelor of Arts degree and a Post-Baccalaureate Diploma and, in 2003, entered a graduate program in Criminology, where she is examining the problems faced by women coming out of prison. Christine, who returned as an "older" student with vast life experience, has been an asset to the education of the younger students. They and I had the benefit of her skills and her quietly assured, open demeanour when she served as my assistant in a course on prisoner autobiographies. In telling her own story she gave the class a vibrant first-hand encounter with someone who has been there.

Christine, Dave and their internationalist companeros, including my brother-in-law, were walking their talk when they laid their own lives on the line to give aid to the El Salvadorans fighting for their freedom from U.S. aggression. The U.S. military, under President Ronald Reagan, trained locals in terrorism to attempt to rid El Salvador of any trace of rebellion and supported a military regime that aided and abetted the monopoly landowners. Death squads were rampant, and mothers were weeping over their sons and daughters who were disappearing by the tens of thousands. Assassinations were par for the course.

I would prefer that we all follow the law, apart from peaceful acts of civil disobedience, and find creative ways to stem the tide of a police state and of global imperialist wars without engaging in coercion, force or violence of any kind. I would prefer that the democratic process lead all good people to the polls, to soundly reject those who would limit their freedoms and human rights. I have the luxury of such preference because I live in Canada, where pacifist beliefs and general respect for the law seem perfectly reasonable to the comfortable majority. However, not everyone has the luxury of choosing pacifism; self-defence against brutal, illegal military and police forces and against poverty, hunger and disease requires every available resource, legal or not. Christine Lamont understood this. She supported the rebels because she saw the suffering, and her conscience and history of political activism dictated her commitment to be of use.

12

FIRST NATIONS WOMEN

PRISON AS COLONIZATION

CANADA HAS BEEN REPEATEDLY placed at or near the top of the United Nations' rankings of the most livable countries in the world, but Canada has also been cited for the oppressive conditions imposed on people of the original nations. Some government reserves, where Aboriginals have been forced to live, lack basic plumbing, never mind other amenities most Canadians take for granted. Most disturbing, since the 1980s more than 500 Aboriginal women have disappeared in Canada (*Redwire*, 2004: 11). Women who work as street prostitutes are particularly vulnerable to being assaulted, kidnapped and murdered, their bodies found in dumpsters and ditches.

The United Nations decries discriminatory treatment of Aboriginals by the Canadian criminal justice system and the severe over-representation of Aboriginal people in prison, as is the situation in most British Commonwealth nations. In January 2004, the Canadian Human Rights Commission responded in the affirmative to a complaint filed by the Canadian Association of Elizabeth Fry Societies (CAEFS), the Native Women's Association of Canada and other groups. The commission concurred that Canadian prisons are breaching prisoners' human rights and that Aboriginal women in particular are vulnerable to abuse.

In 2003, women who were officially registered as Indians constituted only 4 per cent of all women in Canada, but 23 per cent of women in federal prisons were Aboriginal (McIvor and Johnson, 2003: 3), an over-representation that remains constant. In the three Canadian territories and in provincial prisons on the Canadian prairies, Aboriginal women constitute between 70 and 100 per cent of the prisoners (CAEFS 2000; Faith, 1993). Relations between First Nations and the Canadian criminal justice system are adversarial by definition and laden with tragedy.

> I do not know when I am going to pick up the phone and hear about the friend who committed suicide, the acquaintance that got shot by the police, the Native prisoner that was killed in an alleged hostage taking... I do not have any control over the pain and brutality of living the life of a dispossessed person. I cannot control when that pain is going to enter into my life (Monture, 1986: 163).

The Canadian Parliament has counselled the judiciary that First Nations people, in particular, should be sent to prison only as a last resort [Criminal Code Sec. 718.2(e)]. The public purse has not accommodated this intention by funding the social services or community programs that could prevent crime, reduce recidivism and create opportunities for people to offer restitution and to rebuild their lives. In the absence of such alternatives, judges continue to send Aboriginals to prison, as usual, even when the crimes are not serious.

Aboriginal women have higher rates than white women on charges for assault, fine default and public nuisance (Hamilton and Sinclair, 1991: 499–500). The assault charges often come from fights in or outside bars, and the charge is compounded if the accused resists arrest or jerks away in a manner that could be construed as attempted assault of a police officer. Much of what Aboriginals do to get in trouble happens in public. Their communities are under heavy surveillance by police in search of potential suspects, as has been true historically of low-income and political minority neighbourhoods (Mosher, 1998). Conversely, white middle-class residential areas receive more protective policing, such as quicker responses to calls, and residents are not de facto treated with suspicion. Due to discretionary sentencing, penalties are often harshest for those who offend people of higher economic status.

Police brutality is not uncommon. For example, at least two young Aboriginal men have died in recent years, in separate cases, when the Saskatoon police, in sub-zero weather, drove them to the edge of town and left them there without coats. Aboriginals are more apt to be kept in jail while awaiting a hearing and sentencing than are white accused. Some do not know the English language, and Canadian courts are literally foreign to them. The cultural confusions are intense. Women who are normally feisty become subdued. Many plead guilty at the urging of the court, staring at the floor and mumbling whatever they think the court wants to hear. They accept plea bargains that are not in their best interests. I know of at least two individuals, in separate cases, who confessed to someone else's crime, took the rap and did the time to spare their guilty friend the grief. Actually, an equivalent of the word "guilt" does not even exist in most Aboriginal languages.

Sharon McIvor, from the Lower Nicola Band in interior British Columbia, is a respected lawyer, prisoners' advocate, teacher and scholar. We met many years ago in a roundtable discussion, and she has guest-lectured in my university classes. She draws from Western anthropological theories to debunk "drunken Indian" and "dirty squaw" racist stereotypes—stereotypes that are reinforced by homeless people wandering downtown streets of Winnipeg, Regina or Vancouver.

McIvor points out that even though Aboriginal people are over-represented in Canadian prisons, those who get in trouble, or who are alcoholic or lack a home, comprise a minority of all Aboriginals. Most do not get in trouble. Some continue to live traditional lives in the North: hunting, trapping and fishing, far from the arm of Canadian law. Some are fully assimilated in mainstream, urban culture, with little contact with their roots, and they don't get in trouble, either. Many others are able to go back and forth with ease between Canadian and First Nations communities, with one foot in each culture; this group includes a lot of Aboriginal activists. All Aboriginals have been wrenched from their homelands and languages and traditions, most without a safety net, but a minority of them have neither the means nor the will to adapt to Western culture, and they have been torn from their own traditions. They do have one foot in each culture, but they're not at home in either. This is the most vulnerable group, with the fewest resources and the greatest likelihood of getting in trouble.

About language: The large population of people in Canada whose roots are in India confuses the matter of how to refer to the Aboriginal populations. Since the 1970s, the word "Indian" has been rejected by many First Nations as the word of imperialist colonizers who didn't know whose land they had "discovered." Since these new Canadians had to deal with the Native people, they drew up an "Indian Act," in 1876. This act, still in force in 2005 with some amendments, ensured the political subordination of Aboriginal peoples; those on reserves couldn't vote in Canadian elections until 1960, and most treaties have been broken. Many Aboriginal people do call themselves "Indian" to each other, but they may not want to hear it from white people. In public discourse the preferred and most commonly used term is "First Nations." This refers to the 600 different nations that lived for millennia on what is now claimed as Canadian soil, each with its own geographies, languages, economies, religions, music, arts, sports, medicines, ceremonies, rituals, education, social and kinship arrangements, values and laws. The Mohawk, Cree, Haida and so on are each distinct nations, and individuals most often self-identify according to their specific heritage.

The word "Aboriginal," which is inclusive of "Indian," "Inuit" and "Métis," is enshrined in the Canadian Constitution (1982) and is now in common usage by and in reference to First Peoples. "Native" and "Indigenous" are synonymous with "Aboriginal." The word "Native" is used generically by whites, but many Aboriginals reject being

"Native Canadians" because they don't accept Canada's claim to their lands or identities. To complicate matters, some young First Nations activists are defiantly, publicly reclaiming the identity of "Indian," with the irony connoting resistance and empowerment. This resistance rests on the knowledge that all the terms used to identify First Peoples are imposed and are based on the colonizers' views of the world (Monture, 1995).

Millions of white Canadians have small or large traces of Aboriginal ancestry, and my own family is not atypical. On our mother's side, our Cree great-grandmother migrated from Quebec to the prairies. On our father's side, our great-grandmother, of mixed Wyandot heritage, was sent to a residential school for Lakota Sioux children. Other relatives were likewise mixed in their ancestry. When the U.S. Cavalry chased after Chief Sitting Bull and his people, they fled over the border to the grasslands of southern Saskatchewan, where our great-grandparents and grandparents homesteaded. The cultures mingled peacefully and intermarried. Our Norwegian grandfather was made an honorary chief. Our father co-authored a children's book about the positive experience of growing up Métis (Rempel and Anderson, 1987), our official designation. The Métis are blended people, or "half-breeds," who straddle both European and Aboriginal traditions.

Like many people who have some Aboriginal blood, I grew up with romanticized notions about my "Indian" heritage but little knowledge. I feel pride and respect, but I know only from observation what it means to live within Aboriginal culture and traditions. I was raised with primarily European influences and white privilege in a country I didn't even realize was racist. I can't claim an identity for a life I've never lived and haven't earned. At the same time, in my relations with First Nations and Métis people I feel at home, a sense of kinship, affinity, familiarity and ease. My friend Patricia's children know me affectionately as their "krazy kookum," a variation on Cree for "crazy grandmother." I am honoured.

A Chorus of Voices

Aboriginal women have had to fight for their birthright. The 1876 Indian Act [Sec. 12(1)(b)] stopped the matrilineal traditions of many First Nations and imposed patrilineal and patriarchal relations, requiring that women be subordinate to their husbands. A husband would be a woman's only legal identity. If she married a non-Indian she could no longer be considered an Indian herself. She had to leave her community, and she and her children could no longer live with their extended families. She could not participate in cultural activities or be buried with her ancestors (Jamieson, 1978). In a long, determined struggle, women from the Tobique Reserve in New Brunswick appealed to the United Nations Human Rights Commission, which concurred that the act was discriminatory. It was amended by Bill c-31 in 1985 (Silman, 1988). Thousands of women and their children (but not their grand-children) regained their Indian status, which caused housing shortages on the reserves. Other problems ensued, but in the big picture this kind of leadership by First Nations women in recent years is making a positive difference, and some bands are now headed by a woman as Chief.

The title of this book is somewhat of a misnomer, because this chapter is not about one specific woman. Instead, I quote a number of different women, from conversations, interviews, a roundtable discussion, public presentations and publications. The effects of colonization are being challenged by First Nations activists, some of whom are quoted here. The benefit is that you are reading perspectives from various First Nations women. They have had different life experiences and see things from different vantage points, but all give voice to the harm that has come to their communities, and they arrive at the same conclusions. In many respects they are very different from one another, but they speak as one voice.

The reason for this shift in format is the following: Several years ago I set out to find a First Nations woman in prison, or recently released, who would like to tell her story for this anthology. Each woman I approached, or who was contacted on my behalf by a mutual friend, said she would be glad for the chance to tell her story, her own truth. We would do it just as soon as she got out of prison or got resettled. I would wait, but each time something would go wrong, which is symptomatic of the problems and uncertainties an Aboriginal woman often faces when she is released from prison.

Aboriginal women often cannot return from prison to their home communities. They get trapped by the city, in part because of failures in the parole system to provide release opportunities (McIvor and Johnson, 2003). Also, reserves do not always readily accept back those individuals who have served prison terms. This reluctance is based both on lack of resources and on problematic interpersonal relationships. One woman whom I'd arranged to interview got in trouble in the city and moved back north to her reserve, with trepidation. She feared rejection but had nowhere else to run to. Another succumbed to narcotics and got off track. Another, the mother of a young woman whose brain was damaged in prison, had a series of family crises. Another got restless and migrated south to the Dakotas.

And so it went. That is why, instead of focusing on one woman's story, in the following sections I am passing along perspectives and life experience from a variety of sources. They include prisoners and former prisoners, community and court workers, activists, scholars and lawyers, all sharing an interest in prisoners' rights. These women are among the many strong First Nations women who are taking their places as leaders in their communities. They are recovering the respect for women that was inherent to most original societies, but which was damaged by the patriarchal imperatives of the English and French colonizers. My purpose in writing this chapter is both to share these women's experiences and perceptions and to emphasize the connection between three colonizing forms of confinement: foster homes, residential schools and prisons.

Taking the Children

The boarding school was run by nuns. They used to call us savages. To this day I hate the word savage (Sugar and Fox, 1989–1990: 476).

Aboriginal women frequently observe that prison is an extension of residential schools, non-Aboriginal foster homes and reserves (AKA reservations, or "the rez"). The Canadian state has taken people far away from their families and locked them up in hostile institutions where everything is painful, sterile, frightening, lonely and alien. People speak of how the white faces scared them, and of how whites treated them like wild animals that needed to be tamed.

As made clear in the Indian Act, the early Canadian government's purpose was to eradicate "Indians" by causing all First Nations to be entirely assimilated. To this end, in the early 1900s, the state contracted with primarily Catholic but also Protestant churches to run isolated, live-in mandatory schools for Aboriginal children, who were literally stolen from their homes, their families left grieving. At the school in Kamloops, British Columbia, the priest in charge stated the school's purpose:

We keep constantly before the mind of the pupils the object which the government has in view… which is to civilize the Indians and to make them good, useful and law-abiding members of society. A continuous supervision is exercised over them, and no infraction of the rules of morality and good manners is left without due correction (quoted in Haig-Brown, 1988: 30).

A big truck would enter a Native community, and the authorities would sweep up all the children they could find. The children would run, to try to escape, but the white men would catch them and put them in the back of the truck with up to forty other kids. Sometimes the parents cooperated, because they were afraid or because they thought some good could come of schooling.

Generally they did not. The following is one young girl's experience of her separation:

> [T]he kids that are on the truck, they're all bawling because they're seeing us, you know, screaming and yelling... Of course they're all crying because we're crying and Mum's crying and I can remember [saying to her], "What'd I ever do to you? Why are you mad at me? Why are you sending me away?"... She was really heartbroken (quoted in Haig-Brown, 1988: 44).

At these schools, which existed until the 1980s, boys and girls were separated; brothers and sisters couldn't speak to one another. The children were constantly humiliated and called "little savages." Students were identified by their number, which was written in purple ink on their wrists. Punishments for wetting the bed or speaking one's own language included strappings, which drew blood, on the hands or bare body, in front of everyone; having one's head shaven; being locked in a cupboard; being restricted to a diet of bread and water; and having a needle stuck through one's tongue, which was routine in some schools (Haig-Brown, 1988). Most Aboriginal children were not accustomed to physical punishment, so it was not only painful but shocking. Sexual abuse was also commonplace, and since the 1980s many priests and churches have been brought to account in the Canadian courts. Although these trials have been an important part of a healing process, they have also caused grief, because most residential school victims don't want to remember the abuse, much less talk about it.

Lorraine Stick, from the Champagne Aishihik Nation in Yukon, works in youth services in Whitehorse. We became good friends many years ago when we did workshops and ceremonies together on Vancouver Island to promote safety for women in the home. When Lorraine was last in Vancouver and I told her about working on this chapter, she said, "Well, I hope you're including something about the residential schools. They were prisons too."

LORRAINE'S STORY

In December of 1957 I was taken from my home at Otter Falls to Carcross Residential School. I was eight years old. I had no idea where I was going and did not realize I would not be seen by my mother and brother until summer holidays. It was late in the evening; everyone was in bed when I arrived at the school. While I was having a bath, a staff person decided to cut my hair that was very long. I remember thinking that the people helping me are stupid because I am trying to have a bath and there is my hair in the water around me.

I remember having the other girls ask me how to say certain sentences in my language. Of course I would tell them. Because I was new to this environment I was not familiar with the rules against speaking my language. Today I cannot speak my language. I cannot remember what happened. The punishment must have been so severe that I have blocked it out completely.

We were not allowed to speak while in a lineup. We had to eat all the food on our plates. Some of the food was horrid and caused me to vomit. If we talked in line or didn't eat we were punished with a leather strap on our hands. Other punishments were to scrub and polish the hallway and the auditorium. The scrubbing was done on our hands and knees. The polisher was a large machine, which was not easy to handle.

We would get into fights and would be punished for this. We were forced to take square dancing. I would not participate and I was slapped across the face.

The movie that we got to watch every week was about cowboys and Indians, Tarzan or Elvis Presley. This is how we were brainwashed. Can you imagine being in the gym, all the First Nations children cheering for the cowboys or the guys in the blue coats? The Indians were not nice people!

We were not allowed to speak our language or practise our traditions, and no contact with our family while at school was allowed. We had to wear uniforms. We were constantly told that we were dirty Indians and that we had to pray for forgiveness. We had chapel every morning and Sunday school and church service in the evening. Saturday was the only day we had no church service. It was like we were in the army: merits when we did things right and demerits for wrongdoings.

I left that residential school after grade four and was moved to Whitehorse. I was sent to Yukon Hall residence for First Nations children to stay in through high school. We no longer had to eat all the food on our plates, but we still had to line up. We only went to church on Sunday. We could not go outside after 5:00 p.m. during the winter months unless we were involved with a sports team. At Yukon Hall I had to go to the hospital because I cut my arm and the administrator took me. While I was lying on the bed waiting for the doctor to stitch my arm the administrator started to kiss me and fondle my breast and my privates on top of my clothing. I was about eleven.

My relationship with my mother started to go down after the first year of schooling, because I refused to speak our language. I feel we live in two different worlds. The bond between my mother and myself hardly exists, and I feel it is still that way to this day. My mother drinks and I have a hard time with this. I believe I understand her reason for drinking, but yet it hurts. There is little communication between us as I have problems talking to her. I feel it is because I cannot speak her language.

I was home for Christmas, Easter and summer holidays. When I turned twelve my mother thought it was a good idea for me to start working in the summer. After this, I was not home for the summer as I had a job.

When at age eighteen I left that environment, I was a robot, no sense, no feelings and a big chip on my shoulders. I hated the world and everyone in it. I was also a perfectionist and pretty rigid in my ways. Nothing could be out of place in my home. I could do no wrong and I had to be perfect in everything I did, including being a parent. I was not a friendly person to anyone. I expected my children to be perfect also. There was little communication and I hardly expressed my true feelings, like saying, "I love you." That was hard for me. My discipline was harsh. I would scream if my children did not do as they were told and if they broke any items in the house. There was nothing out of place in my house. I would have a hard time communicating to their friends, because I did not know what to say and I just did not know how to speak to them. I was hard on myself if things went wrong. I really had no idea how to be a parent. I have changed, because my children questioned me and I had to think about what they said. I now have a better relationship with my daughters.

To this day the federal government and the churches have not accepted full responsibility for the wrong that was caused to the First Nations people across Canada. We are still treated as third-class citizens in a rich country. We are the First People in Canada. I believe that full compensation should be granted to all First Nations that attended residential schools. No questions asked. Bottom line: we each left the residential school environment a different person than when we came in. Very sterile.

The core of our very being was taken away from us through residential school and the Department of Indian Affairs. When our inner spiritual core has been damaged, it takes generations to heal. We have become dependent on the Canadian government system. We are still struggling to relearn our languages, our culture and our traditions. We were spiritual people, in tune with nature and very proud of who we were. I believe this is slowly returning.

Mary Gottfriedson, a family support worker, also talks about her experience in residential school, on what is now the Kamloops Indian Reserve.

MARY'S STORY

You either fight and survive, or you go along with whatever they say. My mom had all her other sons and daughters in there, and when it came to me and my younger sister, she told us our reserve was going to be no more pretty soon. She said all the people have died off. She told us things were going to be different, so we had to be prepared...

When I first went, it was a nightmare. Seeing a nun for the first time—all in black. Going into the building, smelling it. Coming into the recreation room—300 kids—everybody's looking like Cleopatras, the same hairdos. They stuck you in a tub right away, scrubbed you down with a brush, made sure you weren't filthy. But you never leave your home dirty, that's the way my Mom was. She scrubbed us, clean clothes, the whole bit, to go in. Yet when you get there you're stripped down, thrown in the tub... I didn't understand. One hundred of us in grade one. One teacher... a nun. She had perfect control. You were so scared. Every one of us was petrified... We're all dressed the same and we all have to line up—I'd never had to line up in my life. You got out of line and you got cracked... with a ruler, a long pointed one.

I made sure I learned the ropes because I was an older sister and I knew my younger sister was coming in. She went into shock, she just couldn't handle it... [T]hey strapped you—on the hand. If they couldn't control you with the hands, it was over the legs or on the seat—they stood you up in front of everybody. They'd make fun of how you looked. If a girl was extra pretty, they were always made fun of, to take them down. You wanted to look ugly, didn't want to cause attraction, because they'd pounce on you right away... You had to kneel down... And if the girls didn't cry, if you got 100 straps and didn't cry, they'd give you more, just to try to break you.

[About sexual abuse:] How are these little children, at six or seven, going to know this is wrong? That they could speak up? If you were a loud, noisy kid they never went near you. If you were quiet, that's the ones they picked on. Those were the ones that suffered...

[At home for holidays] you don't know how to act around your mom, you're starin' at her, you haven't seen her for months. And by the time you get used to her again, it's time to go back. The language—you forget.

... They degraded you terribly... And then you'd look at how the people at home fared, when all the kids were taken. They have nothing to do, nothing to work for... This is how alcohol came in real strong... Some of them had ten, twelve kids, and they were taken away (Faith et al., 1990: 180–182).

Parents used alcohol to cover their grief over losing their children to the schools, and the children who grew up in the schools used alcohol when they got out to cover the bad memories.

All Canadian institutions serve the vestigial functions of colonization and have systemically discriminated against First Nations. Like the residential schools, child welfare policy has removed many Aboriginal children from their families in Canada, and they have often been sent to white families in the United States. Patricia Monture, of the Mohawk Nation, is a lawyer, an activist, a professor and an author (1986; 1989; 1995; 1999). She is the mother of four and has raised other children. In the pages ahead her name will come up again in regard to her significant work as an advocate for imprisoned Aboriginal women. Here I bring attention to her pioneering work on child welfare and First Nations.

Patricia observes the serious over-representation of Aboriginal children in the child welfare system, over 50 per cent on the prairies and disproportionately high everywhere else. She states:

Not only are First Nations children more likely to be apprehended, but, once they are taken into care, First Nations children are less likely to be either returned to their parents or placed for adoption. If a First Nations child is placed for adoption or placed in a foster home, it is unlikely that such a home will be a First Nations home. Only 22 per cent of such placements are with First Nations. The effect of the child welfare process is to remove and then seclude First Nations children from their cultural identity and their cultural heritage...

> Removing First Nations children from their culture and plac-
> ing them in a foreign culture is an act of genocide…
>
> The over-representation of First Nations peoples within
> institutions of confinement—be they child welfare institutions,
> provincial jails, or federal prisons—is part of a vicious cycle of
> abuse…
>
> Both the child welfare system and the criminal justice system
> are exercised through the use of punishment, force, and coercion
> (Monture, 1989: 3–5).

Like the residential schools, child welfare and prison separate
individuals from their communities in processes of forced assimilation. The adult is sent away in shame for having done a wrong
act; the wholly innocent child who is taken away or left behind feels
ashamed through fear of being the problem and angry at being
abandoned. The separation harms both the individual taken to
prison or to foster care and those left behind. It throws the community off balance.

I grasped the depth of this harm a few years ago in Saskatchewan when Patricia and I were on a panel together, as we often are,
this time at a women's studies conference. I was moved by her talk,
as always, but a particular image has stayed with me concerning
the devastation brought on communities by residential schools. To
paraphrase Patricia:

> Imagine waking up one morning and it's very quiet and feels
> wrong, and then you remember it's because you don't hear your
> children's voices, because they're gone. Imagine if this happened
> to everyone in your community. Imagine going outside and not
> seeing the children at play or hearing their squeals, shouts and
> laughter. It's empty and quiet. Imagine if there were no children.
> This is what happened to our Nations.

Having reviewed court decisions which repeatedly discriminated against First Nations, Patricia writes:

First Nations distrust the child welfare system because it has effectively assisted in robbing us of our children and of our future. The distrust is further complicated by the adversarial process itself, which is antithetical to the First Nations consensus method of conflict resolution. Judicial decisions on child welfare reinforce the status quo by applying standards and tests which are not culturally relevant. This is a form of racism (Monture, 1989: 12).

It adds insult to injury to lose one's children to the state, then have them placed with white families. In a roundtable discussion in Kamloops with four Aboriginal women (Faith et al., 1990), I heard the following exchange between Cherry Joe of the Lower Nicola Band, who is an Aboriginal court worker, and Mary Gottfriedson of the Kamloops Indian Band, who is a family support worker.

Cherry: It's often quite difficult even to gain custody of your sister's children. They always feel that they have a better place for them, and it's always been most Native people's perspective that, what could be better for them than their aunt, uncle, grandma— their home community? It's a fight that is constantly in the court—trying to maintain control of our own children. Once it gets caught into the Ministry of Social Services and Housing, it's lost. They'll say, "We'll take the children for six months, it's just a short-term contract." And then they get in there, and you have a heck of a time trying to bring [the children] back to their family.

Mary: A lot of our Native women, when they sign the papers, they don't understand what they're signing. If there's not another Native person with them... to tell them "you're really signing away all the rights"—they don't know that. They think, "Okay, as soon as I'm better I can get my kids back."

Cherry: They think the authorities know better, that they know best.

In a study of thirty-nine Aboriginal women who were in the old federal prison in Kingston, Ontario (Sugar and Fox, 1989–1990: 475), it was found that fourteen had been in foster homes, and, of these women, twelve had had negative experiences with their foster parents. Twenty-seven of the thirty-nine were survivors of sexual and physical abuse as children, in both birth families and foster homes, as well as most having been raped and battered as adults. Two women recall their experience of abuse in foster homes:

> I didn't like the way the social worker didn't believe us, she said if you're lying those people won't get foster children ever again, you can wreck their lives if you say they molested you.

> The foster father tried to molest me plus [his] sister would cause trouble for me. I pulled a knife on the foster mother. I thought it was the only way out of there (Sugar and Fox, 1989–1990: 471–472).

The effect of residential schools and foster homes is felt most keenly when that child becomes a parent. Many women lament the loss of parenting skills in the First Nations community, a consequence of taking the children away for several generations. In the Sugar and Fox study, of thirty-nine Aboriginal women, twenty-six were mothers whose children were in foster care, in juvenile detention or with extended family. Each of them testified that her being in prison was having negative effects on her children and their relationship. Upon release, nine of these women were unable to reunite their families (Sugar and Fox, 1989–1990, 480).

The following is from the Kamloops roundtable discussion, when I asked Mary Gottfriedson the reasons for such a disproportionate number of Aboriginal women being locked up.

> I guess lost identity. Take a client of mine on the reserve. She has two children, and two grandchildren she's raising. The money she gets is absolutely nothing. They can't go to the show, they can't do anything. No ways or means of going out and getting a

job, because they're not qualified, they don't have any skills. So of course they'll try something else... A lot of them shoplift—"My kid needs that, by God he's gonna get it" (Faith et al., 1990: 182).

Wendy Leonard, a community health worker with the Kamloops Indian Band, remarked:

If a young girl fought back in residential school—that's the thing that protected her there. When she comes out on the streets, she comes in conflict with the law, she fights back. The correctional system, going into the Prison for Women, is a lot like going to residential school. From one institution to another. A lot of those kids grew up lacking parenting skills. They were in an institution all the time (Faith et al., 1990: 182).

Coping in Prison—or Not

They endured being sent to prison in the same silence with which they had greeted past victimization (Sugar and Fox, 1989–1990: 476).

In the early 1970s in the Ontario region, Aboriginal prisoners began protests and fasts to gain their rights to traditional ceremonies. Art Solomon, from the Anishnabi Nation, was a much-esteemed spiritual Elder who, in the late 1970s, spearheaded policy changes to allow for First Nations' sacred ceremonies and cultural practices inside Canadian prisons. He was very respectful toward women, quoting the old adage of the Cheyenne, "When the women's hearts are on the ground, it's all over." He argued that it was a violation of justice to permit Protestant and Catholic religious worship and ceremonies inside prison but to deny the same right to First Nations. Thanks to his work, Aboriginal women and men inside are now sometimes able to meet with Elders, hold powwows, have smudges, do beading and drumming, burn sage and sweetgrass, have sacred medicine bundles and build sweatlodges with tarps, poles and rocks for purification ceremonies. However, both the Elders and the prisoners have to be vigilant to ensure these rights are honoured in the newer prisons, and often they are not; prison guards are notoriously disrespecful toward Aboriginals.

Sharon McIvor, who is an effective advocate for imprisoned Aboriginal women, spoke at the Kamloops roundtable of how every concession from authorities is tenuous:

> We've put a lot of pressure on the warden and she's allowed just one elder to go in, and then on a really irregular basis. They've put up all sorts of barriers... They've gone into cells and desecrated medicine bundles. It was just another way that the guards could intimidate them. [The guards] will poke in when the women are in the middle of a sweat... After many delays and inconsiderations, they let [the elder] in... and said [sarcastically]: "Well, go on in, and do your elder stuff." They don't have any respect for it at all (Faith et al., 1990: 184).

It is ironic that when young First Nations women were put into the old Prison for Women, often after years on city streets, they encountered their own culture for the first time, through the Native Sisterhood. From other women and from Elders who visited the prison, they learned their history and developed pride in their heritage. Things began to make sense. One of the women who sought counsel with Art Solomon was Fran Sugar, from the Cree Nation, who served eight years there and was active in organizing the first Sisterhood. Fran writes:

> At times when I'd burn my medicine, when we had sweetgrass smuggled in to us because sometimes it was seen as contraband, the sweet smell of the earth would create a safe feeling, a feeling of being alive even though the cage represented a coffin, the prison a gravestone, and my sisters walking dead people. Those medicines were what connected me as a spirit child. One time when I was close to suicide I was told by Mista Hiya that my spirit was

alive and it was housed in my physical shell. And from that hard time I learnt that my spirit was more important than my body because my body was controlled by the routine of life in prison. It was then the connectedness to being an Aboriginal Woman began. I began feeling good about myself even though I had only a few reasons to feel good. I understood there was a spirit within me that had the will to live (Sugar and Fox, 1989–1990: 467).

With support from Patricia Monture, Deb Meness, Linda Jordan, Tony Smith and a number of Elders, Fran and another Cree woman, Lana Fox, organized a research project and interviewed thirty-nine federally sentenced Aboriginal women. Their work comprised a section of a government-sponsored study (Task Force on Federally Sentenced Women, 1990) initiated by the Canadian Association of Elizabeth Fry Societies, with support from the Native Women's Association, to evaluate women's prison conditions and make recommendations to Canada's solicitor general. The final report, titled "Creating Choices," is still the focus of feminist and abolitionist debates on how best to empower women caught up in criminal justice, given the unalterable, punitive functions of prisons. Patricia and the others inspired and ensured a strong First Nations presence in the study, with a focus on Fran's and Lana's research.

As emphasized in their report, Aboriginal women are subject to serious over-classification; they are commonly classified as maximum security rather than medium or minimum. Most women who are classified as maximum are not a security risk and do not pose a danger to anyone, even if they are incarcerated for an act of violence (Hamilton and Sinclair, 2001: 503). They may be considered to be at high risk of attempting to escape, but most often they are restricted and segregated as punishment for being uncooperative and having a "bad attitude." They support each other, and, unlike in the court setting, where they are intimidated and silent, when they're with their sisters in prison these women express themselves and risk defying authority. For example, as Fran and Lana report, women have been transferred involuntarily from provincial to federal prison, "prejudged as violent, uncontrollable, and unmanageable because [they] refused to cooperate with male guards who ordered [them] to remove [their] clothes" (Sugar and Fox, 1989–1990: 469). As of summer 2005, over 80 per cent of women classified as maximum custody were Aboriginal. All in all, Aboriginal women are more likely than white women to be classified as maximum security, to be locked in segregation and to be denied parole.

Joane Martel, a professor at the University of Alberta, completed a study of segregation practices and found that 67 per cent of women in segregation in an Alberta women's prison were Aboriginal. She concludes, "Incarceration practices toward Aboriginal peoples exemplify institutionalized race relations that are a legacy of colonial rule and ongoing coerced dependency in Canada" (Martel, 2001: 200). She describes some of the indignities. Aboriginal women, "in contrast to other women… were not allowed to shower after being tear gassed and maced," contrary to clear prison regulations. They were also confined in the basement section of a segregation unit while the "girls that were white were held upstairs in better-lit, better-ventilated, and better-heated cells" (Martel, 2001: 201). The women were put in segregation as punishment for such offences as throwing things around, cursing, tattooing, breaking things, fighting, being "mouthy," having contraband in a cell (such as salt and pepper or a deck of cards) or writing to a high correctional official to protest the conditions of the prison.

Aboriginal women between the ages of fifteen and twenty-four are eight times more likely to commit suicide than members of the Canadian population as a whole (*Redwire*, 2004: 13). Women who slash themselves or attempt suicide are sent to segregation, where one-quarter of the women self-mutilate almost daily, "to counteract the negated self that results from the subhuman conditions there. It provides women with some sense of their own corporeal existence" (Martel, 2001: 203). The punishment for self-harm is additional time in segregation. Some women have been segregated for as long as nine months, even though the law states a consecutive thirty-day maximum, which is considered the limit before insanity sets in. (For some women, even a day or two in segregation will do it.) In some of the newer women's prisons, women are segregated in cells without cots. They sleep on a mattress on the cement floor, with a blanket but no pillow, and they are not allowed any personal belongings, including grooming supplies—no toothbrush, shampoo or toilet paper. They can't make calls. They are silenced. They are sometimes forced to wear coarse, grey gowns without underclothing (Martel, 2001: 205).

For many reasons, including poor health care and high accident and suicide rates, premature death is common in Aboriginal communities, both in and out of prison. Hepatitis C and positive testing for HIV are epidemic in prisons, due in part to sharing dirty needles. During the late 1980s there was a rash of suicides by Aboriginals in the old Prison for Women, which caused terrible grief to those who remained. On one occasion a group of the newly deceased's friends gathered to mourn her death in a room that was technically off limits to them, locking the door so they could grieve without intrusion. When they didn't open the door to the staff, it was broken down and the emergency response team burst in wearing Darth Vader–like outfits, with dogs and mace at the ready, then took all of the women to solitary confinement (Faith, 1995). When Aboriginal women express valid complaints, some guards say things like, "Why don't you go hang yourself, just like your friend?" When called on it, they say they are joking.

No one knows the exact number of women who have died in Canadian federal custody, because the prison records are obfuscated. However, in the space of a few years, I was personally aware of eight women's deaths by suicide, all but one of them Aboriginal, and one woman committed suicide immediately upon release, in the park across the street from the prison. I'm aware of several other women who died of drug overdose soon after release, and another who died in a car accident related to post-prison trauma. Several others died of serious illness. Another was transferred from the women's prison in Ontario to a men's penitentiary in Saskatchewan, and there she committed suicide in her cell. Prison is often likened to death, and there seems to be a direct relationship; that is, a disproportionate number of people die prematurely while locked up or as a consequence of having been locked up. The prison, any prison, and the attitudes it breeds, are designed to demoralize even the heartiest souls. The wonder is that so many are able to transcend their environment. Many cannot.

SkyBlue Morin, a longtime advocate for imprisoned women, conducted a study of federally sentenced Aboriginal women who have been segregated in men's psychiatric prisons. She discusses the differences between "correctional" practices and the written policies of the Correctional Service of Canada (csc), which purport to "respect gender, ethnic, cultural and linguistic differences and be responsive to the special needs of women and aboriginal peoples" [Corrections and Conditional Release Act, Section 4(h)] (Morin, 1999). The csc commissioner, in a directive to all employees (#702), states a commitment to "traditional Aboriginal healing practices" and "the holistic healing of the Aboriginal Offender." With respect to cultural identity, the commissioner assures prisoners of their right to "revitalize their cultural traditions and customs," including steady access to Elders. These ideals have not been realized in any of the six new women's prisons across Canada, where it is difficult to develop or sustain mental health and spiritual well-being.

Each of the seventeen maximum security women interviewed for the Morin study, many of them in segregation, identified a crucial need for more time with an Elder. They also want culturally appropriate programs for women with alcohol and drug problems, for those with self-harm and suicidal impulses and for victims of battering and sexual abuse; programs devoted to family and parenting skills; couples counselling; formal education; health care; yard space and sports; vocational training; culturally sensitive staff; and peer counselling. Instead these women are subjected to the brutal conditions of isolation in both men's and women's prisons.

Drugging is the common "treatment" of women deemed in need of psychiatric attention, and sedatives are widely prescribed to prisoners as a way to keep everyone quiet. One woman tersely summed up the problem:

> In naïve state believed psychologist/psychiatrist would assist me in achieving release. After first interview of talking about adaptation to prison was put on medication. Did not like the numbing it caused, so did not take it. Medical staff persisted. I refused to take it... couldn't understand why medication was pushed on people. I asked [the psychiatrist] why? It makes women more dependent. How are we going to cope on the outside? (Sugar and Fox, 1989–1990: 474).

The women resented being subjected to psychological tests that were culturally inappropriate, designed by and for white men. Since the 1950s, when the field of psychology was popularized in the Western world, the "psy" professions have taken a great interest in prisons, where they have captive human guinea pigs. The prisoners' common perception is that psychiatric staff are ultimately punitive and incompetent, however much they say they are there to help.

> I said to the shrink: "I don't trust you. I'm only talking to you because I have to." When you see the shrink in there there's always fear that I might say the wrong thing... [The parole board] would just love to keep you in there... (Sugar and Fox, 1989–1990: 478).

The majority of the Aboriginal women in the Sugar and Fox study had been convicted of assault or manslaughter. Typically, the victim was someone well known to them, often an abusive partner, but not a child. (Aboriginal women are more likely than white women to kill their spouses but less likely to abuse a child.) No woman showed signs of being a threat to others; nevertheless, at one point the prison doctors concocted a bizarre plan to send some of these women for "treatment" at the neighbouring men's penitentiary, which houses sex offenders. With legal support from the outside, the women protested and refused to go. As a result, when they came up for parole their applications were denied. They were also sent to segregation, where they were kept under surveillance twenty-four hours a day, with a guard on watch, cameras in the cells and harsh lights on all night. The conditions were brutal, which is characteristic of segregation cells.

> They stripped me down on 8 different occasions. The screws [prison guards and staff] would restrain me and cut off all my clothes with scissors. Each hand was cuffed to the bed, each foot handcuffed to the bed with my legs spread wide open facing where the screw was sitting. [I got] bruises on my arms from the cuffs. That still bothers me. I don't like to show my body. Mr. [guard] knows where every birth mark on my body is (Sugar and Fox, 1989–1990: 472).

> [They maced me], they had me face down on the floor. One of them had their foot on my head. I couldn't move, they were hitting me on the back with billy clubs. To this day I have a scar there three and one half inches long, then the goon squad dragged me to segregation after they beat me in front of the whole range. Now they sent my sister home in a box (Sugar and Fox, 1989–1990: 476).

Fran and Lana discuss the pervasiveness of racism and how it infiltrates every element of women's lives:

> Racism is not simply set by the overt experiences of racism... [being] called "dirty Indians" in school, or in foster homes, or by police or guards, or [seeing] the differences in the way we were treated and [knowing] that this was no accident. Racism is much more extensive than this. Culturally, economically, and as people we have been oppressed and pushed aside by whites. We were sent to live on reserves that denied us a livelihood, controlled

us with rules that we did not set, and made us dependent on services we could not provide for ourselves... [O]ur feeling about
white authority even before we encountered the criminal justice
system mixed passive distrust and active hatred (Sugar and Fox,
1989–1990: 475).

For Aboriginal women, prison is an extension of life on the outside, and because of this it is impossible for us to heal there. In
ways that are different from the world outside, but are nevertheless continuous with it, prisons offer more white authority that
is sexist, racist, and violent... Physicians, psychiatrists, and psychologists are typically white and male. How can we be healed by
those who symbolize the worst experiences of our past? (Sugar
and Fox, 1989–1990: 476–477)

To Heal the Spirit

After Fran Sugar was released, she was in demand as a speaker at
conferences and community gatherings. She appeared as on a mission, a small, energetic woman with large glasses and very long
black hair, eloquently educating white people about the experience
of being a First Nations woman in a Canadian prison. She gave
other Aboriginal women great encouragement.

Regaining their voices is one step toward healing for Aboriginal women who have been trapped by the criminal justice system.
Having contact with their Elders inside, and with First Nations
rituals and ceremonies, can have a positive, healing effect. The
Native Sisterhood can provide a community wherein healing of
the body, mind, spirit and emotions can occur amidst the safety
and trust of one's own cultural family. These are potential benefits
for Aboriginal women in prisons with Native Sisterhoods, but it is
far better to bring someone into the fold in time to circumvent the
crime/prison cycle.

The most important element in healing is the will of the individual. It is only through one's ability to make a mindful, reasoned

decision to act in one's own best interests, as well as in that of others, that the healing process can begin. To be "reasoned" requires recognizing the factor of choice in the midst of what seems unreasonable. Aboriginal women have been subjected to unreasonable conditions and mandates at every turn. If some behave unreasonably, it is because they are reacting in kind and resisting injustice in ways that come naturally in hostile, oppressive environments.

In prison Sisterhoods, where they exist, women have inadvertently discovered their heritage or absorbed it for the first time. They do this in the company of a community of women who are likewise rebirthing themselves as First Nations women. They are hearing the wisdom of their Elders, purifying themselves in sweatlodges and in ceremonies. They are learning to speak their own truths.

Fran Sugar and Lana Fox focused heavily on the need for healing, which manifests most strongly in Canadian society among women who have encountered the criminal justice system. They note that when women have healing experiences in prison, it is as resistance to, not cooperation with, the prison.

> [Healing comes] through the bonds formed with other women in prison, through the support of people on the outside, and from the activities of Native Sisterhood. There are occasional reports of positive relationships with caseworkers, but these stand out as exceptions to the prevailing pattern (Sugar and Fox, 1989–1990: 478).

Because prisoners are so isolated, a Sisterhood becomes a place to find a sense of belonging.

> Because of Native Sisterhood I finally knew the meaning of spirituality. I learned how to pray in a sweat and with sweetgrass. I learned the meaning of the Eagle feather and colours. With that I was even more proud of who I was in my identity (Sugar and Fox, 1989–1990: 479).

Slowly I was changing. Feeling better about myself. My mother was quite traditional. When I got out I went back to my family. The whole reconnection to my people meant my family to me. I wanted life after going to Native Sisterhood, it meant everything to me (Sugar and Fox, 1989–1990: 479).

Sugar and Fox write of the frustration they felt when varied task forces would tour the prison and request to meet with the Native Sisterhood.

We always agreed to meet, somehow believing that there was hope for change... At every meeting someone in our circle was always missing, usually in segregation on some ridiculous charge. And that hope flame raged into a strong fire in our circle because we could speak for each other and those words were strong heartfelt words that were hard to say out-loud, especially to white people who had the political power... "Why are we maximum security?" "Why are we different?" "Why don't we get passes when we apply?"

The circle of chairs we sat in represented the cycle of life from birth to death, and that circle did not exclude anyone. In the ceremony of life that we are told to celebrate, we forgive and accept each person as an individual, as an individual who has made mistakes on their path of learning and teaching, and who can strive to reach a place where their spirit is healed.

The solution is healing: healing through traditional ceremonies, support, understanding, and the compassion that will empower Aboriginal women to the betterment of ourselves, our families and our communities (Sugar and Fox, 1989–1990: 480–481.)

Reasons for Optimism

Sharon McIvor, who has done legal advocacy for imprisoned women, offered the following at the Kamloops roundtable:

I visited most of the prisons in Canada that house federally sentenced women, and we talked to probably every one of the [prisoners]. The Native women who have been in prison, and have successfully completed the term, and are out, and are not going back, have one thing in common—they've gone back to their Native spirituality. [A woman who had] a lot of problems with society in general, with authority figures... in conflict since her early teens... was in and out of correctional places until she ended up in the Prison for Women. When she came out this last time she enrolled in college and her goal is to get a law degree. She's well on her way. [She figured out] that they could lock up her physical self, but they couldn't lock up her spirit, her mind, and her emotions. They couldn't lock that up. That would always be free... She had spent about eight months in solitary because she insisted upon having access to the spiritual teachers and the prison staff refused her (Faith et al., 1990: 185)

Certainly there is reason for optimism, due in large measure to the work of women who are assuming responsibility in their communities for healing, education and preventing further damage. Many First Nations are recovering their history, languages, cultural traditions and spiritual ways (Monture, 1995, 1999). Some communities, especially in the North, are now holding healing circles to resolve community conflicts, rather than bringing in fly-in judges from the south. Some reserves now have 100 per cent sobriety. Increasingly, Aboriginal bands are calling for sovereignty in governing their own affairs. In British Columbia, the Secwepemc Nation has contracted with Simon Fraser University (SFU) to offer an autonomous university program on the Kamloops Indian Reserve. By now hundreds of First Nations people have taken university courses in First Nations studies, anthropology, archaeology, criminology, ethnobotany and other areas, always with an eye to indigenous content. Alongside young people, Chiefs and Elders have earned certificates, diplomas and degrees, or have received honorary degrees, in graduation ceremonies where they wear their elaborate beaded and feathered buckskin regalia alongside university officials from the city wearing staid academic gowns.

The graduation ceremony for students in the SFU program occurs, very symbolically, in the gymnasium of the old residential school on the Kamloops reserve. People incarcerated as children are now running their own First Nations university in that same building, reviving Aboriginal knowledge rather than suppressing it. They were not successfully assimilated. They have reclaimed their space, infused it with the energy of their ancestors. They are adapting the tools and institutions of the colonizing people to relearn and celebrate their own traditions.

Verna Kirkness, a First Nations scholar, observed in 1987 the keen leadership that was building among Aboriginal women, and she stated, "The measure of our success is not 'How much have we acquired for ourselves, as individuals?' but rather, 'How much service have we rendered to our people?'" (Kirkness, 1987: 415)

In this spirit, women are working actively in their communities to ensure their children's future and to keep young people out of lock-up even when they get in trouble. Some of these kids don't know who they are. They've often lost their proper names through encounters with various bureaucracies, who record different names according to what they thought they heard. Sometimes authorities will use the name of whoever was babysitting when the police or welfare came to take the kids, or the name of whoever reported a child desertion. These kids don't usually have identification papers or even know where they're from. They often end up in prison, the depository for every serious social problem. As more First Nations regain their strengths, so have they begun to enfold those who are literally lost, diverting them from a life of going into and out of a cage. Cherry Joe, a court worker, describes the work she began in the late 1980s:

> We are advocates for the people. Meaning, we make the initial contact with Native people, men, women, youth. We act as a referral agency to legal services, community health representatives,

support workers, human resources—wherever the most available help will be for them.

[I meet them] right in the courthouse. We're there every day. Every morning I'm in court—I'll look around the courtroom where the waiting area is and I'll pick out people who look like they don't know what they're doing there... Make contact with them, make the initial appearance in court with them, explain the charges, the procedure, what's happening in court, what's expected of them, where to go for help from there. Sometimes I assist them right through the [entire court process].

What is basically a simple charge in court is much more complex. There are a lot of underlying problems—alcoholism, drug abuse, marital problems, abuse of one sort or another, a lot of low self-esteem type of problems, as someone is on social assistance for a number of years, and they're always living on a low income, and they end up, as a result, not being able to manage their money, not having food for their kids. And then they shoplift, they get picked up, and they end up as a client. We try to backtrack and find out where the problems are coming from, and bring in the other resources to try to assist them from there (Faith et al., 1990: 183–85).

A significant step toward a healing regimen, rather than dead-end punishments, occurred in 1995 when the Correctional Service of Canada opened a Healing Lodge (Faith, 1995). The punitive elements of incarceration will inevitably prevail even if healing is the purported goal. Nevertheless, the Healing Lodge represents a new approach to "corrections." One of the mandates of the 1989–1990 task force on federally sentenced women was to conceive of a way to provide a culturally appropriate centre for Aboriginal women who were sentenced to confinement. With leadership from the Native Women's Association of Canada, a group of Aboriginal women went to work on a vision based on the wisdom of Art Solomon and Alma Brooks, an Elder from the Maliset Nation. Patricia Monture carried their vision to the task force, proposing a place of healing where infants could stay with their mothers. The idea was taken up by Aboriginal women in the prison, who later confirmed:

> It is only Aboriginal people who can design and deliver programs that will address our needs and that we can trust. It is only Aboriginal people who can truly know and understand our experience. It is only Aboriginal people who can instill pride and self-esteem lost through the destructive experiences of racism. We cry out for a meaningful healing process that will have a real impact on our lives, but the objectives and implementation of this healing process must be premised on our need, the need to heal and walk in balance (Sugar and Fox, 1989–1990: 480–482).

A Healing Lodge Planning Circle was formed, including Sharon McIvor, SkyBlue Morin, Fran Sugar and Elder Joan Lavalee (Faith, 1995). With a capacity for thirty women, the Okimaw Ohci Healing Lodge opened in 1995 near Maple Creek, Saskatchewan, situated in a beautiful prairie setting amidst aspen woods and green hills. There was great hope that Aboriginal women who served time there would benefit from the primarily First Nations staff, the regular presence of Elders, and a beautiful tepee-shaped central cedar lodge for smudges, drumming, story-telling and music, and this did occur. The various buildings, including the women's "little houses," are positioned so as to form the shape of an eagle. In addition to doing the day-to-day work of cleaning, cooking, laundry and so on, the women engage in healing circles, receive counsel from the Elders, locate themselves culturally, have ceremonies and begin to recover from years of abuse and mayhem.

Many women who experience the Healing Lodge have benefited from the Lodge's Aboriginal focus. Many others have been discouraged by the prison's lapses back into custody, discipline and security as the priority concerns. The Lodge is on 160 wooded acres belonging to the Nekaneet Band, but the women are confined to the building area. Some guards' rules are petty, arbitrary and unpredictable.

When I visited, none of the women had her children with her. This slide toward punishment has resulted from an increase in non-Aboriginal staff and a system-wide insistence on fences, body searches, lasers, cameras, metal detectors and electronic security gates—all of which create an ambience of fear and control rather than of harmony and communication. Contrary to recommendations from expert advisers, the Lodge is open only to women with minimum security status, and when I was there one-third of the beds were empty. This means that a majority of Aboriginal women prisoners do not qualify for healing. Those most in need are excluded.

The Native Women's Association of Canada (2003) has called for decarceration of Aboriginal women and the establishment instead of "community-based healing facilities for all Aboriginal women prisoners including those classified as 'maximum security'." The goal is to bring "Aboriginal women prisoners under Aboriginal jurisdiction for healing and reintegration back to their community roots" (McIvor and Johnson, 2003: 3–4). This vision is consistent with legislated policy in the Corrections and Conditional Release Act (ss. 81 and 84) and the Canadian Criminal Code [Sec. 718.2(e)], but it is a far cry from existing "correctional" practices.

Problems and limitations notwithstanding, the intended themes at the Healing Lodge of cultural restoration, traditional spiritual guidance and, importantly, being accountable to the community give hope for a more civilized response to wrongdoing by people who have been victims of cultural genocide. In May 2002, I made a visit to the Okimaw Ohci Healing Lodge with Patricia Monture, who helped inspire its creation and is not happy with the shifts toward conventional confinement. Nevertheless, for most of our visit, it was a very positive experience. We were able to visit with the women, play the piano, sing, laugh, dance. We had dinner with some of them together with the Elder, who was very welcoming, as were all of the First Nations staff.

In the evening, spring snow was falling outside as we sat in a cozy benched circle inside the cedar Lodge. No member of the staff was present. A fire was burning in the piped stove at the centre, and six women drummed and sang sacred songs. Others told their stories. We joined the women in a cedar and sage smudge. We saw, heard and felt the reasons why, if a person really must be locked up, a healing lodge that nurtures the spirit makes much more sense than a regular prison. Driving back to town in the night, on an unpaved country road in a heavy snowfall, we counted fifteen mule deer coming out from the woods, which we took as a sign of hope for the universe.

References

Canadian Association of Elizabeth Fry Societies (CAEFS) (2000). "Fact Sheet."

Faith, Karlene (1995). "Aboriginal Women's Healing Lodge: Challenge to Penal Correctionalism?" In *The Journal of Human Justice* 6:2, 79–104.

Faith, Karlene (1993). *Unruly Women: The Politics of Confinement & Resistance.* Vancouver: Press Gang.

Faith, Karlene, Mary Gottfriedson, Cherry Joe, Wendy Leonard and Sharon McIvor (1990). "Native Women in Canada: A Quest for Justice." In *Social Justice* 17:3, 167–188.

Haig-Brown, Celia (1988). *Resistance and Renewal: Surviving the Indian Residential School.* Vancouver: Tillacum Library.

Hamilton, A.C. and C. M. Sinclair (1991). *Report of the Aboriginal Justice Inquiry of Manitoba, Vol. I: The Justice System and Aboriginal People.* Province of Manitoba.

Jamieson, Kathleen (1978). *Indian Women and the Law in Canada: Citizens Minus.* Ottawa: Advisory Council on the Status of Women/Indian Rights for Indian Women.

Kirkness, Verna (1987). "Emerging Native Women." In *Canadian Journal of Women and the Law/Revue juridique la femme et le droit,* Vol. 2: 408–415.

Martel, Joane (2001). "Telling the Story: A Study in the Segregation of Women Prisoners." In *Social Justice* 28:1, 196–215.

McIvor, Sharon D. and Ellisa C. Johnson (2003). *Detailed Position of the Native Women's Association of Canada on the [Human Rights] Complaint Regarding the Discriminatory Treatment of Federally Sentenced Women by the Government of Canada filed by the Canadian Association of Elizabeth Fry Societies on May 05, 2003.* Ottawa: NWAC.

Monture, Patricia (1999). *Journeying Forward: Dreaming First Nations' Independence.* Halifax: Fernwood Publishing.

Monture, Patricia (1995). *Thunder in My Soul: A Mohawk Woman Speaks.* Halifax: Fernwood Publishing.

Monture, Patricia (1989). "A Vicious Circle: Child Welfare and the First Nations." In *Canadian Journal of Women and the Law/Revue juridique la femme et le droit,* 3:1, 1–17.

Monture, Patricia (1986). "Ka-Nin-Geh-Heh-Gah-E-Sa-Nonh-Yah-Gah." [The Way of Flint Women.] *Canadian Journal of Women and the Law/Revue juridique la femme et le droit,* 2:1, 159–170.

Morin, SkyBlue (1999). *Federally Sentenced Aboriginal Women in Maximum Security: What Happened to the Promises of "Creating Choices"?* Ottawa: Correctional Service of Canada.

Mosher, Clayton (1998). *Discrimination and Denial: Systemic Racism in Ontario's Legal and Criminal Justice Systems, 1892–1961.* Toronto: University of Toronto Press.

Redwire Magazine (2004) Vol. 6, No. 3, March.

Rempel, David C. and Laurence Anderson (1987). *Annette's People: The Métis.* Edmonton: Plains.

Silman, Janet (As Told To) (1988). *Enough Is Enough: Aboriginal Women Speak Out.* Toronto: The Women's Press.

Sugar, Fran and Lana Fox (1989–1990). "Nistum Peyako Seht'wawin Iskwewak [First Nations Women]: Breaking Chains." In *Canadian Journal of Women and the Law/Revue juridique la femme et le droit,* 3:2: 465–482.

Task Force on Federally Sentenced Women (1990). *Creating Choices.* Ottawa: Solicitor General.

13

GAYLE

THE POLITICIZATION OF IMPRISONMENT

GAYLE HORII WAS BORN on the Alberta prairie. Her mother's family had migrated from Germany, her father from China, and Gayle was the middle daughter. She doted on her sisters, and when they needed something she was the one who tried to take care of things. By the early 1980s, Gayle was in a successful Vancouver business, blessed with a solid marriage and strong relationships with her two children, her sisters and her father, who had divorced their mother and married a woman from China. Her stepmother bitterly resented her husband's daughters, and this created problems. Despite her good fortune in life, the outcome of hard work and perseverance, Gayle suffered from extreme stress related to work, family responsibilities and suppressed rage from a violent childhood and then four sexual assaults during her teens and into her twenties. For many reasons, Gayle was breaking down. When her father died, the pressures increased; she was losing control and became suicidal. And then tragedy struck. A psychiatrist would later diagnose her condition as masked depression.

On the day she intended to kill herself, armed with a knife and selecting a precise location where she could do the deed unseen, Gayle went first to her deceased father's home to retrieve the family photos. When she asked for them, her stepmother threw a few at her, and Gayle snapped. Her stepmother sat on the couch, refusing to speak about the remaining albums of photos, the heritage Gayle wanted desperately to leave for her sisters. Instead of committing suicide that day, Gayle stabbed her stepmother to death, in an act that was entirely unpremeditated.

To the present, this was Gayle's only act of violence or lawbreaking. While imprisoned, and since her release, she has exercised spiritual discipline to sustain a healthy life that precludes losing one's mind, even momentarily. Her equanimity was achieved only after years of anguish and the hard work of healing. For, indeed, she did lose her mind temporarily; she snapped, acting from feelings of mindless frustration and desperate, blind rage, as is true for those committing most acts of serious violence.

For her crime Gayle pleaded guilty to second-degree murder. She served a total of seven years in four different prisons, two of which were men's prisons in which she was the only woman. She will be on parole the rest of her life, with travel possible only with permission from the National Parole Board, and she is interminably subject to surveillance by the state. There is no question that she has suffered remorse for her crime. She also has been and will continue to be punished by a Canadian system of justice that, short of the death penalty, has adopted the philosophy of the U.S.A. prison-industrial complex, namely, that punishment has no clear limit. People who are incarcerated are routinely denied their fundamental human rights, and for almost two decades, starting in her first year in prison, 1986, Gayle has been actively working to counter the worst of these abuses.

I first became aware of Gayle in the mid-1980s, when I read a series of articles in the *Vancouver Sun* by a respected journalist, Nicole Parton, about Gayle's case. Gayle was then seeking a transfer from the federal prison in Ontario to a prison in British Columbia, so as to be nearer her husband, who had suffered two heart attacks following Gayle's imprisonment. Whereas men's prisons are located across the country, and men are generally incarcerated within reasonable travel distance from their families, women's prisons, because there are many fewer of them, are often thousands of miles from the women's families; this has the effect of gender discrimination. Since the provincial prison for women refused to take Gayle back, she was transferred to a men's prison in B.C. This resulted in her having an opportunity for higher education, something not available in the women's prison. This was serious, clear-cut sex discrimination, rationalized on the perennial grounds that programs for women aren't warranted since there are relatively few women in federal prison (350 in 2004, and approximately 14,000 men).

My interest in Gayle's case had accelerated when her sister called me to talk to somebody with some knowledge of how the prisons operate. Gayle was then at the Prison for Women (P4W) in Kingston, Ontario. She was fasting as a last-resort protest against a system that was refusing to transfer her back to her home province, and she achieved the transfer at some cost to her health. In 1991, at the B.C. men's prison where she completed her sentence, Gayle agreed to my visiting with a video camera, and we conducted an interview for the better part of a day. She was very open, welcoming, articulate, up on current events, gracious, and well informed about the prison system. And I discovered that she was, and is, first of all, an artist. The work she showed me included sculptures of strong, graceful, long-limbed women symbolically moving boulders from their path, as if making way for women's freedom.

Gayle was a rebel from the start of her imprisonment, out of naivete. She tried to keep up her usual routines at the provincial jail, where she was held until her transfer to P4W. For example, she was accustomed to reading the *Wall Street Journal* every morning. She fully expected that the paper would be delivered to her at the jail, and it was. At P4W she exercised her educated propensity for asking questions. Shocked by what she was seeing and experiencing, she persistently inquired into why the prison was run as it was. She didn't get answers, so she did abundant research, managing to obtain and pore over government documents pertaining to the Correctional Service of Canada (CSC). She took note when prison practices went against federal policy, particularly policies intended to prevent undue abuses by guards, and when budget irregularities negatively affected the prisoners' welfare. She was elected by the other prisoners to serve as chair of the Prisoners' Committee, which gave her the responsibility of representing the other women's interests and negotiating with the prison administration for solutions to the women's individual and collective problems.

By the time Gayle left P4W, she had gained a reputation as someone who stood up to authorities in the service of justice. She was, and is, a stalwart defender of imprisoned women's human rights. In 1987, she filed a complaint with the Canadian Human Rights Commission citing discrimination against women prisoners. In 1991 the commission recommended a conciliator be appointed to bring about a settlement of this complaint. In 1992, while at the B.C. Matsqui men's prison, Gayle filed a second complaint after the warden struck her name from the list of nominees to be elected by the population to the Prisoners' Committee. She had also had her recreational privileges removed in the prison's efforts to gain her agreement to transfer to the then new, provincially operated Burnaby Correctional Centre for Women (BCCW). Gail had refused; she was enrolled in university education courses taught at Matsqui, an opportunity not available to women at BCCW.

Gayle's court action resulted in a successful injunction to stop the transfer, pending the outcome of her claim, filed in federal court, of discrimination against women serving federal sentences. In 1989 Kim Pate, executive director of the Canadian Association of Elizabeth Fry Societies (CAEFS), visited Gayle, and in February 1993 Kim arranged for Gayle's temporary release to speak at a conference. For three days Gayle was escorted by three guards to Vancouver for the National Women and the Law biennial conference, where, together with Kim, she gave a dynamic presentation that aroused the crowd of lawyers and legal scholars to declare their support for all imprisoned women. One month later Gayle was released from prison on day parole to a men's halfway house. There weren't any women's halfway houses that would provide her a bed for three years, the time under law she was expected to serve on day parole. She worked at various jobs and took classes at Simon Fraser University, completing a BA in anthropology. Invited to speak at the 1993 CAEFS annual general meeting, Gayle again gave a powerful presentation, with the result that the membership of CAEFS unanimously passed a resolution supporting penal abolition in favour of more practical and constructive responses to people who have broken the law, whether or not they have harmed others. Gayle is able to convey the horrors of prisons without histrionics. She gives the facts and describes the situation, and people come to their own conclusions as to the impractical use of prisons as a response to crime.

Gayle is a good friend of mine, and we've had a running dialogue for almost seventeen years, during which time we've worked together on various Strength In Sisterhood (SIS) projects and public presentations. She has frequently given lectures to my university classes and attention to individual students who are interested in questions of justice. The following is excerpted from an unstructured, taped interview we did a few years ago in a campus recording studio, for off-campus students enrolled in a distance-education course on women and criminal justice. My questions to Gayle appear in italics.

Gayle's Story

I'd like people to try and understand what it's like to first walk into a prison when you've never been to prison before. I was forty-two years old at the time when I was sentenced, and went to a prison called Lakeside Correctional Centre for Women, which was a B.C. provincial prison, but they had federally sentenced women there as well. When I walked in the door it seemed to me like a little schoolhouse, actually. I thought, "This is not as bad as people talk about prisons," because I had in my mind the stereotypical idea of women screaming and beating each other up, and tremendous threats from other prisoners. That's not what I found. What I found was mostly very young women who were unable and ill equipped to deal with a system that was berating them, that seemed to be designed to totally destroy their self-confidence and try to remake them in some kind of image of a young lady with good manners.

One of the things I should tell you, something that made an impression on me, was when I walked into the bathroom one day, and there was blood all over the bathtub. And there was a girl still in the bathtub, and her arm was hanging over the side and blood was dripping all over the floor. I ran to get the matron, as they called themselves, and she was very casual about it; she said, "Oh, that was just a slashing." She said, "You'll see lots of that in your time"—which would be a long time, since I was serving a life sentence. (And I am still serving a life sentence, still reporting to a parole officer.)

That was quite shocking to me, the fact that somebody would consider slashing just a run-of-the-mill activity in prison. The nurse finally came, and they took the girl away and brought her back all bandaged up. She seemed to be okay but in shock. I asked her why she would do something like that, and she said, "Well, I was just so upset, I just didn't know what else to do." A lot of the women couldn't deal with the pain that they were going through emotionally, because of the prison sentence itself, or something that was happening to their family outside and they couldn't do anything about it, or memories of other abuses and the horror of being locked up. Eventually I realized that what these women who slashed all had in common was a lack of family support.

I had tremendous family support, and it made me feel so rich. After I finally realized what the system was about, I felt extremely… well, *rich*, compared to most of the other women who were there. I felt that I needed to really try to help them understand what they were up against.

Lakeside seems like an instant in time, in some respects. I was only at Lakeside for six months. And while I was there, the routine was… well, it was a non-routine, actually. You got up, and you looked on the board to see what your job was for the day. My job was usually washing the hallway floor. I had a huge amount of experience in business, and I offered to teach a class on how to approach a potential employer, or how to do different types of office jobs, but the authorities thought that was "not possible."

At Lakeside, one of the things I thought was really funny, in retrospect, was how it upset the authorities when my *Wall Street Journal* was delivered at the gate. It never occurred to me, at the time, that that was something I should not have done. I was so naive; I thought they would be pleased that I was just carrying on, doing the best I could, and being informed. But the guards and wardens thought that I was trying to show them that I was better than they were. Basically, the other women never paid any attention to it. They had their own thing, and I was reading my paper. They weren't interested in reading the *Wall Street Journal,* but they certainly didn't see anything wrong with it. And actually they got a chuckle out of it, I think.

Do you want to talk about how it is that you were in the prison in the first place?

I pleaded guilty to second-degree murder, for killing my stepmother, and that occurred in April 1985. I was out on bail for a year. It's a long story, like most stories. I think that if you research and look at women who are convicted of murder, most murder, which is a legal term, involves a victim who is a member of the family. I basically lost my mind. That's the only way I can sort of make any sense out of it. And when I recovered, I was in prison. It took about five years to get my head back together again.

Here you are, coming into the prison, very different in background from all these women. Were you well received by them? It sounds as though you didn't find it difficult to get acquainted.

I didn't have any problem at all. One of the reasons was that a lot of people thought I was Aboriginal, because I'm dark. And they automatically assumed that I had been in prison before. I didn't look like the typical person who comes in unaware of the prison structure. After a while they did realize that I came from a different background than they did—in other words, I didn't come from the street—but that I was not above getting on my hands and knees to wash the floor. I didn't think that I was better than anybody else, and that's all they were concerned with. I think it's like any circle of women. If you go into a circle of women as an outsider and try and take over the place, and try and tell everybody what to do, and put on some kind of air, you're not going to be well received. And I went to prison thinking that I would try and treat it like a job. To me that meant reading and learning everything I could about it, to try and understand it.

I was extremely suicidal, struggling with my own personal demons. I finally did come through that time and realized that that wasn't the way to solve anything or make anything better. I realized that I had to make myself useful and do the best I could in the situation. That meant doing it like a job, because that's what my background taught me. I looked at the rules and the regulations from a point of view of logic and law. What did the law say? What was the reality of what was going on in the prison? They were totally different.

Could you tell us about your transfer from Lakeside to P4W?

Moving from one prison to another is a really, really horrible experience. First you have to strip search, which is one of the most degrading things anybody can go through, and I think that different protestors have found that out now. Being forced to strip search. Well, everybody has the right to say no. I didn't know that, but one of the conditions for travelling was that you had to strip search. You're in a room with four or more strangers, and you have to take off your clothes and perform all sorts of different poses, extremely degrading. Then you are handcuffed and shackled, a chain goes around your waist, and your handcuffs are chained to that chain, to your waist. For the whole trip you can't really eat, because you can't get your hands to your mouth. And your feet are shackled. This is standard procedure for any prisoner who is transported.

Then they put me into a van and drove out to the Abbotsford airport. It was like a movie about the aliens, or the Star Wars thing. It was about five in the morning, still dark. And there at the airport were all these vans, lined up and parked alongside the runway. All the headlights were on, quite bizarre. And then, there's the plane, you see the plane. I go up the stairs with guards on both sides, sort of like a red carpet treatment, but the reverse. They're making sure you don't run away. But where could you run to? The whole place is covered with guards, and these guards are standing there with guns. And at the same time there's a movie camera going. Because they record everything, to make sure that if there's any violence they can cover their butts and rationalize it. Just getting up the stairs was difficult, because the stairs are quite high and you can't get your legs apart wide enough to get up. So I'm basically hopping. Meanwhile, the guards are making sure that I don't run away. It's totally ludicrous. All these people and all this expense, for what? There were only two of us being transported back east, another woman and myself, both frail little things. It's insanity.

The plane made stops to pick up other prisoners across the country on the way to Ontario, Quebec and the Maritimes. Just outside Prince Albert, Saskatchewan, it was bright sunlight by then. Three men were coming out of the van, which is pitch-black inside, so they couldn't see in the bright light and were trying to shield their eyes, stumbling, falling around. There must have been fifteen guards for those three bumbling men in chains, off to some prison. When they got on the plane and came along the aisle, I was trying to make eye contact, but there was no eye contact. They didn't look anyplace. They looked just straight ahead. And that was my reality check about what it's like to be a prisoner. They had been used to being prisoners in a maximum security segregation facility, an SHU. That's where they were coming from, a Special Handling Unit for men who are considered to be extreme risks. Most of the men incarcerated there are not convicted of murder. But they're there because they have assaulted a guard or tried to escape. Or been found to have had problems with other people in the population, other prisoners.

But they weren't necessarily violent?

They may have been violent while they've been in prison, but they weren't necessarily convicted of violent offences. They may have been defensive, or reactive against something in the prison, but not aggressively violent. Later on in my incarceration at Matsqui, I met quite a few men who were in SHUS, and I had some really interesting conversations with them about it.

We landed in Kingston, with the prison van waiting for us. And then, immediately, because we got in about 8:00 p.m., after the check-in time, I was taken straight to segregation. It was so filthy, it's hard to describe. The cell that I was put into, there was so much dirt on the floor—you have to give up your clothes right away and put on their pajamas. Which are mismatched, have no buttons. It's hard even to keep them on. You have nothing on your feet; you have nothing with you. All there is in the cell is this thin mattress, which was so filthy, it had every kind of stain you can imagine on it. The walls were covered in graffiti, and some of it was actually quite funny. But there I was, and they handed me four pieces of toilet tissue. The sink and toilet was a one-unit affair, all rusted out, only one push-button, from which you could get a little bit of cold water. There was no hot water at all. The floor was so bad I didn't want to step on it in my bare feet, so I used two pieces of the toilet tissue for the two steps it took to get from the bunk to the sink. And the dirt was coming through the tissue. It was just unbelievable. I was freezing. And I had a headache. It was a scary situation. You're on a wooden slab bolted into the wall, that's the bunk; the mattress is about three inches thick, one blanket. I asked, "How long am I going to be here?" And they said, "We don't know; we can keep you here as long as we want."

I was at P4W nearly three years, separated by a two-month jaunt out to Mission, B.C. I had fasted to try and come out to see my husband, who had had a bad heart attack, another long story.

How did you come to do time in different prisons?

When I got to Prison for Women I was suicidal and pretty depressed. I'd been told a lot of lies about Prison for Women by the authorities. They said I had a choice of staying at Lakeside or going to the federal prison in Kingston. There was nothing in Lakeside; the school only went up to grade ten. It certainly wouldn't have kept me occupied for a life sentence. I was told that at P4W I could take university classes [a lie], and that really appealed to me. And they said I could have private family visits with my husband and my family, whereas the visiting restrictions were terrible at Lakeside. You had to visit in the gym. You couldn't even touch each other.

So were things better for you at P4W?

Yes and no. No because I was so far away, and staff were a lot more cruel. But the women were all serving federal time, long sentences like myself. Because of that, I got involved with the Prisoners' Committee. And that was quite an experience. I was able to read back through all the correspondence in the committee files, about what had gone on at Prison for Women before I got there. And I got into the library and realized that in fact we did have some rights.

The library was available to all prisoners, with very restricted use. You didn't have access during your "work day," but being in the Prisoners' Committee, since the committee office was right next to the library, I could get in there.

A lot of women didn't want to know what the rules were, because it was just a bunch of bafflegab to them. To them the rules were not interpreted in any way that they could understand, so they didn't want anything to do with them. Also there were a lot of Aboriginal women in the prison who, for one reason or another, did not want to learn about "white man's laws" because all those had done was bring them hardship.

I also found documents on the correctional law review, which was very enlightening to me. I learned about different policies being considered and how people outside of the system were trying to reform the system itself. Through the work on the Prisoners' Committee I got a lot of support from the other women. We had a true sisterhood going. We helped one another through a lot of difficult times.

At this point you have become an activist and advocate within the prison, learning the technicalities of how the laws were constructed and where the loopholes are, and where the opportunities for appeals and grievances might exist within prison policies. How did this happen?

One of the first things I tried to do was return to B.C. after I was told that, in fact, I could return if I didn't like P4W. I applied to go back to B.C. and was denied very quickly. From then I realized that there was no way I was going to get back to my home province. And through that, I started to research the Commissioner's Directives. They're supposed to be, under law, accessible by every prisoner. There are also Regional Instructions written by every regional headquarters, and Standing Orders by the warden of every prison.

So you discover the intricacies of the possibilities, and you start putting it together, and then your husband has major problems, a heart attack, correct?

I applied for a pass to go back home to see him. I had appealed the denial of my transfer and reapplied, and also had requested an escorted absence, a temporary absence from Kingston to visit my husband, and all these things were denied. At that time I had been at P4W for a little over a year. I decided that I was going to fast in protest of my transfer being denied. The federal authorities had no problem with me being transferred and had actually recommended my return, since all my family and community support were in B.C. But the provincial authorities were happy to get rid of me and didn't want me back. They said they wouldn't have me back because of overcrowding. But in reality, here's what happened.

When I was at Lakeside there was no electricity in the cells, so any woman who had a TV or a radio had to use a battery to run it. Of course it was very expensive, and no one could afford it. So I said, "Well, there's obviously electricity in the building, so I think we should put some outlets in the cells so the women could have electricity in their cells." And the authorities said, "Well, no, it's too expensive, we can't afford it, blah blah." First they said the power wouldn't work because it was an old building and there wasn't enough wiring for it. So I did a study of the electric wattage usage by taking meter readings every day. I brought to their attention the fact that when the laundry and kitchen stopped operating for the day, there was ample wiring to handle any usage in the cells.

So then they said they couldn't afford it. I said, well, the prisoners have what's called the Inmate Welfare Fund—every woman has to put in a dollar every pay period to this so-called fund, which is supposed to fund social activities. There was only bingo at Lakeside. Also, there was a 20 per cent mark-up on all the canteen supplies, and that money was supposed to go to the Inmate Welfare Fund, to be used for prisoners' activities. I calculated that there should have been at least seven or eight thousand dollars going into the fund annually. It certainly would have been adequate to pay for the wiring. I asked to see the books, but nobody knew where they were, or knew how much money was there or was supposed to be there. Or what happened to it. Obviously the money was used for other things. I think my stirring up that trouble was the main reason they didn't want me back in B.C.

So you had started prison life as a political activist when you were still in British Columbia, before ever getting to Kingston.

It never occurred to me that I was being political. Most people in prison have never understood that they had rights. Never accessed them because they never understood they had any. When I went to prison it never occurred to me that I didn't have rights. That was a huge difference between us.

The women at p4w helped me survive my sentence. I couldn't have done it without them. Their kindness, their understanding. Times when you'd get depressed because there was way too much to deal with—another strip search, another lockdown. One of the women would say something, you know, just wonderful. Like, "Hey, it's a great day, who cares?" Just a small phrase, and it would change your whole state of mind, and you'd get through to the next moment and the next day. I owe those women a tremendous debt. I helped them as best I could, but they helped me tremendously, too. Women came from all over the country. At that time there was no other place a federally sentenced woman could go. Everybody was far from home, and we shared that in common, like being together in a war.

When my husband had a second heart attack, I decided I was going to fast. They put me in segregation because they determined that when you're fasting you're at risk to yourself. They consider it like a suicide, to which I said, "Nobody's going to commit suicide by fasting to death." There are other ways; it's ridiculous. I said, "This is a protest. I have a legal right to protest in a non-violent manner, which I'm doing, and I'm determined to stay in this fast until you transfer me." And I said, "I won't accept a transfer without other women from B.C. being able to have the same opportunity."

Then my husband had another heart attack. They offered me a thirty-day transfer, but no other women. I backed down and said I would go for the thirty days because he was in critical condition. I was transferred to Mission, a men's prison; I went by regular flight with two guards escorting me, again a huge expense.

Were you in chains and handcuffs?

I was handcuffed the whole time, but they let me carry a sweater over my chains so people didn't stare. The two women guards weren't in uniforms, although, at the airport, two RCMP met the plane and escorted the guards and myself through the airport onto the plane.

When I got to Mission it was incredible, because I was able to see the stars for the first time in two and a half years. Seeing the night sky. At six in the morning the doors were cranked open and the prisoners could walk out and have their coffee outside. It was just mind-boggling to me. The Mission bells [from the nearby monastery] used to peal. You could see deer through the fence. There were two huge yards, tennis, a huge gym with a racquet-ball court, a massive canteen where you could buy ice cream and things like that.

You make this prison sound like a wonderful place.

I know it's going to sound like a picnic. But compared to Kingston Prison for Women, it was. What was striking to me was that men would have facilities like this, when women don't. The excuse is that there are not enough women to justify the expense of having facilities like this. I was determined, after seeing Mission, that I was going to try and do everything I could to make sure that federally imprisoned women had facilities that were better than what we had at Kingston.

I ended up staying in Mission for two months, but I had to agree to not protest, nor to file any legal injunctions et cetera, for thirty days, which I didn't. But on the thirty-first day I filed an injunction to stop them from sending me back, while I was trying to get transferred to Lakeside. In the interim period Lakeside denied my transfer request again, and the warden at Mission said that they were going to have to send me back to P4W involuntarily. I said, "Well, I'm going to make a fuss, I'm not going to go, you're going to have to carry me, because you're violating my rights." In my opinion they were. I should have had the right to appeal the transfer denial.

Since it was near the Christmas season, they didn't want a big ruckus on their hands, publicity-wise. They couldn't send me on a regular plane because they knew I was going to kick and scream. There were no charters going at Christmas, when the crews have time off. So I stayed there for another month. And in the meantime I had tried to file an injunction to stop them from transferring me back, but Supreme Court Justice Reid, her name was, suggested that I was raising a good question, but it would have to be fought in court. So she couldn't grant me a temporary injunction. And in the middle of the night of December 31, actually about four in the morning of New Year's Day, I was awakened from a deep sleep in my cell at Mission. I saw that I was surrounded by guards, and the movie camera was rolling. They said, "Get up and strip, you're going back to Kingston." I said, "I'm not moving, you're violating my rights." They said, "Okay, we're taking you like this." And they just handcuffed and shackled me, right on the bed, lifted me up and took me to a van that was waiting outside. There were two p4w guards waiting there, and a Lear jet, imagine, a huge expense, again. They literally threw me into the jet and did not uncuff me or take my shackles off because I'd refused to strip search. The theory was that I could have had some kind of a weapon hidden inside my body.

In the Winnipeg airport, they stopped the plane to refuel, and they let me out to have a cigarette, still cuffed and shackled. We were way down the runway, so there was nothing around, no other planes, nothing. It was a clear night and it was snowing, the snow swirling around my slippers. The guards took off to get some coffee, leaving me standing there in the snow in my pyjamas, having this cigarette, looking up at the sky and saying to myself, "Happy new year." It was quite a moment, really, something that I will always remember.

I was back at p4w in Kingston for another year, a year of horror. A year of extreme violence against the women. The year that Marlene Moore [a prisoner] choked herself to death, in a long line of suicides. There were twenty-eight women in segregation and we fought very hard to try and get them out. It was a terrible, terrible time.

The year passed, not easily, and it was December 31 again, 1988. The regular lock-up at P4W was at 11:00 P.M., but the custom at that time was that on New Year's Eve women were allowed to stay out of their cells until midnight, to wish each other a happy new year face-to-face. At 10:50 that night, ten minutes before regular lock-up, the warden came over the intercom saying that since we'd been rude this year, the regular lock-up time was going to be enforced, and everybody had better get into their cells. About a dozen women decided they weren't going to do that. These women had been denied any recreation by the prison. The authorities shut the gym down, and we hadn't had any recreation for three months. So the women decided that they were going to at least wish each other a happy new year. They'd had enough, and they weren't taking any more.

It's a classic scenario for triggering a prison riot, to arbitrarily change the rules or the routine, to withhold what little pleasures are available in a prison, to punish everyone across the board, because some prisoners may have been "rude."

Yeah. This is such an important thing. You hear about "corrections" when you're out there in the world. Well, "corrections" corrects nothing; all it does is err. I have a long list of "correctional" euphemisms. One of them is "cell-extraction." When the women decided that they weren't going to be locked in their cells, I pleaded with them, and said, "You know, you're going to get hurt here. We'll protest this tomorrow, we'll file grievances—please lock in." But they wouldn't. I went upstairs to my cell, locked in, while about twelve women stayed out of their cells, just leaning against the wall. That's what it meant to be "out" of your cell, because there was no place to go with the end barrier already locked.

So they're just standing in the corridors, in front of their own cells?

Yes, right in front of their own cells, leaning against the window, against the concrete. At about fifteen minutes to twelve, in come the ERT, the Emergency Response Team from the men's prison. We call them the Goon Squad; armed, they had their batons raised, cans of mace, their hooded helmets on, their chest protectors, their big boots, their big gloves and two Dobermans. Suddenly the women were running and dashing into any empty cell they could find, before they got maced or beaten. The guards dimmed the already dim lights, so we couldn't see a thing. We can hear the guards making sure all the cages are locked, and then they start to drag the dogs upstairs to the top tier but, and it was sort of funny, the dogs didn't want to go along the top tier. I don't know why, but they seemed to be afraid of the top tier.

So now you've got all these men in Darth Vader costumes—

Yeah, men and dogs, and they're banging their sticks on your bars as they're going by. A lot of women are throwing water out at them, throwing water from their sink as the only way they could say, "Get out of here," and of course they were using a lot of different words.

After they made sure everybody was locked in, you could hear them taking women out of the cells, one by one, and these were the "cell-extractions." We could hear their heads being banged against the wall. You could hear the screams. You could hear the women trying to hold onto the bars, the ones who were resisting. Or the women yelling out, saying, "I'm not resisting, I'm not resisting, you don't have to do that. Don't kick me." This went on for about an hour and a half, maybe two hours.

What was the ostensible purpose of the cell-extractions?

No purpose given. They don't have to give a purpose.

In fact it was punishment, because these women had been—

Because they had decided to stay out. But think about this: fifteen minutes they had left. And the women would have locked in, no problem. They would have said "happy new year" and locked in. That's all they wanted. No, they had to bring in the Goon Squad from across the street, from Kingston Penitentiary for men, and you know, liven up *their* New Year's. I'm sure they were really happy about it. It gave them something exciting to do.

They took all the protesting women to segregation that night, and the next day we yelled through the vent to find out if they were okay. They were, even though there were a couple of macings and some women got roughed up. But nobody was stringing up yet, so that was pretty good.

Meaning that no woman was hanging herself?

Yeah. The next day, New Year's Day, we were all locked down, couldn't leave our cells. But what's it got to do with us? They'd taken all the women who were involved in that to segregation. Now the whole range was locked down. When the guards came by I asked, "Why are we locked in?" There was no answer. We were not told, which is a violation of their own rules.

You have a right to an explanation, correct?

We have a right to at least know what we're being held for. It's just like if you are arrested on the street, you have a right to know what you're being accused of. Nobody was being spoken to; we didn't get a morning meal. There was a lot of fear on the range, about how long we were going to be locked in. For me, I didn't really care, because I knew eventually they were going to have to let us out, and talk to us, and when they came by I'd be reading out from the [Canadian] Charter of Rights and Freedoms.

We learned that the authorities had decided to take every one of us, one at a time, down to the unit manager's office and find out who instigated the women standing out there. Now, I mean, this is a big investigation. It was so stupid.

They want you to name the ringleader who instigated the New Year's rebellion. There always has to be a ringleader, by their logic.

That's right. Now there were thirty-two of us who were locked in. We persisted in asking for a reason. "What justification have you got for keeping us in here?" Well, there was no reason given. I tried to organize a protest, passing a message cell to cell, saying, "This is wrong, they're violating our rights, and everybody needs to stand together on this issue and refuse to go down to the unit manager's office. We did nothing wrong, we don't have to answer to their demands. They're wrong." And we'd fish each other things. Fishing is where you throw out a blanket with a note attached, or a bottle of water in it, or a chocolate bar, or whatever the person needs, passing it cell to cell, down the range and to the cells beneath.

Well, naturally, what happened was that a lot of women went down to see the unit manager, because they're afraid, they're just terrified. A lot of women didn't have the skills to fight verbally or with their pen and file grievances, or realize that you could call a lawyer. So a lot of them did go down. But a few of us refused, so the authorities said, "Okay, if the whole range doesn't come down, the whole range will be locked up." In other words, those who refuse will be keeping everybody else locked. So I decided that I would just go to segregation and check in there. And then they could unlock the range for the other women. About five of us went to segregation in protest.

In the meantime I had decided to start another fast. I had basically had it. I just couldn't deal with P4W anymore. I believed at the time that I couldn't do any good there, that things were not getting better even though I did everything I could. I wrote letters until they were coming out of my ears. I wrote just about every Member of Parliament, all sorts of women's groups, colleges, you name it. And nothing changed. Nobody came to help. Things were getting worse and worse there. So with all the loss of privileges, with the suicide of Shaggy [Marlene Moore] and with the attempted suicides of four other women just prior to that, I thought that the best thing I could do for them is try and get myself out of there, and try and get them some help from outside. So I decided I was going to fast to the death totally.

As a way to get out of the prison one way or another?

As a way to get back to B.C. I just made the assertion: "I'm fasting. I'm drinking water right now, but on January 12, which is my sister's birthday, I will stop drinking water." After that I would only last about a week because I was already pretty thin. I knew that once you stop drinking water your liquids go very quickly, dehydration, and then you go into cardiac arrest and they can't bring you back because there's no fluids in your body.

But when you went to segregation you weren't planning to die, were you?

Oh, no. I didn't want to die. But I didn't want to live any longer, either, like that. And yet I was lucky, because I had a tremendous base of social support in B.C. and all over the country. It was amazing how people had written me about my other fast. And people I didn't know. Men and women. It was just amazing to me, the people that saw the injustice of the treatment of women in prison. How unjust it was, and how wrong it was, to take women away from their families, three thousand miles, when they didn't do the same thing to men. That's what my case is about.

I fasted fifteen days, the last three without any water, so I was pretty close to dropping, and basically the warden gave in. I was transferred to Matsqui, where I did four years with men.

How did that work?

I was separated out, they put me in the hospital unit. But I got to go to university classes with the men, I went to the hobby shop, and I got limited time in the gym to work out. There was no problem at all.

Compared to what you had been experiencing at P4W, you were able to live a fairly planned-out life.

Fairly productive existence.

Where you could be useful to other people, including your family.

Right. When a person goes to prison, it's not only them who goes, it's their whole family. So you can say, "Well, you should punish the person, they've done this terrible thing." But should their family be punished? My family still loved me very much. Their hardship at having me 3,000 miles away was huge. So for me to be back here was great for them.

But there was still more drama for you to live through.

When I was in Matsqui, they planned to move me to Burnaby [Correctional Centre for Women] when they finished construction of that new prison for women. I refused to go, because I knew the conditions would be horrendous. My lawyer filed an injunction to stop the transfer since it would interrupt my university education. Which is sort of funny. And we won. I still have to get the CSC [Correctional Service of Canada] into court to address my charges of unequal treatment under the Charter, which guarantees equal benefits and equal protections under the law.

Reflections

In 2002, when Gayle's case against the Correctional Service of Canada was finally settled, she won again, with CSC stating that they are "committed to substantive equality, under section 15 of the Canadian Charter of Rights and Freedoms, for all federally sentenced women offenders through the provision of facilities and services." As urged by Gayle's suit, CSC was advised to heed the recommendations of Madam Justice Louise Arbour, who conducted an official inquiry into violence against women in P4W. Echoing Gayle's own complaints, Arbour strenuously criticized the lawlessness of the prison and recommended that the judiciary take responsibility for monitoring prison practices. Typically, judges never see the insides of the prisons to which they routinely send people, nor concern themselves with prison policies and practices.

When Gayle calls for equality between men and women in the prison system, she is not idealizing men's prisons, most of which are extremely oppressive. Indeed, she is a penal abolitionist, recognizing the human rights infractions that cause further damage to prisoners and their families and compromise the law and the integrity of society at large. In calling for the equality protections of the Charter, Gayle is asking only that the CSC provide women prisoners with a minimum standard of decency, as is found in the best of the men's prisons such as those in which she completed her sentence. P4W, by contrast, represented maximum indecency.

The Prison for Women in Kingston, constructed in 1934, was closed in May 2000, and federally sentenced women are now generally sent to one of six new regional women's prisons across Canada. (Some women, most of them Aboriginal, have been involuntarily segregated in men's prisons.) These new prisons have somewhat eased the problem of women's distance from their families. Another positive feature is that when you get past the walls, barbed-wire fences and laser beams, the buildings look more like condominiums than cellblocks. Moreover, when I speak to some of the new wardens and guards, I get the idea that they are being instructed to think constructively about how best to assist a woman toward a better future, rather than inflict further harm beyond the fact of confinement. Nevertheless, most of the new prisons have adopted the same punitive practices that governed P4W, including the excessive use of segregation; tighter security than is mandated for minimum and medium security prisoners, so as to accommodate maximum security women in prisons holding all classifications; the over-classification of women as maximum security, particularly Aboriginal women; pointless strip searches; lack of meaningful educational programs or vocational training; severely inadequate medical services; lack of effective programs to heal from drug or alcohol dependency or from childhood sexual abuse (both of which are problems most imprisoned women have experienced); frequent, arbitrary abuses of power by "correctional" officers and administrators; and so on.

In the years following her release, Gayle has not been taking it easy. Her husband's health has improved in part due to her care. She has assisted with her son's business, she worked at a women's centre, and she is a dedicated grandmother. Her balanced life and strong family ties have been key to her healing, as has her artwork and her advocacy on behalf of women in prison through Strength In Sisterhood. For example, she coordinated a SIS-sponsored study of community services that are available, or more often *not* available, to women leaving prison. She also received funding on behalf of SIS and activist group Joint Effort to open a Vancouver community office to coordinate activity related to justice for women, staffed by former prisoners. Gayle was politicized by her prison experience, and she has sustained her commitment to making changes in a criminal (in)justice system that is destructive to those who enter it but which can be constructively resisted.

An event occurred at the Prison for Women in April 1994 that resulted in the official inquiry chaired by Madam Justice Arbour and the rapid construction of new women's prisons across Canada. During the night of April 27, 1994, six men (and one woman who in riot gear appeared to be a man), all of whom were dressed in the Darth Vader–like uniforms of the csc Emergency Response Team, burst into the p4w segregation unit. They jerked women from their cots, forced them face down onto the cement floor, forcibly removed their clothing, crushed one woman's glasses under a boot and otherwise tormented and degraded the women while ostensibly in search of contraband, of which there was none. The ert assault was videotaped, and a clandestine copy found its way to the Canadian Broadcasting Corporation (cbc). It was televised in February 1995, causing a national scandal. What was not shown was that, after their cells had been completely stripped, the women were lined up and, one by one, subjected to vaginal searches. For weeks or months following, they were not allowed phone calls, visits with lawyers, paper or pencils, clothing, mattresses, bedding or any basic physical amenity. As Gayle found out when she first arrived at p4w in 1986 and was put straight into segregation, "When a woman in seg needed toilet paper, she was handed two, three or, if she was lucky, four squares. The rationale is that if they give a woman a whole roll to herself, she'll clog up her toilet, as unruly prisoners are wont to do. And of course prison authorities, with their eye to economy, would not want to waste good toilet paper on the likes of women in segregation."

The following is from an article Gayle published in the journal *Under the Volcano* (Fall 2004), wherein she alludes to the ert assault and ongoing harms.

Who would have predicted [in 2004], after the February 1995 national airing by the cbc's *Fifth Estate* of the videotapes taken by the Correctional Service of Canada on April 27, 1994, inside Kingston's Prison for Women that exposed the egregious sexual assaults of eight women, that some of these same women would still be getting brutalized inside Canada's prisons?

Many of you [who saw the assault on cbc] will recall those black eyes crammed with horror and the piercing, defenseless pleas of these women as one-by-one, their naked bodies were exposed by helmeted, baton-wielding, male members of the emergency response team from the men's Kingston Penitentiary—men who ripped or cut away their few, thin pieces of clothing as these eight [primarily First Nations] women lay or knelt on the concrete floors of P4W.

Many Canadians believed the immediate outrage that resulted in the April 1996 Report by the Honourable Justice Louise Arbour Commission of Inquiry [authored by Kelly Hannah-Moffat and Tammy Landau] would ensure that the CSC would correct its criminal-like behaviour. Unfortunately, the many criticisms leveled by Justice Arbour, such as, "There is nothing to suggest that the Service is either willing or able to reform without judicial guidance and control" (1996: 198) and "The Rule of Law is absent, although rules are everywhere" (1996: 181) are still relevant. The CSC continues in its unabated cruelty and sticks its finger in the air to those who raise alarms.

The parliamentary-appointed Correctional Investigator is still frustrated with the lack of humanity displayed by the CSC following the transfers of mostly Aboriginal women, beginning in 1994, to units in four men's penitentiaries (two in Saskatchewan, Springhill in Nova Scotia, and Ste. Anne des Plaines in Quebec). One woman had already been in P4W's segregation for over a year prior to being stripped by men on April 27, 1994. She was then forced to endure nine years under segregated conditions in two penitentiaries for men in Saskatchewan!

In 2001, the Elizabeth Fry Society of Saskatchewan filed a complaint with the Canadian Human Rights Commission about the treatment of this woman and other mostly Aboriginal women also held in men's penitentiaries in Saskatchewan. In 2002, the Canadian Association of Elizabeth Fry Societies garnered the support of sixteen national equality-seeking women's organizations and added their voices in charging the CSC with systemic discrimination in their treatment of women prisoners. [In December 2003 the commission ruled that the Correctional Service of Canada was indeed guilty of discriminatory treatment against women prisoners.]

GAYLE HORII HAS BECOME a recognized and respected expert on Canadian prison policies and practices. A persistent, informed critic of the Correctional Service of Canada, she is acknowledged by them as an expert and, as such, is invited by them to serve as a consultant. She is driven by empirical, documented facts, experiential knowledge and a generous spirit. She recognizes the links between prisons and social inequities, and she is fluent in statistical language.

In 1995, Gayle made a strong impression when she testified before the commission of inquiry into violence by guards against women in P4W. The commission was chaired by the Honourable Madam Justice Louise Arbour, an Ontario Appeals Court judge who, following the inquiry, went to the Hague, in the Netherlands, as chief justice of the international war crimes tribunal for Rwanda and the former Yugoslavia. She was subsequently appointed to the Supreme Court of Canada and is now the United Nations high commissioner for human rights. During the hearings, which took place in Kingston, Ontario, across the street from the infamous Prison for Women, Justice Arbour took the opportunity to visit P4W and speak with women there, as did other commission members.

Touring P4W with Justice Arbour was an emotional experience for Gayle, returning to the place she had worked so hard to escape from. It was also emotional for the women who had known and admired her when she was locked up with them and were inspired to see her again. When they last had seen Gayle she was seriously weakened from her fast. Now she was strong and among the advisers to the esteemed judge. She was still representing them.

Gayle submits briefs to various agencies, is a close working ally of Kim Pate (Canada's primary advocate for imprisoned women), keeps abreast of official prison-related documents, corresponds with authorities and receives calls from women at present or formerly in prisons and responds to their cries for help. For example, she combed city streets and finally located and took care of the runaway daughter of another former prisoner, who had called from the prairies in fear for her daughter's safety. When Jo-Ann Mayhew, a close friend from P4W, was stricken with ALS soon after her release from prison, Gayle arranged for her to have a computer she could operate with her impaired muscles. When Jo-Ann died, Gayle and two other women who had also done time with Jo-Ann flew to Nova Scotia to assist with the memorial service. When a woman in Saskatchewan was being severely over-drugged and otherwise abused in a segregation cell of a men's prison, Gayle brought pressure to bear and there was some easing up. She gained the support and respect of Svend Robinson, a longtime New Democratic Party Member of Parliament. At her behest, Robinson intervened in human rights abuses of prisoners on several occasions. She maintains contact with the independent correctional investigator who identifies human rights abuses in federal prisons. She has built a network of women, many of whom, like herself, are lifers, which means that they must report their every move to the state for their entire lives. She publishes articles and speaks to university classes, at conferences and public forums and in the media. She is a founding member and a recurrent coordinator of the Strength In Sisterhood society, a model national support network and advocacy group composed primarily of women still inside prison or on parole that works in coalition with Joint Effort and other activist groups for women's rights.

Gayle had the skill, persistence, courage and legal support to take her case against the Correctional Service of Canada just one step from the national Supreme Court. At that point she agreed to settle, and she and her lawyer, John Conroy, won the case. The government conceded gender discrimination, and the settlement included the requirement that CSC thereafter consult with Gayle before making structural decisions concerning incarcerated women. They don't have to agree with her comments or follow her advice, but they have agreed to solicit her opinion and appear to consider it. In this capacity Gayle has been appointed to the Program Advisory Council to ensure that a new federal women's prison in British Columbia will incorporate the principles and practices of providing resources needed by women if those women are to have choices in their lives.

Gayle's energies and commitment are joined with those of Sylvie Bouchard, Brenda Blondell, Ann Hansen, Christine Lamont, Kris Lyons and other Canadian and Quebecois women who extend their hands to women newly recovering from prison. They share a vision of a world where punishment is replaced with lending a hand.

Reference

Arbour, the Honourable Louise, commissioner (1996). *Commission of Inquiry into Certain Events at the Prison for Women in Kingston.* Ottawa: Solicitor General.

CLOSING REFLECTIONS

AMONG THE WOMEN WHOSE stories are told here, those who harmed someone or took a life suffer deep regret but sustain their appreciation for life. Those whose crime did not hurt anyone are not remorseful. No matter what the crime or the problems they face, some women exhibit an irrepressible spirit, even in confinement. In the details of their stories, these women are all different from one another: Diane, Angelique, Lia, Kathy, Norma, Vicki, Marie, Mattie, Betty, Ann, Christine, Gayle and the First Nations women whose words appear in these pages. Yet each story is a parable about the fragility of life, about how easily plans fall apart, how we can be overtaken by harms that come our way as well as by our own wrong actions and stupidities. Each is also a story of resilience, of bouncing back, not letting setbacks get us down, facing the world bravely and seeing the light, learning the lessons.

Each story is unique, but these women also share certain strengths and grievances. A number of them have in common (with each other and with other imprisoned women) the experience of poverty, of violence against themselves and of the indignities of racism. Like a majority of imprisoned women, a number have been battered. Eight are mothers who endured being separated from their children. For women, this is commonly the most painful and frightening aspect of incarceration. Before incarceration, some of these women suffered the stresses of trying to take care of too many other people. Almost half of them used illegal drugs to alleviate stress, to feel normal, to experience pleasure or the absence of pain—or to just relax in the manner to which youth became accustomed in the late 1960s. The law is often slower to change than are social customs and attitudes, which is why Diane, arrested for selling a small quantity of marijuana in the 1960s, and Norma, who was a lesbian in the 1950s, had such hard times. Of course, in many parts of the world, including Canada and the U.S., there are still many people in prison for possessing marijuana, and same-sex relations are still illegal in many places.

From encounters with the police to being sentenced in the court to serving time, people who come into contact with the criminal justice system are prejudged according to their perceived social status. Those without material resources or employment and those who are members of racialized minorities, especially if they live in low-income neighbourhoods, are more vulnerable to surveillance, arrest, conviction, imprisonment and parole denial than are middle-class people who break the law, white middle-class people in particular. Mattie, who was returned to prison again and again, and Marie, who served almost five years on a six-month sentence, are strong examples of how prison time is extended gratuitously for those who dare confront, criticize and defy the status quo.

Of all the categories of crime, "suite" (white-collar) crime is the least likely to be prosecuted, whereas street crime produces the greatest number of individuals processed through the criminal justice system. Crime rates in the U.S. and Canada have been going down consistently for two decades because, in addition to economic and social factors, the group that commits the most crime, young men, is diminishing in population. And yet more people than ever in the U.S.A. are being incarcerated. In Canada, incarceration rates for men have gone down, but more women are being locked up.

It is predicted that one in ten people in the U.S.A. will soon be involved with criminal justice. California locks up more people per capita than any *nation* in the world, with the exception of China. One in every eight U.S. prisoners is in California. As noted in the introduction to this book, Canada has about 350 women in prison. California, with close to the same population, has more than 11,000. In California, in 1997, almost 2,000 black people per 100,000 people in the black population at large were sent to prison, compared with the white rate of 215 per 100,000. "California locks up more people, per capita, than France, the United Kingdom, Spain, Italy, Switzerland, Sweden, and Finland combined... These countries are inhabited by approximately 240 million people, compared to California's 32 million" (Koetting and Schiraldi, 1997: 40, 44). "While the United States has five per cent of the world's population, it now has 25% of its prisoners," to the tune of about $40 billion a year (Platt, 2001: 140). In 1994, California "was spending more on its prisons than it did to educate students in all its 20 state universities and 107 community colleges combined" (Platt, 2001: 145).

Women constitute over 10 per cent of the incarcerated population in the States and less than 4 per cent in Canada. People sent to prison have not generally finished high school. As noted elsewhere, they are not less intelligent on average than the population at large; however, most lack the resources to advance their education, and they lack the social contacts that could steer them toward opportunities. By contrast, a number of the women whose stories are told here, including Angelique, Lia, Mattie, Christine and Gayle, have been resourceful in achieving relatively high levels of education. A number of the women are natural leaders, and that includes the women incarcerated for political crime.

In addition to the higher-than-average educational level of some of these women (albeit achieved following imprisonment), as a group they are not representative of women in prison for several other reasons. It wasn't feasible logistically to include in this book a representative from every cultural group. For example, I would like to have included someone from Quebec, where the prison experience has been often made worse by language barriers, given that so few English-speaking women (whether prisoners or staff) are bilingual. With a new federal prison in Joliette, francophone women now have the dubious benefit of a prison within their own cultural and language milieu. Also omitted from the book is a story from someone whose native language is Spanish. In the 1970s there were fewer Hispanics, Latinas or Chicanas in the California women's prison than there are now; by the mid-1990s they constituted just over 30 per cent of women's prison populations in California, with African Americans at about 35 per cent.

Almost one-third of the women in this book were incarcerated for crimes involving violence, which is out of proportion given that women are convicted of under 15 per cent of violent crime. The majority of women's crimes relate to theft or drugs, and several of the stories here are focused on these activities. This collection also includes the stories of three women convicted of crimes intended to promote social and environmental justice. Very few women in North America are in prison explicitly for politically motivated crimes, although many are politicized by the experience of being incarcerated.

With four decades of exposure to both men's and women's prisons in California, Canada and elsewhere, I am struck by the consistency of punishment systems across time and place. Prisons in Canada and California, like prisons globally, operate on the principles of confinement, deprivation, labelling, discipline, subordination and retribution. Likewise, the crimes being committed today are basically the same as in the past. The new Canadian prisons are more attractive than the old P4W fortress, once you get past the walls, fences and coiled razor wire. But cosmetic improvements cannot alter the fundamental purpose of prisons for over 200 years, which, in effect, is to degrade the wrongdoer and enforce submission.

The internal dynamic of prisons changes very little from one prison to another. Universally, and over time, these are small, totalitarian communities in which the administration and guards have complete control over the lives of the prisoners. Abuses are inevitable, as are prisoners' resistances. In the 1970s there was considerable rhetoric concerning the need for rehabilitative programs in prisons. It was this message that allowed us to take the university program into the California Institution for Women and to have open access to the workings of the prison. The staff believed in a "correctional" philosophy and wrongly presumed that people from the university would think the same way. They were never apologetic or defensive when we would witness a disturbing event, for example, a woman being roughly hogtied by two large men in uniform, then carried off in chains to segregation. Her offence? She played her guitar in the corridor a couple of minutes past count time, when she was supposed to be in her cell to be counted. She wanted to finish her song. One minute she was singing a mournful folk song, the next she was screaming.

With fleeting historical exceptions, such as the Healing Lodge in Saskatchewan when it first opened in the mid-1990s, the overriding concern of so-called correctional systems has never been to provide women with the resources that could help them build or rebuild their lives. Prisons operate on principles of custody and retribution: "Lock 'em up and make 'em suffer." The social and economic factors related to crime are ignored by the courts, and women who are convicted of crime (or who are victims of violence) are pathologized. When paroled, they are usually returned to the circumstances that prompted the lawbreaking, often losing their children in the process and with no new skills or resources to enable them to create a stable life for themselves.

I oppose prisons for all but truly dangerous individuals, for all the preceding reasons and many more:

- Prisons are horribly expensive to taxpayers (in Canada in 2005, as much as $100,000 per year per woman), and taxes support an immense, expanding punishment industry at the expense of education, health care and social benefits. Private prisons, which provide punishment for profit and must constantly replenish their "work force," are not the answer.

· Prisons are the dead end of a discriminatory system, confining people according to race and economic status.

· Locking up people who are good parents, no matter what they've done, causes untold harm to over 10 million children on this continent who have been displaced when their parents were incarcerated.

· Victims are generally excluded from the prosecution process, and when the person who harmed them is sent to prison the victim is left without restitution.

· Contradictorily, even though the rate of serious crime has been dropping for over twenty years (in 2005), there has been a severe increase in prison populations in the U.S. due to the war on drugs.

· Prisons don't rehabilitate; rather, they feed the growth of a subculture of people living on the margins of society, with inadequate resources and often no qualms about breaking a law.

· Prisons don't prevent crime; even those who are locked up find ways to break laws.

· Prisons don't deter people in general from crime, because people inclined to break one law or another don't usually expect to be caught.

· Prisoners suffer dehumanization and degradation, and punishment for its own sake doesn't induce feelings of responsibility or accountability, but rather anger and frustration.

· Prisoners are denied basic human rights and are often subjected to brutalities and cruelties that stem from guards having complete power over them.

· Prisons successfully infantilize many of those who are locked within them, and when such prisoners are released they lack the ability to rebuild their lives without significant support.

· Prisons support a capitalist hierarchy of human value based on material acquisition.

IN SUM, PRISONS ARE not helpful to victims, lawbreakers, communities or society at large. On the contrary, they cause considerable damage to a great many people, at great cost monetarily, and also damage the moral fibre of a nation. It has been said by many that you can ascertain a nation's level of civility according to how that nation treats its prisoners. It is my belief that there is no such thing as a good prison. I certainly agree that people who we have good reason to believe are likely to inflict violence need to be confined, but they don't need to be brutalized—with physically abusive practices, drugging or psychological games-playing. Instead, they need opportunities to make sense of and heal from their own violence, whether it is related to social conditions, home life, a health problem or rage at having been abused as a child, humiliated by a patronizing boss, unable to find work, never getting a fair shake, or experiencing a personal tragedy. There is always a reason. Being able to explain the behaviour is no reason not to confine a dangerous person, but if our aim is harm reduction, it *is* a reason to take a more holistic approach in responding to people who cause harm.

Retribution and restorative justice are at the polar ends of justice ideologies, the one based on revenge and punishment, the other on accountability and healing. Those who advocate punishment follow the mainstream adherence to age-old disciplinary traditions and techniques established by militaries and religions. Proponents of restorative justice are commonly prison abolitionists, and they would do things very differently by keeping the focus on healing, which includes encouraging accountability and providing restitution if a victim is involved.

People who hurt other people need to unlearn those patterns of thinking and reacting, and that requires being confronted by those whom they've harmed or others who have been similarly harmed. For example, when women who have been raped go into prisons to confront men who have raped, everyone benefits. The women are vindicated and empowered. The men are held accountable and appropriately shamed. Everyone is re-humanized.

Prison serves no useful function for people who do not pose a danger. The majority of incarcerated women fall into this category, including most of those who have violence on their records. Retributive justice requires a penalty, an act of revenge, a payback. Punishment is an end in itself—except, in fact, it isn't, because it's a self-perpetuating cycle. The person who is punished wants to retaliate and is more often angered than repentant. The person who offends is more likely to re-offend as a consequence of imprisonment. Revenge only builds on itself. Rarely do both injured parties say, "We're even now."

It is much to her credit if a woman, upon release, succeeds in overcoming the stigma and other negative effects of imprisonment, which may include poor health; a craving for alcohol or other drugs; a lack of money; worry about children; and all the social barriers to finding a home, a job and a community. Success is much more likely if a woman has a support system of family, community or friends who can help her make the transition. Most of the women who tell their stories in this book had that advantage, and they won't be going back to prison. In turn, some of them now give support to other women exiting from prison. They are in the international vanguard of former prisoners who are organizing with one another, pooling their energies to collectively seek human rights for prisoners and to serve as advocates for women seeking life in a free world.

Certainly there is no single solution to the problems created by competitive, individualistic and materially unequal societies, apart from working with others toward more cooperative and equitable social arrangements. Meanwhile, education is the best way to prevent street crime, reduce recidivism, and strengthen an individual's chances for self-reliance and contributing to her community. The women in this book who formally advanced their education after release from prison found that far more useful than punishment as a way to improve their choices in the wider world. Getting an education is both empowering and equalizing in the job market. Likewise, the recovery of Aboriginal languages and cultural practices is a strong deterrent to unlawful activity among First Nations.

All around me I see the ordinary valour of unselfish people who are committed to a better world and who do their part to create it. In the past thirty years, some parts of the world have improved for many people because of social movements. I also see self-serving people in high places whose greed and abuses of power obstruct progressive social change. I dream: If only... If only politicians were to invest as much in education as they now invest in punishment, they would correspondingly reduce street crime. If corporations didn't control governments, we could focus on corporate and state crime, which cause much more damage. If men were not violent toward women, there would be many fewer women in trouble. If children weren't abused, they would not so often grow up to be abusive or depressed. If single mothers had access to skills training, health care, decent wages and childcare, even fewer would be stealing, drugging or taking frustrations out on their children. If people came before profits, we would be closer to justice.

It no longer surprises me that some of the most talented, intelligent and generous people I meet are people who have been imprisoned for one crime or another. All kinds of people take risks and form habits that get them in trouble; or are loyal to family or friends in ways that are not in their own best interests; or react impulsively in rage against injustice; or suffer a temporary loss of sanity; or have been beaten down by the system and don't care any more; or do what they do for lack of perceived alternatives; or act against the law with clear planning, intent and deliberation, based on their principled convictions. All kinds of people break the law, and most of them are never apprehended. Those who are caught and punished include some remarkable women. I am glad, with help from Anne Near and others, to have shared some of their stories with you.

References

Koetting, Mark G. and Vincent Schiraldi (1997). "Singapore West: The Incarceration of 200,000 Californians." In *Social Justice* 24:1, 40–49.

Platt, Anthony M. (2001). "Social Insecurity: The Transformation of American Criminal Justice, 1965-2000." In *Social Justice* 28:1, 138–155.

Karlene Faith (left) *and Anne Near*

KARLENE FAITH, *born and raised in Saskatchewan, is a long-time community activist who does advocacy for prisoners' human rights. The mother of four and a grandmother, she earned her Ph.D. in the History of Consciousness at the University of California at Santa Cruz, where she cofounded the Santa Cruz Women's Prison Project in 1972. In 1982 she joined the School of Criminology at Simon Fraser University in British Columbia and is now Professor Emerita. Her many publications include the award-winning* Unruly Women: The Politics of Confinement & Resistance *and* The Long Prison Journey of Leslie Van Houten.

ANNE NEAR, *born and raised in New York City, has been an activist citizen in rural northern California for the last sixty years. She was one of the cofounders of Plowshares, a community centre that provides meals and services. She has been a longtime critic of war, a supporter of education, a feminist and a member of the cultural education committee of* SPACE (*School for the Performing Arts and Cultural Education). She is the author of* Dubious Journey: From Class to Class. *Married to a rancher, she raised four children and is also a grandmother. She is now retired.*